TOMBSTONE

ST. MARTIN'S PRESS
NEW YORK

TOMBSTONE

The Earp Brothers,
Doc Holliday,
and the Vendetta
Ride from Hell

TOM CLAVIN

First published in the United States by St. Martin's Press, an imprint of
St. Martin's Publishing Group

TOMBSTONE. Copyright © 2020 by Tom Clavin. All rights reserved.
Printed in the United States of America. For information, address
St. Martin's Publishing Group, 120 Broadway, New York, NY 10271.

www.stmartins.com

Frontise: OK Corral courtesy of the Arizona Historical Society

The Library of Congress Cataloging-in-Publication Data is available upon request.

ISBN 978-1-250-21458-4 (hardcover)
ISBN 978-1-250-27246-1 (signed edition)
ISBN 978-1-250-21459-1 (ebook)

Our books may be purchased in bulk for promotional, educational, or business use.
Please contact your local bookseller or the Macmillan Corporate and
Premium Sales Department at 1-800-221-7945, extension 5442,
or by email at MacmillanSpecialMarkets@macmillan.com.

First Edition: April 2020

10 9 8 7 6 5 4 3 2 1

TO MY BROTHER,
JAMES CLAVIN

Contents

Author's Note

When I was on tour to talk about my two previous books set in the American West, *Wild Bill* and *Dodge City*, an inevitable question was, "What is your next project?" When I said I was working on a book about Tombstone, the reaction was usually enthusiasm, but a few people were puzzled, too. Let me focus on the enthusiasm for a moment.

As I researched the events in Tombstone, Arizona, from 1877 to 1882, I realized that the so-called Gunfight at the O.K. Corral and the Earp "vendetta ride" are our *Iliad* and *Odyssey*, two separate but connected events that are big parts of the foundation of our mythology. The shoot-out in a vacant lot has often been viewed as the classic confrontation between good guys and bad guys, and its participants have become legendary figures in American history and popular culture. The "bad guys"—Ike and Billy Clanton and Frank and Tom McLaury—weren't all bad, and the "good guys"—Virgil, Wyatt, and Morgan Earp and Doc Holliday—weren't all good, but that is beside the point. They were two opposing forces representing the past and future of the American West who clashed on that cold late-October afternoon, and law and order and the future won. To our way of thinking, that was how it should be. And it was a heck of a gunfight, too—thirty shots in thirty seconds, leaving three dead and three wounded. So, a new version? Bring it on!

But why were some people puzzled? Because of the perception that the Gunfight at the O.K. Corral story has been told. Of course it has, in books by a range of writers as well as on the big screen: *My Darling Clementine*, though highly fictionalized, is considered one of John Ford's best westerns; *Tombstone* remains a western-fan favorite more than a quarter century after its release; and two of Hollywood's biggest stars who were at their peak, Burt Lancaster and Kirk Douglas, teamed up to play Wyatt Earp and Doc Holliday in *Gunfight at the O.K. Corral*. What more can be told about the Tombstone story?

Answering that question was my challenge. One reason I wrote *Tombstone* was to gain a sense of completion. *Dodge City* had been written first, then *Wild Bill*, and suddenly there needed to be a third volume of an unanticipated but apparently welcome "Frontier Lawmen" trilogy. With these three books there is an arc from the post–Civil War years, when the prototype of a frontier lawman was established by Wild Bill Hickok as the lone gunman with two six-shooters, to the mid- to late 1870s, when Wyatt Earp and Bat Masterson cleaned up Dodge City as peace officers trying to avoid gunplay, to Tombstone, when the famous gunfight in 1881 can be seen as the last gasp of violent lawlessness in a closing frontier as "civilization" took hold in the West.

But a more powerful reason is that the Tombstone story is so rich with colorful characters and delicious details . . . and exaggerations and outright fictions. Some have been included in previous versions, some have not. Each writer, whether it be of a nonfiction book or a screenplay, makes choices based on the research, material gathered, and sometimes personal biases. I wanted to tell *my* version of the Tombstone story, to have it refracted through my lens, and along the way provide new and previously overlooked characters and details.

That does not mean that in the pages to follow I simply winged it. A lot of sifting of material had to be done to present a version that is as accurate as possible. I was blessed with a wealth of material, topped by the works of several inspiring authors. Their books are cited in the text, but I want to give them extra credit here. One is Casey Tefertiller's indispensable biography of Wyatt Earp, another is Gary L. Roberts's engaging biography of Doc Holliday, and a third is Jeff Guinn's *The Last Gunfight*, the most comprehensive treatment of the Tombstone shoot-out that forever branded the Wild West.

I hope to have many opportunities to give *Tombstone* talks and meet readers . . . and this time, fingers crossed, the only reaction will be enthusiasm.

Prologue

On the morning of Sunday, March 26, 1882, a week after his brother Morgan had been murdered, Wyatt Earp gazed at the outskirts of Tombstone. He wondered if this was the day he would be saying good-bye to it forever. If so, good riddance. Years later, he would reflect on events during his two-plus years in Tombstone and say, "This was where a lifetime of troubles began."

There was no nostalgia for this already aging boomtown and now no hope for the future of making a life there. It was over, this Tombstone venture, the only time in his thirty-four years that he and Virgil and Morgan and James and their wives, and at times Warren, had all lived in the same town together. Well, that was done—Virgil crippled and in California, Morgan dead. Now, it was all about unfinished business.

The members of Wyatt's posse were saddled up and ready to go that morning when Harelip Charlie Smith rode out of Tombstone and joined them. The other members of Wyatt's posse were his younger brother Warren, Texas Jack Vermillion, Turkey Creek Jack

2 ★ TOM CLAVIN

Johnson, Sherman McMasters, and of course Doc Holliday. He did not know about the others, but Wyatt was sure that if more killing was to be done, Doc would be in on it. Until a few days ago, Doc had had a lot more experience at it.

There were plenty of people in and around Tombstone who were calling this posse illegal, that it was no more than a gang of vigilantes bent on executing instead of arresting. In recent years, Wyatt would have taken that as an insult to his honor. He had done his best at lawing. In fact, on that morning and since the day in December when Virgil had been ambushed, he was a deputy U.S. marshal, so appointed by U.S. Marshal Crawley Dake, who had the federal and legal authority to do so.

But there was another, overriding fact: he no longer cared about the technicalities. As Casey Tefertiller would state in his classic biography, "Wyatt Earp was making his own law."

The seven men rode northeast into the Dragoon Mountains. Somewhere out there, or behind them, or wherever they were, was Johnny Behan with his posse. The sheriff of Cochise County was looking not for the men who shot Morgan Earp but for the Earp posse, the ones who truly were going after the cowards who killed Morgan. Not that it mattered, because "wherever" was probably more like it. Most everybody knew that Sheriff Behan did not really want to catch up to Wyatt and his bunch because then he might actually have to try to arrest them. Possibly take a bullet for his trouble to boot. Behan would become just one more casualty of the so-called vendetta ride, joining Frank Stilwell, Indian Charlie Cruz, and Curly Bill Brocius in Hell, where they belonged.

Behan wore the badge, though. It didn't fit him too well, but he'd schemed and finagled and back-slapped and betrayed hard enough for it. If he sat safe in his office and didn't go after Earp's crew, even the few friends Johnny had left would turn against him. Irony was, if it had been cowboys Behan was after, he'd have quit looking by now and be facing a lot less grief. But there was that other motive: Wyatt had stolen his woman. When this was all over, the beautiful Josephine Marcus would be waiting for Wyatt, not that peacock of a sheriff. Johnny could be past tense in more ways than one, but maybe almost by accident he could wind up doing something about it.

In the Dragoons, Wyatt and Doc flagged down a westbound passenger train. The engineer at first might have feared a robbery, but the seven men were not wearing masks and as the train drew closer he recognized at least Wyatt and Doc. The engineer and the crew waited patiently as the two grit-covered men looked through the cars, probably making the passengers nervous—anywhere Doc was, people got nervous—but they had nothing to fear. It was true that they were searching for a man with money, but this was money friends in Tombstone wanted Wyatt to have. No such man existed on this train, however. Time to get back on the trail before it grew any colder.

Later in the day, the posse reached the ranch owned by Jim and Hugh Percy. It was customary in the more remote parts of the territory that when riders showed up, you fed them and their horses and gave them a place to sleep. Even adversaries put hostilities aside so as not to break the unwritten rule of frontier hospitality. But the Percy brothers were too frightened for that, what with all the killing lately.

As he spoke quietly to the ranch owners, Wyatt was unaware that Barney Riggs and Frank Hereford had secreted themselves in the barn. It was possible they contemplated an ambush, perhaps waiting to see if the posse would bed down for the night. However, it was unlikely the two men, one of whom had been deputized by Behan, would have been brave or foolish enough to take on the seven guests, especially with two of them being Wyatt Earp and Doc Holliday.

A few hours later, the posse rode on. Wyatt was disappointed but not angry with the Percys. Legitimate ranchers had a hard enough time with the cowboys, with all their cattle rustling and other stealing, and that wouldn't change even with Curly Bill taken off the map. Being seen as giving aid and comfort to the Earp posse would make things even warmer for the Percy boys. It might be different at the next destination, because the owner of the Sierra Bonita Ranch, Henry Clay Hooker, was of another stripe.

Hooker greeted Wyatt and the others with handshakes. His 250,000-acre ranch had been victimized repeatedly by the cattle-rustling cowboys, so any enemy of theirs was a friend of Hooker's, and he welcomed them into his spacious ranch house. Doc, especially, was surprised when Wyatt accepted the offer of a drink. Except for the very occasional small beer, his close friend's drink of choice since their Dodge City days had been coffee. Now, as Wyatt sat at Hooker's dinner table, he nursed a whiskey. To Doc and Warren, this was a clear indication of the stress Wyatt had been under since the week before when he had watched his younger brother die in a Tombstone billiards parlor. The visitors were given a good meal and beds for the night.

But Wyatt had underestimated Johnny Behan. While he and his companions slept, the sheriff and his own posse were on their way.

Behan had not suddenly gotten any braver. It was more that the election the following November had gotten another day closer. Being sheriff of the new Cochise County had brought with it many more headaches than he had anticipated, especially in the aftermath of the October 26 gunfight, but Behan wanted to keep the job. Letting Wyatt Earp and his party get clean away would not play well among voters—especially those who disliked the Earps, and they were the sheriff's core supporters.

So, on that same day that the federal posse had ridden northeast into the Dragoons, the county posse traveled the same route. With Johnny Behan were a collection of cowboys, including Johnny Ringo, who could very well shoot Wyatt Earp on sight; Phin and Ike Clanton, who had their own dead brother to avenge; and the undersheriff Harry Woods, whose newspaper, the *Tombstone Daily Nugget,* had been gleefully anti-Earp. They would eventually find their way to the Hooker ranch, whose name translated to "Beautiful Mountain." Before closing in on it, though, they bedded down and tried to sleep, planning on arriving at the ranch at first light.

Wyatt figured the smart way to think was not if Behan and his force would show up, but when. In the bright morning, the lanky deputy U.S. marshal sat with Henry Hooker to discuss courses of action. Sometimes the easiest was best, and that would be for Wyatt and Doc and whoever wanted to go along to ride east into New Mexico or south into Mexico. Either place, Behan had no jurisdiction. Everyone would live at least another day.

No surprise, however, that the easiest way was not Wyatt's way. He could not stomach the thought of the sheriff returning to Tombstone boasting he had booted Wyatt and Warren Earp and Doc Holliday and their equally well-armed friends out of Arizona. That would be too much of a victory for Johnny, and he did next to nothing to achieve it.

No more running. Wyatt told his host that he was not about to be chased off. Hooker offered to back him up, and the posse could make its stand right there at the easily defended ranch-house compound. Again, Wyatt shook his head. Any bloodshed on Hooker's property put the older man in serious legal jeopardy because he was aiding fugitives. Anyway, this wasn't Hooker's fight. Wyatt went outside and he and his men, their bags containing fresh supplies, mounted up and rode away from the compound.

Sheriff Behan just missed them. When his posse arrived, Hooker barely tolerated their presence and refused to answer questions about Wyatt's whereabouts. The Cochise County posse was left to its own devices to track their prey.

Wyatt and his men came to a halt about three miles away. He considered a bluff and the vantage point it offered. This was a better place than most to stand and fight. It would cost Behan dearly to get close. When he turned in the direction of the ranch compound to view it from atop the bluff, Wyatt could see the other posse leaving. He had to assume the sheriff was on his way to him.

The two Earp brothers, Doc Holliday, and the four other men took up good firing positions. Their rifles and their pistols were fully loaded. When Behan and his boys got close enough, bullets would fly. Wyatt had never been a man-killer, and it may have sickened him a bit that in the last few days he had begun to get the hang of it. He expected on this day to send more men to Hell . . . and maybe he would be joining them.

ACT I

THE TERRITORY

Hauling ore from mines, 1879.
(COURTESY OF ARIZONA HISTORICAL SOCIETY)

We fought one war with Mexico to take the Southwest. We should
fight another war to make them take it back.
—GENERAL WILLIAM TECUMSEH SHERMAN

Chapter One

---◆---

"MEN OF RESTLESS BLOOD"

hree years before that day in the Dragoon Mountains, in 1879,
Wyatt Earp had bade farewell to Dodge City. It had also been
time for Bat Masterson and Doc Holliday to move on from the
Kansas cattle hub that had been called the "wickedest town in the
American West." The three friends would reunite in Tombstone.

While Bat would not stay away from Dodge City long, in November of that year he had essentially been told it was time to leave.
Bat had been the sheriff of Ford County for the previous two years
and believed, with justification, that he had done a good job. Jim
Herron was a younger resident of Dodge City then, and years later,
after he himself had become a lawman in Oklahoma, he recalled,
"Bat Masterson was a splendid peace officer, never took it all too
seriously, and when it looked like there would be real trouble he
had what it took to stop it. He was a young man and seemed to get
all the fun out of living that he could."

Bat aimed to remain in the job for at least two more years . . . but
the voters did not endorse his plan. He was a popular man in some

circles, especially in the saloons, and had proved to be an effective sheriff. He and Wyatt were the best of friends and had worked well together at lawing, their efforts complemented by Charlie Bassett, Bat's brother Jim Masterson, and other city and county peace officers. But Bat had figured he would be reelected handily and had not campaigned, and thus on November 4 he learned he had figured wrong when the Ford County voters elected George Hinkle. Worse, it was not even close: Hinkle collected 404 votes to Bat's meager 268 votes.

To say he was irritated would be an understatement. R. B. Fry reported in *The Spearville News*, "We hear that Bat Masterson said he was going to whip every s__ of a b____ that worked and voted against him in the county." This was not true, and in fact in a letter to the editor published in *The Dodge City Times* the following week, Bat insisted the story was "as false and as flagrant a lie as was ever uttered."

However, he needed to get out of Dodge and breathe some fresh, apolitical air. After finishing up his few remaining responsibilities, Bat set out for Leadville, Colorado, trading in his badge for the gaming tables. He was confident he could make good money gambling.

Not that it would have mattered, but Bat did not get Wyatt's vote in that November 1879 election because Wyatt had already left. While he had never intended to make lawing a career, there had to be a few fond memories of the times when he, as an assistant marshal, and Bat, as a deputy marshal and then sheriff, were fast friends and still in their twenties and learning on the job, patrolling the Dodge City streets, having each other's backs. And being a lawman in the wildest of Kansas cow towns had been a generally good and certainly formative experience for Wyatt.

As Casey Tefertiller observed, Wyatt "had matured markedly from the boy who found himself in trouble in Indian Territory. He had become a most self-assured man who stoutly believed in right and wrong—and in his ability to determine which was which. He loved to be amused, yet almost never laughed; his dour countenance covered an air of supreme confidence in his ability to deal with just about any problem."

And there were plenty of problems to deal with during his time in Dodge City, thanks to the regular arrivals of thirsty and feisty cowboys finishing the long cattle drives up from Texas. There were times when Wyatt had to draw his six-shooter, but what made him an especially effective lawman was his ability to subdue trouble-makers without gunplay. He and Bat Masterson took the "peace" in "peace officer" literally and knew that the way to tame the notorious town was not to outkill the bad guys but to intimidate them, sometimes with the help of a gun barrel to the skull. By the end of the cattle-drive season in 1879, the local calaboose had fewer inhabitants and Boot Hill had become mostly obsolete.

Wyatt foresaw that if he remained in Dodge City, he would become bored. It was no longer all that wicked. He and Bassett and the Masterson brothers and a handful of others had done an effective-enough job the past several years that killings and robberies had become rare. Jailing inebriated cowboys did not make for a stimulating occupation. And there were fewer drunken drovers. Dodge City was no longer the capital of the cow trade, and the cow trade itself was dwindling. Many cowboys were moving on to New Mexico Territory.

This presented Wyatt with a couple of immediate challenges. One was with less lawing to do, his income would dwindle, too. The other was leading a life too uninspiring for an active and ambitious thirty-one-year-old man. "Dodge City," Wyatt said, "was beginning to lose much of its snap which had given it a charm to men of restless blood."

But where was the next frontier for such men? For Wyatt, Arizona beckoned. His brother Virgil was already living there with his wife, Allie, and he had written letters about the territory, extolling its virtues. One of them reported that the area was booming. Gold and silver strikes were attracting new settlers and businesses. The southeast corner of Arizona had become a magnet for those looking to get rich quick or who saw a longer future as business and family men.

Wyatt was not looking for a town to raise a family in. He had come close to that once. Two months shy of his twenty-second birthday, and with his father, Nicholas, performing the ceremony, Wyatt had married Aurilla Sutherland in Lamar, Missouri. She soon became pregnant and he bought property with a house on it to be their home, at least until the family grew out of it. Wyatt became a town constable in Lamar, where both parents and at least four siblings also lived. But late in her pregnancy Aurilla, barely out of her teens, died, probably from cholera, and the baby did not survive.

A grieving Wyatt began wandering, getting into trouble along the way. Tefertiller's reference to Indian Territory is that was where Wyatt was arrested for stealing a horse, which, until the immediate aftermath of the Tombstone gunfight, was the most serious charge brought against him. He avoided dire punishment—some accounts have Wyatt busting out of an Arkansas jail with several other prisoners—but being locked up for a long stretch seemed in the cards for this angry young man.

Wichita was a shot at redemption for him. James and Bessie

Earp, his brother and sister-in-law, operated a brothel there, and in 1874 it was as good a city as any to stop and earn a few dollars before moving on. Wichita became more than that, though. Wyatt was appointed a part-time assistant marshal and his skills at fist-fighting and "buffaloing" plus a cold, intimidating gaze went a long way toward keeping the peace.* He also met his second and third "wives," Sarah Haspel and Mattie Blaylock, during this time, so he earned a measure of domestic peace, too, though the situation would become less peaceful and more complicated.

When a new administration in Dodge City reached out to Wyatt in 1876, he was ready to put Wichita behind him. He would be given a steady salary as assistant to the corpulent marshal Lawrence Deger, who much preferred to ride a desk than a horse (a choice the local horses appreciated). Wyatt saw himself as least as much a gambler as a lawman, and thus the gaming tables in the saloons in the booming Dodge City offered the opportunity for bigger earnings.

Three years and a few deaths later—with Wyatt probably being responsible for just one of them, the cowboy George Hoy—it was time to move on from Dodge City. He had been told there was money to be made in Arizona. Wyatt was done with lawing. He was about to become a full-time businessman, and he expected to be successful at it . . . even though he hadn't found success in similar pursuits so far.

Wyatt had gotten from his father the desire to be successful

---

* "Buffaloing" entailed drawing a gun and cracking a man atop the head with the barrel of it. Wyatt, taller than most men and with strong hands, was a particularly effective practitioner of this skill, which helped him subdue rather than shoot someone who was misbehaving.

and make money. And like Nicholas Earp, Wyatt had not managed to do that. Once he had established himself in Dodge City, Wyatt had given a couple of side jobs a try. During winters when there were no cattle drives entering blizzard-strewn Kansas, he had headed into the Dakotas to gamble; however, while he was pretty good at it, especially faro, lightning did not strike. He had also given bounty hunting a try. Again, it was a lot of traveling for not much gain, other than during one pursuit in Texas when he found a man who was going to become a steadfast friend: Doc Holliday.

The allure of Arizona was, according to Virgil, that it was fertile ground for those looking for a fresh start and infused with an entrepreneurial spirit. An added incentive for Wyatt to move on was that the Dodge City Council, citing reduced income during the 1878–1879 off-season, lowered the salaries of the peace officers. Clearly, this was an occupation with high risk and little reward.

He wouldn't be going it alone in the Southwest. There was Mattie. She had been born Celia Ann Blaylock in Iowa in 1850 and raised on a farm. This apparently was not a stimulating enough environment, because sometime during her teenage years she and her younger sister, Sarah, ran away. Sarah returned, but Celia Ann did not.

How she made her way in the world is not known, but it is known that by the time she was twenty-one she was living in Fort Scott, Kansas, because a photograph of her was taken there. It is believed that it was in Fort Scott that she first encountered Wyatt Earp. Celia Ann was by then known as Mattie, which implies that she may have hidden her real name because she worked as a prostitute. "Some women willingly turned to prostitution because they earned quick money and retired into a comfortable life," writes

Sherry Monahan in *Mrs. Earp*. "Others became prostitutes because they needed to eat."

Conceivably, by the time Wyatt was fixing to leave Dodge City, he and Mattie had been together for eight years. Whether she wanted to pick up and move did not matter. She was dependent on Wyatt for financial security and she had to go where he went. And especially in the case of the Earps, their women went along, like it or not. Allie would experience this when the time came for her and Virgil to leave a comfortable life in Prescott, Arizona, and head south to Tombstone.

It would be there where the most Earps would be together since the Lamar days. Virgil waited, Wyatt was winding up his duties in Dodge City, James and his wife, Bessie, would go along, young Warren would probably show up as he always did so other Earps would feed and shelter him, and Morgan must have been mighty tired of cold and remote Montana by now. Accepting the inevitable, Mattie packed up her belongings, which by then may have included bottles of laudanum, to which she would soon be addicted.

For John Henry Holliday, the decision to leave Dodge City had to be a wrenching one, because it meant leaving Wyatt behind. By the time Wyatt and Mattie were loading up a wagon, Doc had already hit the trail. After its initial promise, he had found Dodge City an inhospitable environment and gotten out before he was thrown out.

Clear evidence of the "taming" of the city had come in August 1878, when lawmakers banned both gambling and prostitution. The latter did not matter much to Doc, but it may have curbed an occasional source of income for his companion, "Big Nose" Kate Elder.

She had been born Mary Katherine Harony, the first of seven children, in Hungary in November 1850. Ten years later, the Haronys immigrated to the United States, finding a welcoming Hungarian community in Davenport, Iowa. At age sixteen, after both parents had died, Mary Katherine ran away from the family who had taken her and her siblings in. Renamed Kate Fisher, she was living with other prostitutes in a house in St. Louis by the time she was nineteen.

It was there that she first met the young dentist who had grown up in a somewhat aristocratic family in Georgia. Her dalliance with Holliday did not last long, and when he returned home she made her way west. It is believed that Wyatt first met Kate—soon to change her name again, this time to Kate Elder—when she worked with or for Bessie Earp in Wichita.

Kate drifted in and out of the life of a "soiled dove," as such women were often called, and then reunited with Doc Holliday, whose bouts with lung ailments had forced him west. With Kate's help, he had barely escaped being lynched in Griffin, Texas—where he had first met the moonlighting bounty hunter Wyatt Earp—and they had fled to Dodge City. The imposition of the restrictive ordinances, especially the one outlawing gambling, in 1878 resulted in Doc and Kate trying to find a more accommodating town.

By this time, being twenty-seven years old and sickly, Doc was past any hope of making a living as a dentist. He would not have been able to stand it as a full-time occupation anyway. Gambling was Doc's life, that was his "snap," and life was no good without it. He had pretty much worn out his welcome there as far as others were concerned. From time to time he had been accused of cheating at cards and insulting citizens and even burglary, though not to his face. Especially when drunk, which was often, Doc had a hair-trigger temper and was quick to go for his gun. The body count attributed to Doc Holliday would have been higher, except he was not a very good shot. Even at close range he could miss a target, and, amazingly, opponents had failed to dispatch him, too. And Doc was not one to mind much what people thought of him. He was a disagreeable and unlikable and dangerous man, but as long as Wyatt had his back, he could get along.

The tipping point for Doc, as if the gambling ban were not enough, was his worsening health. He had initially been spurred west by medical advice that a warm, dry climate could extend his life. But north Texas and Kansas were not warm and dry enough, especially in the winter and spring. Rain and bitterly cold winds and blizzards sweeping across the prairie were not for the faint of heart or the faint of lung.

In his thorough biography, Gary L. Roberts suggests that while in Dodge City, "Doc was moving into the 'second phase' of consumption in the inhospitable climate of Kansas. His voice began to develop a deep hoarseness as a result of throat ulcers that would periodically make it difficult for him to speak above a whisper or to eat. His cough became more severe, constant, and debilitating, producing a thick dark mucus of greenish hue with yellow streaks and laced with pus."

Even if townsfolk had liked Doc, few would have wanted to be in his presence given his gruesome illness. Lingering in Dodge City was most likely a death sentence and, according to Roberts, "the hollow rattle of Doc's cough and the frequent pallor of his face suggested that his condition was worsening as the fall snows began to blanket Dodge City."

He and Big Nose Kate traveled west.* The trip so wearied Doc that they had to stop in Trinidad, Colorado, until he had regained some strength. They climbed into a train and took it south to New Mexico, disembarking only when the railroad ran out of track. The couple joined a freight wagon train that shuddered and shook its way over the rough and dusty roads to Las Vegas.†

During the war with Mexico in the 1840s, an army hospital had been built in nearby Gallinas Canyon, and in 1878 it was the Old Adobe House, a treatment center for people with ailments like Doc's. During that winter he took advantage of the hot springs and his health improved to the point that he could resume gambling and even have a few dentistry patients. However, reform movements were on his tail, and New Mexico Territory lawmakers also issued a ban on gambling. Of all things, Doc, with renewed energy, returned to Dodge City, where he was recruited by Bat Masterson to fight in the Royal Gorge War in Colorado.

It didn't turn out to be much of a war, but Doc was paid and he and Bat were able to enjoy another adventure and to some extent each other's company. Doc returned to New Mexico, and for the next several months he gambled, got arrested for it, shot and killed at least one man, drank and fought and fought and drank

---

* Kate did not have a particularly large nose. She probably acquired the nickname during her "soiled dove" days. Most women used fake names and kept them simple for the cowboys, like Alice or Sally or Kate. Inevitably, there were many women with such names, and even a slightly noticeable feature was seized upon. One was Big Nose Kate, and another Dodge City resident was Squirrel Tooth Alice.
† This town in New Mexico had been founded in 1835 and prospered as a stop on the Santa Fe Trail. The Las Vegas more well-known today, in Nevada, was in the late 1870s known as "Las Vegas Rancho," where the entrepreneur Octavius Gass made wine that he sold to thirsty travelers on the Old Spanish Trail.

with Kate, reportedly had dinner with Frank and Jesse James at the Las Vegas Hotel, and was falsely connected to a stagecoach robbery. Doc Holliday did not have to find trouble, it found him wherever he was.

In September 1879, Wyatt Earp found him, too (again). He had officially resigned as assistant marshal and set off for Arizona with Mattie, James, and Bessie. As many such travelers did, they stopped off in Las Vegas. One day Doc was crossing the plaza there and found the tall and lean Wyatt wearing one of his rare smiles.

His explanation to Doc was probably the same as what he later told an interviewer: "I decided to move to Tombstone, which was just building up a reputation."

Wyatt Earp, the reluctant lawman, could not have imagined how much he would contribute to the establishment of that frontier town's most enduring reputation.

Chapter Two

"SUNLIGHT INTO OUR HEARTS"

The reputation of Tombstone that exists to this day as the epicenter of the Wild West was established on October 26, 1881. However, the forces and events that characterized Tombstone began centuries before, when the region was first explored, and later during the early days of the Arizona Territory.

The story of the initial exploration of North America has tended to favor the voyages of Christopher Columbus, the subsequent European "discoveries" along the Atlantic and Caribbean coastlines, and early settlements. However, as the western historian Odie B. Faulk points out, "The Southwest has a long history, for Spanish explorers were crossing the region less than four decades after Columbus discovered America, many decades before the East Coast of the United States was opened. The Spanish empire had planted permanent outposts here well before Jamestown and Plymouth Bay were colonized."

In 1519, more than a century before the Pilgrims landed in

Plymouth, Massachusetts, Alonso Álvarez de Pineda and his four ships sailed around Florida into the Gulf of Mexico and on to Mexico, stopping along the way at the mouth of the Rio Grande to name it "River of Palms." Eight years later, Álvar Nuñez Cabeza de Vaca was a high-profile member of the first significant exploration of the Southwest, and, thankfully, he kept a journal of his adventures.

Cabeza de Vaca—which, unfortunately for the courageous nobleman, translates to "Head of Cow"—was by 1527 an experienced military officer. He had participated in Spain's conquest of the Canary Islands, fought in Italy and Navarre, and earned several medals of honor. He was thirty-seven when he served as treasurer and marshal of an expedition that began in Florida and was led by the conquistador Pánfilo de Narváez. It seems not all his men shared the leader's explorer spirit, because when Narváez's five ships stopped on Hispaniola for supplies, 150 of them refused to leave the island.

This was but the first of many setbacks. The next stop was Cuba to find more men and supplies, and there the small fleet was hit by a hurricane, resulting in two ships sunk and more men lost. The following April, the Narváez expedition finally made it around Florida and up to present-day St. Petersburg. There they heard of a city named Apalachen filled with food and gold. Since they needed one and desired the other, off they went. Thus began what must have seemed an endless saga that involved trudging through swamps, fending off harassing Indians and insects, encountering and destroying villages and stores of food, slaughtering and eating their own horses, and a litany of demoralizing deprivations.

Accepting at last that there was no gold to be discovered, what

was left of the expedition constructed five primitive boats in hopes
of sailing to Mexico. The small flotilla, with fifty men per boat,
hugged the coast of present-day Florida, Alabama, and Louisiana.
Upon arriving at the mouth of the Mississippi River, the boats were
pushed out into the Gulf of Mexico, where they were struck by yet
another hurricane. One of the lives lost was that of Narváez, surely
one of the unluckiest of New World explorers. Cabeza de Vaca took
command of the two boats and eighty men left. They took refuge on
what is now Galveston Island, which the new inhabitants presciently
named Malhado, or "Island of Doom." Winter set in, and when it
was over Cabeza de Vaca's command was reduced to fifteen men.
Some good news was they were found by a band of Indians who provided food; the bad news was they became the Indians' slaves.

After at least a year of harsh living, the indefatigable Cabeza de
Vaca and three other men escaped. Incredibly, the thirst for exploration had not been quenched by their nightmarish experiences.
They traveled through Texas, northeastern Mexico, and parts of
New Mexico and Arizona to the Gulf of California coast. During this eight-year trek, they lived for periods of time with Indian
tribes, eating their foods and adhering to their practices and rituals.
Eventually, after hiking south and east, Cabeza de Vaca's party
reached Mexico City. From there, in 1537, he sailed back to Spain.*

Next up in the rotation of Spanish gold seekers and would-be
conquerors was Francisco Vásquez de Coronado. He had arrived in

------

* The undaunted Cabeza de Vaca would set sail for the Americas again in 1540,
becoming an official in Spain's colonies in South America. He undertook new
explorations, which allowed him to encounter many wonders and indigenous
peoples, but he remained unable to stumble upon a cache of gold. He died in
Seville, Spain, in 1560.

the New World in 1535 and enhanced his prospects by marrying into a wealthy family in Mexico. This helped him to underwrite the largest land expedition so far in that colony, which stepped off in February 1540 with 336 men led by Coronado wearing gilded armor. From Compostela they traveled to Culiacán and then to Sonora and into Arizona. That July, the expedition was met by Indians who did not welcome the interlopers, and a furious battle ensued. After defeating them and gaining a pledge of obedience to the Spanish crown, Coronado moved on. He sent a smaller expedition on a side trip to verify a rumor of gold, and those men wound up being the first Europeans to visit the Grand Canyon.

The larger expedition continued to roam about, and by March 1541 Coronado was in west Texas, killing buffalo and enduring a journey through what would become known as the Staked Plains. Subsequent searches for that elusive reservoir of gold brought Coronado as far to the east and north as present-day Wichita, Kansas. By the summer of 1542, after suffering such painful indignities as a broken arm and being trampled by a horse, the unsuccessful treasure seeker was in Mexico City.

There were other, smaller expeditions by Spanish military and civilian leaders into the Southwest, but the region was not judged very hospitable. Most important, no precious metals were there to be easily found. Instead, it was religion that led to the establishment of the first enduring European settlements, especially the journeys of Father Eusebio Francisco Kino.

He first appeared in Arizona in 1691, ministering to and converting Indians and founding missions. His ongoing travels brought him as far north as Colorado at least twice, and the maps he created were welcomed back in Spain. Those rudimentary but enlightening documents, plus his writings and assurances of a large number of pacified Indians, made the Southwest more appealing to Spanish colonizers and other settlers. The region became a prominent part of the expanding Spanish Empire. The tens of thousands of Indians who lived in the area were only a minor inconvenience, except when friction flared. Even then, as European weapons became more sophisticated and deadly, natives ended up on the short end of the gun barrel.

As decades passed, the tribes learned that survival depended on geography. In southeast Arizona, the aboriginal inhabitants knew every hill and gully, crevice and cave entrance, mountain range and stream. They knew the wildlife and what roots and plants were edible. Crucial to their survival and eventually that of Tombstone was the Dragoon Mountains.

Not very tall compared with more well-known mountain ranges in the Southwest, the Dragoon Mountains are seven thousand feet at their highest point, and they extend northwest for thirty miles. Folding and faulting created the passes in the mountain range. It was through one of these passes that the Southern Pacific Railroad laid down tracks in 1880. By then the range was named, because fourteen years earlier a troop of U.S. dragoons had ridden through, and that was apparently good enough for a name to use by those who came after.

According to Lynn Bailey, "It was Cochise who endowed the Dragoons with an almost mythical quality." She reports in her book on the range, "Every foot of the range bears evidence of native Americans. Petroglyphs and pictographs decorate rock slabs. Prehistoric villages mark canyon entrances. There are even ancient turquoise mines. At a later date the range was a favorite hunting and gathering locale for the Chiricahua Apaches."

It is not far-fetched to think that if there had not been a completely unexpected silver strike in the area, there never would have been a town called Tombstone. The harsh terrain and climate and its proximity to a foreign country—just thirty miles to the Mexican border—would not have appealed to settlers such as ranchers and especially farmers. And without them, there would not have been businesses opening, not even a saloon. Putting an exclamation point to the unlikelihood of settlements was the presence of the Chiricahua Apache.

It is believed Apache Indians first arrived in and around the Dragoon Mountains in the late 1500s or early 1600s. If the earlier estimate is correct, they would have encountered, or at least observed, those Spanish expeditions that first explored Arizona and New Mexico and beyond.

For the most part, the Spanish expedition leaders had not been foolish enough to try to engage the Chiricahua Apache in battle. The Dragoon Mountain Range was a natural stronghold. The Apache certainly could not be surprised, because any intruders could be spotted while still a day's march away. Even if such a force approached unmolested, once they got into the range it was easy for the Chiricahua to rain arrows and spears down on it from a higher elevation, or they could choose to hide out beyond the ability of pursuers to catch up to them.

The Apache had another big advantage: leadership. Well before, during, and after the establishment of Tombstone, the tribe was led by three strong men who reluctantly made southeast Arizona a bloody battleground to maintain their land and way of life.

The first was Mangas Coloradas. Born sometime around the turn of the nineteenth century, the six-foot-four-inch, 250-pound Chiricahua, known as Red Sleeves because of his colorful shirts, was obviously a physically imposing man. One army officer described him as "a truly striking figure with a hulking body and dispropor-tionately large head [and] possessing a cunning as impenetrable as the thick mat of hair that hung down to his waist." He was also a fierce fighter in the tradition of his tribal predecessors, who had been raiding and battling the Spanish Mexicans since Francisco Vásquez de Coronado's expedition.

By the mid-1800s, Coloradas's name struck fear among the "White Eyes." One explorer claimed that he was responsible for "the most atrocious cruelties, the most vindictive revenges, and wide-spread injuries ever perpetrated by an American Indian." Coloradas had gone to great lengths to unify the various Apache denomina-tions. Eventually, however, eleven years of raids, skirmishes, and battles against enemies on both sides of the border proved too costly a burden for Coloradas.

He was recovering from a bullet wound one morning in early 1863 when he called a tribal council to announce his plan to request a peace parley with U.S. military leaders under a flag of truce. Instead of meeting Coloradas on the promised terms, however, his American hosts betrayed him. He was chained and locked in a guardhouse. That night the army officer overseeing Coloradas's "surrender," Gen-eral Joseph Rodman West, left no doubt as to his intentions. The general told the sentries guarding Coloradas, "Men, that murderer has got away from every soldier command and has left a trail of blood for five hundred miles on the old stage line. I want him dead tomor-row morning. Do you understand? I want him dead."

Coloradas, sensing the inevitable, accepted his fate stoically. After being goaded with red-hot bayonets, he finally attacked his persecutors. This gave the sentries the excuse they needed. Colo-radas was shot and killed "trying to escape," as official U.S. Army logs put it. His corpse was then beheaded and boiled and his skull shipped to a New York City phrenologist for study.*

As can be imagined, this did not sit well with Coloradas's son-in-law Cochise, who somewhat reluctantly inherited his war bonnet. Despite the fact that the man believed to be his father, Pisago Cabezon, who had several wives and thirteen children, was killed by scalp hunters in 1845, Cochise was not keen on war with the white soldiers. This should not imply he lacked courage.

A handsome man with deep-set eyes and sharp cheekbones, Cochise from boyhood had eagerly participated in raids and skirmishes against the Mexicans. But having personally witnessed the overwhelming strength and weaponry of the Americans during a brief stint working as a woodcutter for the Butterfield Overland Mail Company,† Cochise considered resistance against this new, powerful enemy self-defeating. But even before the death of Mangas Coloradas, he had been provoked. One day in 1861, after a separate band of Apache cattle rustlers kidnapped the child of a white rancher, an American cavalry detail arrested Cochise and his wife and two children, as well as his brother Coyuntura and Coyuntura's two sons. It was soon apparent why Cochise's Indian name translated to "Strong as Oak."

---

* It is believed that the skull of the Apache warrior, after being put on display, wound up in the Smithsonian Institution. However, to this day searches for it there have been unsuccessful.

† John Butterfield was the owner of express companies in New York State. His entry to the American West was signing a six-year contract worth $600,000 with the U.S. postmaster general to provide mail service between St. Louis and San Francisco. One of Butterfield's other achievements was cofounding the American Express Company.

While being questioned in an army tent, he attacked and subdued his interrogators, grabbed a knife, and hacked his way through the thick canvas. Though shot three times during the struggle, Cochise managed to escape—a feat still remembered by the Chiricahua warrior's descendants, who refer to it as the "Cut the Tent" incident. Not waiting to recover from his wounds, Cochise retaliated immediately by organizing a raid during which he captured a dozen Mexican and American teamsters. He killed the Mexicans but offered the white men to the twenty-five-year-old lieutenant George Bascom in exchange for his incarcerated family.

Instead, in what notoriously became known as the Bascom Affair, the green lieutenant ignored the advice of a veteran Indian-fighting sergeant to make the trade. His response instead was to hang Cochise's brother and his two nephews. This sealed Cochise's destiny. He joined his father-in-law's resistance, and upon Coloradas's murder, though still respecting the firepower and growing number of white soldiers, he took over as leader.

To add insult to injury, before being recalled to Washington for bungling the Cochise incident and intensifying the Apache wars, the preening Bascom ordered the court-martial of the sergeant who advised him against killing the war chief's family. Cochise may have had the satisfaction of learning of Bascom's death from a Confederate bullet a year later.

Meanwhile, much as on the Northern Plains, by 1861 the American Civil War had siphoned regular Union army troops from the southwest territories. Unlike in Sioux and Cheyenne country, however, that void was quickly filled by a force of three thousand volunteer California militiamen ostensibly sent to the area to repel a Confederate invasion. But as the rebels never mounted any serious incursions, the Californians took to hunting Cochise and his Apaches. Over the next decade, a furious Cochise and his warriors raided throughout the region, using the near-impenetrable Dragoon Mountains as their base.

During the few occasions that Cochise encountered white people, they were impressed by his clarity and gravitas. "You must speak straight so that your words may go as sunlight into our hearts," he once told an Indian agent. "Speak, Americans. I will not lie to you; so do not lie to me."

Despite his eloquence, however, the attacks orchestrated by Cochise were both violent and effective. "I have killed ten white men for every Indian slain," he taunted one American frontier commander through an intermediary, and he was not far off. The War Department had assigned a series of incompetent and venal officers to hunt down Cochise, but by 1871, frustrated by the Apache's continued success, it called on the Civil War veteran George Crook to assume command of the Department of Arizona. Colonel Crook was one of the many Union generals who had to make do with a lower rank after the war.

At forty-one years old, Crook was a man with something to prove. With the Civil War concluded, opportunities for American officers seeking military honors were thinning. Crook's appointment immediately created intramural enemies throughout the army, not least because he had bounded over several superior officers with this new assignment. His peers sniped that he had graduated West Point ranked only thirty-eighth in his class of forty-three, and even General William Tecumseh Sherman opposed Crook's appointment. But he had caught President Ulysses S. Grant's eye with his steady if unspectacular leadership during the War Between the

States and was also close to General Phil Sheridan, which included agreeing with the latter's assessment that the only good Indians were dead Indians.

A seasoned fighter with pronounced idiosyncrasies, Crook preferred civilian clothes to his uniform, insisted on riding a mule instead of a horse, and was so conservative with his speech that some soldiers initially wondered if he was mute. All this, however, was balanced by his respect for his Indian adversaries' fighting abilities, a trait infrequently shared among the army's racist officers' ranks.

Crook was also a man respectful of the army's chain of command. His Apache campaign was interrupted early on by the unexpected arrival of General Oliver Otis Howard, who outranked Crook by one star. Though Howard had been awarded the Medal of Honor for actions during a battle in the opening months of the Civil War in which he lost his right arm, he was best known for the humiliating defeats he suffered at Chancellorsville and Gettysburg that had earned him the nickname "Uh-Oh Howard." Also referred to as the "Christian General" because of a belief that military campaigns should be conducted in accordance with his fundamentalist religious piety, Howard ordered Crook to suspend his hunt for Cochise so that he might personally find him and, calling down the word of God, convince the Apache leader to surrender.

As Crook looked on in astonishment, Howard set off into the wilderness accompanied by Lieutenant Joseph Sladen and a small party of guides and interpreters, one of them being Tom Jeffords. After weeks of traveling and negotiating with various Cochise emissaries, the group was allowed to visit Cochise's base in the mountains. Upon meeting the famed Chiricahua, Howard fell to his knees and began praying as loud as he could. Believing that this strange white man was summoning some sort of evil medicine, several of the Apache warriors jumped on their horses and scattered. Cochise himself was more amused than cowed.

The devout general, presuming his deliverance was an act of Providence, reported to Crook that he had parleyed a peace treaty. And he turned out to be correct. As Jeffords wrote about Howard, "I doubt if there is any person that could have been sent here that could have performed the mission as well; certainly none could have performed it better." Howard returned east but would later be involved in fighting Indians, this time the Nez Percé, which resulted in the surrender of Chief Joseph.

Cochise had become painfully aware that despite his ten-to-one arithmetic, the influx of whites into the territories would soon overwhelm his people. When he surrendered in 1872, he said, "No one wants peace more than I do. Why shut me up on a reservation? We will make peace; we will keep it faithfully. But let us go around free as Americans do. Let us go wherever we please."

Naturally, Cochise's plea fell on deaf ears. He was forced to retire on a reservation. He died there, probably from stomach cancer, two years later. He was buried in the rocks above one of his favorite mountain strongholds, with only his immediate family and Jeffords aware of the location of his final resting place, a secret they took to their own graves.

If Cochise sensed the futility of doing battle with the white invaders from his earliest days, his successor, Geronimo, never recovered from the inner rage fired by the murders of his family. Sometime during 1858, an unprovoked attack launched the twenty-nine-year-old Apache into a lifetime of war. While he and others were gathering supplies in Janos—a town just down the road from what would become the Mormon colony of Colonia Dublán—a company of four hundred Mexican soldiers attacked their unguarded encampment. Recounting the raid in his 1905 autobiography, Geronimo wrote, "When all were counted, I found that my aged mother, my young wife, and my three small children were among the slain." More than one hundred Apache women and children were killed, but only Geronimo's family was destroyed so thoroughly.

Geronimo had ridden and battled side by side with Cochise, though the two men had different fighting styles—Cochise was a blunt force, Geronimo was a guerrilla tactician. Upon Cochise's death, the younger man assumed the lead role in what would be the last act of Apache resistance.

Of the many grievances the Apache had, a major one was that four years after the treaty Cochise had agreed to, the tribe was forced off its familiar land designated as a Chiricahua-only reservation and ordered to be relocated to the San Carlos Reservation, 175 miles due north. There they would encounter an Indian agent named John Clum. As will soon be related, he would not only play a significant role in the early days of Tombstone and the lives of the Earp brothers, but represent a type of adventurous and enterprising young white man who in the years after the Civil War was moving into the promising new territory of Arizona.

Chapter Three

"I'LL GET EVERY SON OF A BITCH"

The U.S. Army and officers such as George Crook and Otis Howard would not have risked their men and stretched their military district's thin budget on lower Arizona if it had not begun to attract settlers after the Civil War. The handful of soldiers and prospectors and railroad visionaries who traveled through what was then the New Mexico Territory between Texas and southern California found a land that had changed little from the days of the Spanish explorers.

Much of the topography was dry, flat land, and when the wind picked up, dust clouds were a common sight. Water was often scarce; however, when it rained, it rained hard, especially during monsoon season. As the Arizona historian Richard Shelton notes in his memoir, *Going Back to Bisbee*, storms "are usually brief, violent, and incredibly dramatic, with enough thunder, lightning, and hard-driven rain to make life exciting, even precarious. After the clouds build up into great white cathedrals, the desert turns suddenly dark and still. The light is dim, green, and eerie. Everything seems to be holding its breath, waiting. The air becomes languid, palpable with humidity. Low thunder begins to roll around in the distance. . . . Then somebody up there starts flipping light switches."

American soldiers and early visitors had little protection from the ensuing deluge and flash flooding. One saving grace of a storm's intensity was its brevity and aftereffects. Shelton reports that "a half hour after the first real clap of thunder, the storm is usually over, leaving the desert bedraggled but the air soft and aromatic with the smell of wet greasewood."

Traveling when it was not monsoon season typically meant mile after mile of thirsty slogging for man and beast. The ones who were not prepared for such a vast and arid landscape perished, their white bones to be found months afterward by the next batch of adventurers. Mostly, southern Arizona was much more suitable for the hardiest of creatures, such as spiders. And of the spiders, perhaps most feared was the tarantula. It had a bad reputation because in the Italian seaport town of Taranto in the sixteenth century, residents suffered repeated bouts of a disease that produced a form of frenzy. What was named "tarantism" was believed to be from the bite of a particularly ugly spider. The inaccurate perception persisted into twentieth-century Arizona. Worse, it was viewed as a deadly enemy of humans, even though the fact is a tarantula rarely bites, and if it does, the bite is no more fatal than a bee sting.

So, the New Mexico Territory was not the most appealing place to explore, let alone settle and raise a family, but what it had going for it was that the vast territory connected California to the rest of the country and thus was caught up in the Manifest Destiny migration west. The pace of this picked up in the Gold Rush of 1849 after the discovery made in California the previous year. The

New Mexico Territory was not the best way to get to Sutter Creek and its immediate surroundings, but inevitably, more people came through.

To help them along the way, some influential business-oriented individuals envisioned a railroad that would link the southern states with California and its ports, and it could carry passengers in addition to freight. One of those men was Jefferson Davis. The future president of the Confederate states was the secretary of war in the administration of President Franklin Pierce, who had been elected in 1852.* Davis advocated that the time had come to take a big chunk of the Southwest off Mexico's hands. Pierce listened and negotiations between his administration and that of President Antonio Lopez de Santa Anna began.†

The result was the Gadsden Purchase, so named because James Gadsden, the U.S. ambassador to Mexico, signed the treaty on December 30, 1853. When it took effect the following June, Mexico received $10 million for the southwest corner of New Mexico and the lower third of Arizona. Having fared poorly in the war that

---

* Among the many peculiarities about Franklin Pierce as a man and a president, such as being a New Hampshire lawmaker against abolition, was that his vice president, William King, died only a month after being sworn in, and during his four years in office Pierce did not replace him because the Constitution did not require that he do so. If, say, Pierce had died in office in December 1854, almost midway through his term, the southerner Linn Boyd, of Kentucky, the Speaker of the House, would have become president.

† Yes, the same Santa Anna who had wiped out Davy Crockett, Jim Bowie, and other supporters of Texas independence at the Alamo in 1836. Despite essentially losing Texas at the Battle of San Jacinto that same year and the Mexican-American War in the 1840s, and the volatility of Mexican politics through much of the 1800s, Santa Anna remained in power into 1855 and died a month before his eighty-second birthday in Mexico City.

had ended five years earlier, Santa Anna apparently concluded it was better to sell off land than wait for it to be taken. The Gadsden Purchase was the last land acquisition of its size or larger in the Lower 48 states. And it completed what became the permanent border with Mexico.* Now it was time to fill in the gaps in the southwest population map.

Settlers did not come flocking to the region, and the proposed railroad was snail slow to be built, especially as the South inched toward the Civil War. However, strikes of precious ore west of the Missouri River reawakened the interest of prospectors and others seeking to get rich quick anywhere in the West. The first big one that had many people strapping on picks and shovels was the Pike's Peak Gold Rush, which got under way in 1858. This was before there was a designated Colorado Territory, so Pike's Peak—named after the intrepid early-nineteenth-century explorer Zebulon Pike—was actually in western Kansas Territory or southwestern Nebraska Territory. Prospectors were not particular about what territory it was in. "Pike's Peak or Bust!" became the motto of those heading toward the hills that, more precisely, were eighty-five miles north of the landmark mountain.

The next strike to turn more attention on the American West was the Comstock Lode, in 1859. A large lode of silver ore was found on the eastern slope of Mount Davidson in the Virginia Range of Nevada, then part of Utah Territory. The miner Henry

---

* The Mexican garrison at Tucson was the only military outpost in the area, and its troops did not leave until March 1856. Residents actually begged them to stay longer rather than leave them without protection from Apache raiders.

Comstock gave his name to what would be the first major discovery of silver ore in the United States.*

Predictably, once the discovery was made, news traveled fast and a new rush west was on, the most intense one since the California Gold Rush. More than a few fortunes were made by those who staked the better claims and did so quickly. The Comstock Lode was also notable—and would have a direct impact on Tombstone— for the advances in mining technology it inspired, among them square-set timbering and the Washoe method of extracting silver from ore.

For the most part, the Comstock Lode was played out by 1874. However, at first blush it had excited the national imagination and encouraged the belief that there were similar discoveries to be made in the American West.

Far from the Washington, D.C., and Richmond, Virginia, corridor, the New Mexico Territory was not terribly interested in the Civil War. Much of the territory was abandoned by federal troops, making residents more vulnerable to Apache raids. The timing could not have been worse, because of the Bascom Affair, detailed in the previous chapter. With Cochise's thirst for revenge at its peak, 1861 was not a good year to have federal

---

* The lode named after Comstock turned out to be sadly ironic because the eccentric prospector was not a successful man and the discovery did not make him rich. Fellow prospectors called him "Old Pancake" because he could not be bothered to bake bread. One of his idiosyncrasies was never leaving the house for any occasion unless he was wearing at least seven belts. Comstock came into knowledge of the enormous silver lode that is named after him but sold out his interest too early to reap its riches. He later worked as a surveyor and miner, again failing to make his fortune. He shot himself and died on September 27, 1870, near Bozeman, Montana.

troops withdraw. And eventually, the Confederacy did control a portion of Arizona.

The reaction in Washington, D.C., was to separate Arizona from New Mexico. Arizona became its own territory on February 24, 1863, when President Abraham Lincoln signed the bill passed by Congress. As the war ground on in the East, it was comparatively calm in the Southwest. When it was over in the spring of 1865, military attention could finally turn to eliminating the ongoing threats from Apaches.

Soon, though, there would be enough white people in the New Mexico and Arizona Territories that they could fight among themselves. Perhaps the most well-known conflict, one that would have an impact years later on Tombstone, was known as the Lincoln County War. In the early 1870s, that New Mexico county was the largest one in the United States, covering 20 percent of the territory. The only store that mattered in Lincoln County was Murphy & Dolan Mercantile and Banking, owned by Lawrence Murphy and James Dolan. Over time, the two men, with a third man, John Riley, as partner, created and acquired large cattle ranches. They also prospered from military contracts issued to them at Fort Stanton.

Soon, the Murphy & Dolan firm was being referred to as "the House" because it controlled so much of the Lincoln County economy as well as its law enforcement. The virtual monopoly on goods and money caused anger among the farmers and smaller ranchers, who suffered the double hardship of paying for goods and selling their harvests and cattle for whatever prices the House set. In 1877, when a lawyer, Alexander McSween, and a wealthy English banker and cattleman, John Tunstall, created H. H. Tunstall & Company to challenge the Murphy & Dolan array of operations, conflict was in the cards.

The newcomers, however, had an ace in the hole: John Chisum. The Tennessee native turned fifty-two in the summer of 1876. His family had moved to Texas when he was thirteen, and a few years later he went to work for a large rancher, learning the business from the hoof up.* Chisum was able to raise and grow his own herd, and by the Civil War it consisted of at least one hundred thousand head of cattle. He branched out, establishing a ranch in the Bosque Grande area of New Mexico Territory. After the war, he became partners with Charles Goodnight and Oliver Loving. After the latter was killed by Comanches in 1868, Chisum and Goodnight continued the partnership, prospering by driving herds to Fort Sumner and Santa Fe.

In 1875, Chisum created his own ranch south of Roswell, and it became the headquarters of a cattle empire that covered more than 150 miles on the Pecos River. It was while living on his South Spring Ranch that Chisum became friends with Alexander McSween. When the Lincoln County War erupted, Chisum loyally provided sanctuary and money to those supporting McSween and his partner, John Tunstall.

However, Chisum's protection was not enough. The first act of violence of the war occurred on February 18, 1878. William Brady, the county sheriff, sent a posse out to seize horses belong-

---

* During this time, in the 1840s, Chisum encountered people bound for California and purchased from them a mulatto named Jensie, who was fifteen years old. He fell in love with her, they had two daughters, he built a home for his family in Bonham, Texas, and the rancher freed all his slaves.

ing to Tunstall to resolve an outstanding debt—or so the House had contended to a local judge. Tunstall resisted and was shot in the head.

One of Tunstall's employees was Henry McCarty, later William Bonney, also known as Billy the Kid. He was eighteen at the time of the shooting, five years after being orphaned and a year after killing a blacksmith in Arizona Territory. He had found a refuge in Lincoln County and a friend in Tunstall. At the funeral, Billy swore, "I'll get every son of a bitch who helped kill John if it's the last thing I do."

And he did. Billy joined with several other men who had worked for Tunstall and named themselves the Regulators. Sure enough, the following month the band killed William Morton, the deputy who had shot Tunstall, as well as another deputy, Frank Baker, and even one of the Regulators who had tried to prevent the killings. On April 1, they finished off Sheriff Brady and another of his unfortunate deputies.

Soon, though, there was a new sheriff in Lincoln County, George Peppin. In July, he and a new batch of probably nervous deputies surrounded McSween's house and set it on fire. As people ran out of it they were shot and killed, including the owner. Two months later, President Rutherford B. Hayes appointed Lew Wallace as the new governor of New Mexico Territory with a mandate to end the Lincoln County War, which had attracted national attention and embarrassed southwest lawmakers and businessmen.* Wallace declared amnesty for everyone involved if the murders stopped, and

---

* Wallace had served with distinction in the Mexican-American War and as a Union general in the Civil War but is best known for writing the novel *Ben-Hur: A Tale of the Christ.*

that gambit worked, though by then the war had taken a total of nineteen lives.

Actually, there was one more murder. The widow of Alexander McSween hired an attorney to pursue legal action against James Dolan. That effort ended when the attorney was murdered. Dolan wound up buying the Tunstall property. The former Murphy & Dolan Mercantile building is now the Lincoln County Courthouse.

The events of the Lincoln County War illustrated the unavoidable conflict between ranchers and rustlers and a growing number of farmers who wanted to fence off properties. Similar tensions were emerging in southeast Arizona, exacerbated by friction with ranchers on the Mexican side of the border and, very soon, a rapidly expanding population of prospectors.

A direct consequence was that some families who wanted to get away from the hostilities—among them the Clantons—left New Mexico, looking west for a safe place to work and profit. Also leaving the territory were cowboys and outlaws looking to escape the law-enforcement crackdown. They could not go east, where the Texas Rangers reigned, so the only option was to work their way west.

When miners and others came to the Tombstone area, they found it, as Indians had centuries earlier, more habitable than expected if based solely on its geography. "Springs exist on both sides of the [Dragoon] range, sycamores indicating presence of water near the surface," writes Lynn Bailey. "Well watered canyons sustain thickets of manzanita and pinon, as well as three species of oak, the acorns of which were gathered, roasted and pounded into a groul by native Americans. Prickly pear, yucca, bear grass, as well as a variety of wild berries grew on canyon sides. Deer, bear, and other game were plentiful, and the surrounding plains teemed with antelope."

By this time, miles upon miles of railroad track had been laid in Arizona. In July 1866, the Atlantic and Pacific Railroad company had been authorized to construct a railroad line from Springfield, Missouri, to San Diego, California, cutting across the territories of New Mexico and Arizona. However, no progress was made, and during the Panic of 1873, the company went under. The Southern Pacific Railroad company got going, building south through California to San Diego, then going east across the state to Needles . . . where work ground to a stop. Another company, the Texas and Pacific, had a charter for railroad construction in Arizona and New Mexico. Pretty much ignoring this, lawmakers gave the Southern Pacific a similar charter. Work resumed eastward.

By this time, the New York financier Jay Gould had taken over the Texas and Pacific Railway, and he was not about to roll over and let a competing company take his territory. He hired General Grenville Dodge (for whom the "wickedest city in the American West" would be named), who had formerly run the Union Pacific Railroad company, to charge ahead with construction west by the Texas and Pacific. The Southern Pacific arrived in Tucson in March 1880 and pushed on. More interested in making money than spending it on feuding, the two railroad companies reached an agreement and their tracks met each other at Sierra Blanca, ninety miles east of El Paso. Both companies would continue with their respective projects and gain a railroad monopoly in the Southwest.

While most migrants traveled in wagons hauling their possessions, expanding rail transportation did make it easier for men, especially those who could afford to buy equipment and supplies at their destination, to arrive in Arizona. Trains also made travelers feel safer, with Indians not known to launch attacks against what they initially called the Iron Horse. However, according to Jeff Guinn in *The Last Gunfight*, cross-country wagon trains had indeed been dangerous, but not because of Indians, as popular culture would have us believe: "Between 1842 and 1859, about thirty thousand Western emigrants died while en route by wagon train, but fewer than four hundred were killed by Indians. The wagon train death rate was 3 percent, compared to the 2.5 percent average among all Americans. Ninety percent of wagon train fatalities came from disease, with cholera the leading cause."

Whichever way they chose to head west, the Desert Land Act of 1877 provided even more incentive to do so. In May 1862, President Lincoln had signed the Homestead Act, designed to encourage westward migration. For a modest filing fee, a man could claim up to 160 acres on the frontier, and if he worked them for five years, he became the legal owner of the property.

It was a different story, though, in the Southwest, with its vast expanses of land, some of it including desert that could not be cultivated. The 1877 legislation allowed settlers to purchase as many as 640 acres for $1.25 an acre, with only 25 cents per acre due up front and the rest payable in three years when the property was to be irrigated. The act proved irresistible to many who were or intended to become farmers and ranchers, though some found the conditions so harsh and the hot work so hard that they did not last the three years required for ownership.

What about the Apaches? George Crook may have made his peace with Cochise before the latter died, but there had remained plenty of cleanup work to do. In a battle at Skull Cave in December 1872, seventy-five Yavapai Apaches were killed. By the following April, virtually all denominations of Apache had surrendered and allowed themselves to be moved onto reservations. For his successful campaign, Crook was promoted and would later play a major role in the campaigns against the Lakota Sioux in 1875 and 1876 . . . before being forced to return to Arizona.

It was one of those reservations, at San Carlos, that drew John Clum to Arizona. He represented a type of ambitious and adventurous white man moving into the territory—like the Earp brothers. Clum had been born in Claverack, a community of farmers of mostly Dutch descent in upstate New York. Obeying his parents, when the time came Clum enrolled at the divinity school at Rutgers College in New Jersey. There he played a new game, football, for the college. An injury forced him back home to recuperate. Once on his feet, Clum realized he did not want to be a minister; in fact, he did not want to return to college at all, he wanted adventure. Just turned twenty, he joined the U.S. Army Signal Service, which needed men to staff the fifty weather stations being established throughout the country. He received six weeks of training as a weatherman in Virginia, then Observer Sergeant Clum was assigned to the new station in Santa Fe, New Mexico.

He proved to be industrious. The results of his daily measurements were telegraphed to Washington, D.C., and he opened a school. He earned $3 per pupil, and when the student body climbed to seventy-five children, he hired an assistant teacher. Then Clum grew restless again. He learned that the San Carlos Indian Reservation, near the Gila River and founded in 1872, needed an agent to supervise it. In August 1874, just a month before his twenty-third birthday, Clum assumed the position. The Apache residents named the already balding agent Nantan-betunnykahyeh, "Boss with the High Forehead."

Right away, Clum did two things previous reservation agents

had not done—he learned as much of the Apache language and culture as he could, and he did not invite soldiers on the reservation to resolve issues. Instead, he created an Apache police force and appointed a white man named Clay Beauford to lead it.* Additionally, Clum created a rudimentary court system with Apaches as judges who ruled for or against defendants who had been brought in by the native police force.

George Clum, John's older brother, was brought to San Carlos to teach at the reservation school. To help the Apaches support themselves, encampments were established near streams so that the inhabitants could till the surrounding fertile bottomland, with corn being the most-produced crop. For the Apaches, however, this was not the preferred living situation. Not only were they prohibited from traditional roaming and hunting practices, but they could not leave the reservation at all without permission, no Apache could own a firearm, and there were daily counts of the men and weekly counts of the women and children. While John Clum was more enlightened than most Indian agents on the entire frontier, he was essentially supervising an internment camp.

Over time, given that the San Carlos Reservation was a relatively peaceful and productive place, other Apache bands were brought

---

* Born in Maryland as Welford Bridwell, Beauford changed his name to avoid recognition when enlisting underage in the Confederate army. After the war, he enlisted again, this time in the U.S. Army, and served with the Fifth U.S. Cavalry during the Indian Wars against the Plains Indians. Beauford also acted as a guide for George Crook in his campaign against the Apaches, receiving the Medal of Honor for his actions. Beauford and Clum were credited with the capture of Geronimo at Ojo Caliente in 1877, and Beauford was largely responsible for turning the San Carlos police into one of the most respected law-enforcement agencies in the Southwest. He was later elected to Arizona's territorial legislature.

there from elsewhere in Arizona and even New Mexico. The native population leaped from eight hundred to more than four thousand. The mistake made by the approving Bureau of Indian Affairs was to assume that all Apaches were the same. As Neil B. Carmony points out in his introduction to Clum's autobiography, "The people we call Apaches were not a unified nation with a single leadership structure, but were a collection of autonomous groups loosely linked by language and other cultural traits. Some of the bands had long histories of mutual antagonism, and old disputes resurfaced when they found themselves living close together."

The most dramatic "dispute" occurred in the spring of 1876 when three hundred Chiricahuas were ordered to San Carlos. Instead, the Apaches headed into Mexico to hide out in the Sierra Madre Occidental. Their leaders were Geronimo and Juh. It would be a year before Clum and Beauford and a hundred Apache policemen found and arrested the renegades.* Geronimo was put in shackles, and Clum would have prosecuted him aggressively if, in July 1877, he hadn't resigned as the San Carlos agent. He now saw his future as a husband and father and businessman in Tucson.

Though Geronimo would periodically cause trouble to the surrounding settlers and army forts, the Indian presence in the Dragoon Mountains became something of an afterthought when silver was discovered. Though Tombstone was to become one of the more famous silver-mining locations in Arizona, if not the most famous,

---

* During this interval, Clum and two dozen Apaches led by Taza, son of Cochise, traveled to St. Louis as the first stop of a "Wild Indian Show" Clum produced. It was not well received in the wake of the Little Bighorn victory by Indians, and during the Washington, D.C., run, Taza died from pneumonia. A bright spot for Clum was stopping off in Ohio to be married to Mary Ware, whose uncle had been governor of the state and postmaster general in the Lincoln administration.

it was not the first. A former trapper named Joseph Rutherford Walker* discovered deposits in 1862 and 1863 in northern Arizona, and the Walker Mining District was established.

The Silver King deposit was found in 1873, east of Picket Post Mountain. It would eventually yield $6 million worth of ore. A few years after that, attention shifted to the southeast corner of the territory, where a robust discovery was made by one of the most peculiar characters in the history of the American West.

---

* Walker was in his mid-sixties by then and had been a scout and guide for many expeditions heading west to California, including with John C. Frémont, who named the Walker River and Walker Lake in Nevada after him.

Chapter Four

"THE ONLY STONE YOU'LL FIND"

It can be said that the founding of Tombstone originated in Germany in 1702 when Johann Jacob Schieffelin was born. He visited America in 1743, found Philadelphia to his liking, and six years later returned to it with his wife and children. Johann had a son named Jacob who had a son named Jacob who had a son named Jacob who had a son named . . . Clinton. He was born in 1823 in New York City and was the first Schieffelin to head west.

That adventure began in 1852 when Clinton and the brother of his wife, Jane Walker, who had emigrated from Ireland, set off for California to see if there was any gold left in them thar hills. There was not, so Clinton and Joe Walker went north to Oregon and purchased a claim on the Rogue River. That is where Jane was reunited with her husband when she finally made the perilous continental crossing in 1857, perhaps wondering, as she shuddered along the rutted roads, if even a potato famine back in Ireland was a better fate. The couple would have nine children, with the oldest to achieve adulthood being Edward Lawrence Schieffelin. He had been born on October 8, 1847, in Pennsylvania, which meant that he made the long journey west with his mother.

Ed's first taste of mining life came when he was nineteen and visited camps along the Rogue River. He found the mechanics of the primitive hydraulic systems used to search for gold in the river fascinating. But Schieffelin was a restless man, and by the early 1870s he was in southeast Nevada, where silver was being found. He explored more of that territory as well as parts of Utah and Arizona. On most if not all of these sojourns, he traveled solo, and it is remarkable that he survived the dangers he faced, including hostile Indians, hostile whites, and hostile weather events.

"If you want to get really badly scared, just get caught in a box canyon once during one of those thunderstorms or cloud bursts, as they are usually called in Nevada and Arizona," Schieffelin wrote in a memoir published years later. "Once will do you, and you always afterward will take good care to be out of them whenever there is one of those storms coming up."

He went on to describe his own experience of "every jump digging the spurs in to the flanks of your horse trying to make him increase his jumps. And looking back over your shoulder, see that roll of water, mud, logs, sticks and rocks making a wall six or eight feet high, tumbling and rolling, sweeping all before it, and knowing that at least half a mile had to be made over the rocks, cactus, brush and such things before you would have a chance to escape."

Despite the risks, it was during this time that his hunger for a big strike formed and over the years became ravenous. One of Schieffelin's prospecting trips took him to the Grand Canyon. However, with that site offering little in riches other than visual ones, in 1877 he was employed as a scout operating out of Camp

Huachuca. This was actually a pretty ideal situation, because as he roamed the area on the lookout for renegade Apaches he could also be searching for signs that indicated an ore deposit. One has to wonder how dedicated Schieffelin was to his official duties with the distraction of the next big strike constantly on his mind. It is also beyond fortunate that he did not get picked off by renegade Indians during his far-and-wide wanderings, which he continued to do alone so as not to tip anyone else off if there was ore to be found. "Not once did I build a fire," Schieffelin boasted.

He made sure his mule was with him wherever he paused to do some prospecting. "She was always on the alert, better than a dog, and seemed to have a realization of the danger she was in, always saddled with the bridle hanging to the horn. Rifle in one hand and pick in the other, cartridge belt and six-shooter around me day or night just the same. After doing so for a while, I would pack up and go off to some other part of the country for a week or so, return and try it again and so on all summer."

Eventually, Schieffelin found his way to the Dragoon Mountains. He later contended that he had a hunch about this range. One day he found "float ore," pieces of ore found in water. They could mean nothing, or they could have been washed away from a substantial deposit. Ever a patient man, on his daily treks Schieffelin traced the source, which he hoped would be a mother lode of silver. Back at the camp, a few soldiers saw the "stones" of float ore, and Schieffelin admitted that he was prospecting during his outings to scout for Indians. They told him, "The only stone you'll find out there will be your tombstone." Thus, we can thank a handful of anonymous troopers for one of the most famous town names in American history.

He brought his float ore to Tucson but found no takers. "I had been carrying it around town to see if I couldn't get somebody interested," Schieffelin reported. "But it was no go. With very few exceptions they wouldn't take a look at it and those that did pronounced it very low grade. And a man that at that time would have put up $150 or $200 would have owned half of Tombstone, for with that much money then I could have found any mine there was in Tombstone, because there was no prospectors in the country and before anybody had found them out, I would have them all."

An unhappy irony for Schieffelin was that he might have a financial tiger by the tail but could be too broke to do anything about it. The prospector, by then soon to turn thirty, roamed through Tucson with all of thirty cents in his ragged pocket. "I found that Tucson was no place for a prospector," he lamented. His first claim, which he had named Tombstone, might well be his last.

His solitary wanderings in the Dragoons had not improved his appearance from previous years. The early Arizona historian James McClintock, whose brother Charles published *The Phoenix Herald,* described the visitor as "about the queerest specimen of humanity ever seen in Tucson."*

This was saying something on the southwest frontier. McClintock further detailed that Schieffelin's clothing "was worn and covered with patches of deerskins, corduroy and flannel, and his old slouch hat too, was so pieced with rabbit skin that very little of the original felt remained." McClintock estimated his age as forty. "His black hair hung down below his shoulders, and his full beard,

---

* The future military career of the journalist and farmer James McClintock included serving as a captain in the Rough Riders commanded by Colonel Theodore Roosevelt. McClintock was severely wounded in action in Cuba in June 1898. He later became the president and historian of the Rough Riders Association.

a tangle of knots, was almost as long and he appeared to be a fur-bearing animal."

Accompanying the odd-looking prospector was a man named William Griffith, whom Schieffelin had at least partly confided in and who offered to pay recording fees in return for a piece of any claim. This became moot when no one in Tucson was impressed by the samples the two men had brought, and there was no assay office there anyway to examine and verify that silver ore was present. That was enough for Griffith—he quit as a partner and went off to find a job on a ranch.

Schieffelin turned north, to Globe. There he expected to find his brother Al, who he hoped would underwrite a proper prospecting expedition. But Al had moved on to Signal City to labor in the McCracken Mine. By now flat broke, Ed essentially took his brother's former job in the Silver King Mine. Ed's job was to spend every night cranking a hand windlass to hoist tons of silver ore. When he had earned what he hoped was enough, Ed pushed on to Silver City.

He got lucky. Not only was Al still there but so was Richard Gird, the McCracken Mine's assayer. His later claim to fame was as the founder of Chino, California, but at the time Gird was a respected assayer and, more important to Tombstone, he did not dismiss Ed Schieffelin based on his disheveled appearance but agreed to examine the samples he had brought. His jaw-dropping conclusion was that the ore not only was the real deal but could be worth $2,000 a ton. The peculiar prospector was right after all.

The Schieffelin brothers and Gird hurriedly formed a partnership and then gathered supplies and a mule for the trip south. To reduce the risk of being followed, the trio waited until dark to slip out of town. The brothers were not missed during the next few days, but some prospectors wondered what was so important to persuade Gird to leave his position at the McCracken Mine.

It was not until late February 1878 that the trio entered the San Pedro Valley. Ed was disturbed, to say the least, to find other prospectors working near the two sites containing silver ore that, tongue-in-cheek, he had named Tombstone and Graveyard. Further digging and examining confirmed that there was indeed a mother lode of silver in this section of the Dragoons, with new estimates by a giddy Gird being as high as $15,000 per ton. This was indeed the "Eureka" strike that Ed Schieffelin had always sought.

As the partners were digging and assaying and recording adjacent claims, word of the discovery spread like a prairie fire. Other prospectors arrived in the area, trailed by those who would make money off them. The first town to be created was Goose Flats, on a mesa overlooking another one of the Schieffelins' claims, called Tough Nut because it had been more difficult to find.

Soon the hills were crawling with competing prospectors, and investors were drawn to the area to underwrite new ventures. According to Jeff Guinn, "Almost everyone camped in tents; they had no time or inclination to build anything more substantial. Comfort was secondary to the near-hysterical urge to strike it rich fast, before the fellow camping nearby beat you to it."

The first miners' meeting was held in 1878, and the Tombstone Mining District was created. This confirmed that the area was bursting with silver, with one estimate as high as $85 million worth. What had happened in California, in Nevada, and in Colorado was now happening in the southeast corner of Arizona—the boom was on.

The original Goose Flats site grew until March 1879, when a man named Solon Allis laid out the grid for what was to be a new and bigger town. This would be named after Ed Schieffelin's first discovery, Tombstone.

The indefatigable prospector did indeed become rich, and his persistence and discovery spawned what would become one of the most famous towns in the United States. However, except for in Tombstone itself, the name of Schieffelin would be lost in the mists of history. The name that truly put Tombstone on the map was Earp.

ACT II

THE BROTHERS

Allen Street, 1880.

That nothing's so sacred as honor and nothing's so loyal as love.
—WYATT EARP

Chapter Five

"DESPERATE CHARACTERS"

The Earps in America propagated in almost biblical proportions. Walter Earp, born in 1787 in Maryland, was descended from men who hailed from Ireland and England, with one of them, Thomas Jr., born in 1665, being the first Earp to cross the Atlantic Ocean. His great-great-grandson Walter married Martha Ann Early and the couple moved to North Carolina and had nine children.* One of them, the second son, Nicholas, greeted the world in 1813.

Born that same year was Abigail Storm. Soon after she and Nicholas married in 1836, she gave birth to Newton and Mariah (who would live only ten months). Newton would later be called, especially by Earp family detractors, "Newton the Good" because he had little to do with the rest of the family and spent most of his life farming in California. Abigail died at only twenty-six, and

---

* As if fulfilling a family requirement, Walter and Martha's first two children, Lorenzo and Elizabeth, each had nine children.

when the widower met Virginia Ann Cooksey, eight years his junior, they soon married and Nicholas set back to work matching his father's output. In fact, he exceeded Walter by one. Nicholas had eight more children with Virginia, for a total of ten. The youngest, Adelia, was born in 1861, and by living to 1941, she spanned the presidencies of Abraham Lincoln to Franklin Delano Roosevelt.

Nicholas's second son and first child with Virginia was James, who during the first half of his life would spend a lot of time with his brothers, though not as a lawman. The next child was Virgil, then came Martha, named after her paternal grandmother. She was only eleven when she died, perhaps from cholera. Wyatt was Nicholas's fourth son, born on March 19, 1848, and he was followed three years later by Morgan and four years after that by Warren. The second youngest, Virginia, died in 1861 at just three years old.

To support Texas remaining in the United States, and find glory while he was at it, the thirty-four-year-old Nicholas joined the army when the war against Mexico began in 1847. He did not last long. While it did not curb his reproductive efforts, Nicholas was kicked in the groin by a mule, an injury severe enough to put him in the hospital in Vera Cruz, where he was discharged in December 1847. He returned to what increasingly became a life full of real and perceived grievances—perhaps understandable for a man who went off to fight for his country and got kicked in the nuts for his trouble. With all his wanderings and ambitions that lasted into old age—Nicholas died in 1907, at age ninety-three—he never attained what he most wanted, money and stature.

The chronic frustration churning in Nicholas was seen in his displays of anger. "Nicholas Earp beat his sons," reports the historian and novelist Mary Doria Russell. "He cowed and terrified his wife and daughters. He always had some dispute going with their neighbors. He repeatedly packed up his family and moved on, to escape unpaid debts."

And to find that brass ring. Nicholas was at varying times a farmer, moonshiner, justice of the peace, shopkeeper, constable, bartender, and whatever else was handy to put food on the table. Wyatt was one of the Earps born in Illinois, but the family also lived in Pella, Iowa. It was there that the first of the Earp sons enlisted in the Union army. At twenty-four, Newton signed up in November 1861, becoming a member of the Fourth Cavalry of the Iowa Volunteers.

James was nineteen when he enlisted, also in 1861, joining the Seventeenth Illinois Infantry Regiment. It was only five months after becoming a soldier that James was severely wounded. On October 31, there was a battle near Fredericktown between the Seventeenth Illinois and the Missouri State Guard. More than sixty troops were killed or wounded, including James. Although he was wounded in the shoulder and temporarily lost the use of his left arm, he remained in the army for over a year and was discharged in March 1863 as disabled.

Virgil may have had a patriotic motive for enlisting, which he did in July 1862, becoming a member of the Eighty-third Illinois Infantry Regiment, but he also was getting himself out of a hasty marriage. Apparently, facing Rebel bullets was preferable to a pregnant wife, and off Virgil went to war. He saw some combat, not much, and unlike his unlucky brother James, he went unscathed, mustering out—still only a private—in June 1865 in Nashville. By this time, his father-in-law, his hopes overcoming reality, had reported Virgil killed in action, and his wife and daughter had moved on.

To link up with his father and other family members, Virgil traveled not to Illinois or Iowa but to California. In 1864, Nicholas, restless again and perhaps thinking there was a perpetual gold rush, led a wagon train out of Pella headed for San Bernardino, California. Along for the bumpy ride were his wife and five of his children: James, Wyatt, Morgan, Warren, and Adelia. Nicholas was officially the journey's wagon master, and he took the position very seriously. That the train passed through hostile and inhabitable lands to reach its destination safely was a credit to Nicholas's dedication—or disinterest on the part of the Indian tribes along the way—but still, it did seem that for him "stern" was an understatement.

Among the travelers were Dr. J. A. Rousseau and his wife, and the latter kept a diary. Among the actions she recorded were angry outbursts by the wagon master, including: "This evening Mr. Earp had another rippet with Warren fighting with Jimmy Hatten. And then he commenced about all the children. Used very profane language and swore if the children's parents did not whip or correct their children he would whip every last one of them. He still shows out more and more every day what kind of man he is."

When Virgil returned from the war, Wyatt was seventeen and by then even more restless than his father. Several attempts to run away and join the Union army had been unsuccessful. Wyatt was happy to leave his parents and younger siblings behind (James by then had struck out on his own) and especially the farming life to join Virgil as a freight hauler and stagecoach driver. Their sojourns took them between southern California and Salt Lake City and Prescott in Arizona. At mining camps especially, Wyatt learned how to box and that he could not drink alcohol without getting sick. By the time he returned to his parents' home, they were living in

Lamar, Missouri.* It was there he met and married Aurilla Sutherland, the daughter of transplanted New Yorkers who had opened up a hotel in Lamar.

It was also in Lamar that Wyatt for the first time served as a lawman. In March 1870, two months after his marriage, Wyatt was appointed constable. There was very little crime in Lamar, but still, he represented the law. He and the pregnant Aurilla bought a plot of land with a small house on it for $75. It is certainly possible that the name Wyatt Earp would not be a well-known one in U.S. history if he had continued to live a quiet family life in southwest Missouri.

Even more encouraging was that in November he was elected to retain the constable post in what would be the only time he ran for office. Then, as mentioned in Chapter 1, life changed dramatically: Aurilla died. The cause most often cited is typhoid or while delivering a stillborn baby.

A devastated Wyatt sold off his property and within a few months was gone from Lamar. During his subsequent wanderings he found himself on the wrong side of the law, particularly when he was arrested and imprisoned for stealing a horse. He and two other men had taken two horses in Arkansas and were convicted of it. In May 1871, seven men, all referred to as "desperate characters" in the local paper, escaped from the prison. Wyatt Earp was one of them, and he took off and never looked back.

It was around this time that he found employment as a buffalo hunter, and at one such camp he first encountered the brothers Ed

---

* The city was named for Mirabeau Lamar, the second president of the Republic of Texas. Its main claim to fame is thanks to another president—Harry Truman was born there in 1884.

and Bat Masterson. In the summer of 1873, Wyatt was in Ellsworth, a Kansas cow town. Also there were the gamblers Ben and Billy Thompson and a county sheriff named Chauncey Whitney.

The lawman was in the process of defusing a confrontation between the Thompsons and two of his deputies when Billy's shotgun went off. The younger Thompson rode out of town, leaving Ben behind. There are embellished accounts of what happened next, but it does seem to be the case that Wyatt approached Ben Thompson and persuaded him to surrender. He later recalled of the confrontation, "I just kept looking him in the eye as I walked toward him. And when he started talking to me I was pretty sure I had him. I tried to talk in as pleasant a voice as I could manage and I told him to throw his gun in the road. He did and that's all there was to it."

Word that Wyatt Earp had faced down the known man-killer Ben Thompson circulated through the Kansas cow towns. According to one account, Wyatt was hired as a deputy sheriff in Ellsworth but returned his badge when Ben Thompson's punishment was only a $25 fine. (Billy was later found, brought back, and acquitted of murder.) "Ellsworth figures sheriffs at $25 a head," Wyatt fumed. "I don't figure the town's my size."

Wichita was more to his liking. Wyatt took up residence there because his brother James had fallen in love and married Nellie Bartlett "Bessie" Catchim, a native New Yorker, and the two had opened a brothel in that southeast Kansas town.* Now twenty-six,

---

* While many legal marriage ceremonies were performed along the frontier, it was not uncommon for men and women to live together as man and wife and to claim that status or be recognized as a married couple. With Wyatt, for example, of his four "wives," the only woman he officially married was Aurilla. Bessie brought to her marriage with James (which endured until her death) two children from a previous relationship.

Wyatt worked as a brothel bouncer and gambler. "Despite his relative youth," writes the biographer Casey Tefertiller, "he had an aura of authority about him, a solemnity and bearing that commanded a situation. He rarely laughed or even broke a smile. He was all business when he was going about his business."

Despite his dubious occupations, Wyatt was on his way to being a frontier lawman. This would be furthered along when he served as a summertime deputy in 1874 and then in April 1875 became an official member of the Wichita police force.

Wyatt did well as a peace officer there, receiving praise in the local press. He was, however, fired for beating up the man running against his boss for the marshal's job. The challenger, Bill Smith, had made a comment about Wyatt's brothers that he deemed insulting. Thus, he was free and available when Dodge City came calling.

Cupid's arrow found Virgil when he was in Council Bluffs, Iowa. At the time, he was employed as the driver of a stage that went back and forth through Iowa and Nebraska. Alvira Sullivan was a waitress at the Planters House restaurant. She was sitting at a table with other employees having an early supper when a tall man with a red mustache entered. She was interested and was told his name was Virgil Earp.

"Virge saw me too," she told her nephew Frank Waters decades later. "He always said I was just getting ready to take a bite out of a pickle when he first saw me. When I was mean he used to say I was just as sour. But mostly he said I was not much bigger than a pickle but a lot more sweet. I can't say I liked him particularly right off. For one thing, he wasn't the looks of a man I'd figured to fall in love with. I'd always fancied myself somebody my own size. But Virge was handsome, and he always sat straight on a horse."

Virgil and the woman everyone called Allie would be together for more than forty years. No time during their marriage was as exciting and painful as the years in Tombstone, when five of the Earp boys found one another.

Chapter Six

"THREE PEAS IN A POD"

Becoming governor of a territory growing in population might seem like a ripe plum of an appointment. However, for John C. Frémont it only further confirmed his backwater status in American politics. At one time, he had been one of the country's most famous frontiersmen, with his nickname, "the Pathfinder," uttered with awe and admiration. Now, he was relieved to have the Arizona job and he aimed to keep it until something better came along.

Born in 1813 in Savannah, Georgia, Frémont grew up in Charleston, South Carolina, and set out from there on a life of adventure. He taught mathematics aboard a U.S. warship, was an assistant engineer working on railroad surveys, and at twenty-five was commissioned a second lieutenant of topographical engineers in the U.S. Army. His first assignment was to assist the French scientist Joseph Nicolas Nicollet on an expedition to survey the upper Missouri and Mississippi Rivers that would last three years.

Frémont's expanding desire to see more of the American West

coincided with his friendship with Thomas Hart Benton, a senator from Missouri who wielded a lot of influence in Congress and was an ardent proponent of Manifest Destiny. (He had his own nickname: "Old Bullion.") The two became even closer when the twenty-eight-year-old officer married the senator's daughter, Jessie . . . after Benton got over his anger that the bride was still only sixteen. With the political and financial support Benton provided, Frémont conducted mapmaking missions that would allow him to explore the lands between the Mississippi River and the Pacific Ocean.

In 1843, he teamed up with the scouts Kit Carson and Thomas "Broken Hand" Fitzpatrick on a mapping trip that ended at the mouth of the Columbia River in the Pacific Northwest. Frémont turned south to explore Nevada, then crossed over the Sierra Nevada into California, a journey that almost killed him and his men when they were trapped in snow. His survival brought Frémont national acclaim as a fearless (and fortunate) explorer.

He headed another expedition that became involved in international politics. In 1846, Frémont and his troops supported the Bear Flag Republic, which was an attempt by California to break away from Mexico. When war between that country and the United States began, Frémont combined with General Stephen Watts Kearny and Commodore Robert Stockton of the U.S. Navy to push out the Mexican military, paving the way for California to become the thirty-first state four years later. However, Frémont's attempt to be governor of the new American territory without authorization from Washington resulted in a court-martial. He was found guilty and sentenced for dismissal. President James Polk stuck the military court's verdict in his back pocket, but an insulted—and more popular than ever—Frémont resigned from the army anyway.*

Frémont could not have picked a better time to enter private life. He returned to California, to a ranch he had established in the foothills of the Sierra Nevada. When the gold rush began and landowners went looking for what might be in their backyards, Frémont found rich ore veins worth millions of dollars. When California entered the Union in 1850, he became one of the state's two senators. Undaunted when he lost his bid for reelection to a pro-slavery candidate, Frémont set off on another exploration, this time to Utah, and his subsequent account of the adventure caused a fresh surge of popularity. In 1856, a new major political party, the Republicans, nominated Frémont for president. His defeat by James Buchanan not only saddled the nation with an inept chief executive but was the beginning of the end of Frémont as a hero in the eyes of the American public.

Early in the Civil War he served as a Union major general but was removed by President Lincoln when he insisted on confiscating the property of Confederate sympathizers in Missouri and declaring that all the state's slaves were free. After another command in the Appalachian region was beaten and embarrassed by forces under General Stonewall Jackson, Frémont once again resigned. He sat out the rest of the war, and after it, he lost much of his money investing in railroads and the rest of it in the Panic of 1873.

---

* Though uncredited, Jessie Frémont wrote much—and possibly all—of her husband's travel books and memoirs, which were bestsellers in the 1840s and 1850s. In addition, the fervent abolitionist and political activist wrote six books of her own.

By 1878, Frémont needed a job. He still had a few friends left in Washington, and they persuaded President Rutherford B. Hayes, a Republican, to appoint the former Union general governor of Arizona Territory. His tenure has a direct bearing on Tombstone, because by then Frémont had lost most of his luster as well as his ambition and ability to govern. To him, Arizona was little more than a stepping-stone to another, more high-profile and enriching venture. He spent as much time traveling and living away from the territory as in it. Frémont's disinterested, hands-off approach allowed the conflicts between cowboys and townsfolk to fester and then burst into the open, and lawlessness proliferated. Tombstone and eventually the climactic gunfight in October 1881 were one result of Frémont's ineffectiveness.

In 1890, at age seventy-seven, Frémont was reappointed a major general in the U.S. Army. There were no more campaigns or explorations, though. He and Jessie had been living a rather destitute life in New York City, and the presidential appointment by a sympathetic Benjamin Harrison and Frémont's immediate retirement allowed him a pension. He enjoyed it for only three months, however, dying that July. Jessie continued to write about her faded hero husband until her death in Los Angeles in 1902. Though one of the pivotal figures in opening up the American West, John C. Frémont resides in a cemetery in upstate New York.

Eschewing a marriage ceremony, Virgil and Allie began living and traveling together, probably in 1874. He continued to work as a stage driver and freight hauler and did not have much contact with the rest of his family. Allie would remember this as a blissful time because she had left a life of drudgery behind and she had the tall, handsome Virgil Earp all to herself.

Things changed when Nicholas Earp again grew restless. It was time, he declared, to give living in California another go. In 1877, a new wagon train was formed, with of course Nicholas, though pushing sixty-four, as the leader.* If he'd had a rearview mirror then, Missouri would be reflected in it. Nicholas and Virginia were accompanied by their youngest surviving children, Warren and Adelia. Also driving a wagon was a man named Bill Edwards, who optimistically saw a cross-country trek through varying weather conditions and Indian lands as an opportunity to woo Adelia.

Their first stop was Hutchinson, Kansas. Nicholas's oldest son, Newton, and his wife, Jennie, were farming there but were undergoing a fierce grasshopper plague that had soured them on such a life. California was clearly a case of the grass is greener on the other side of the Continental Divide. As luck would have it, Virgil and Newton had been corresponding, and the latter had—before the insect apocalypse—invited Virgil and Allie to come live in Hutchinson for a spell. The timing was such that when the couple showed up in their wagon, it became the eleventh one lined up at the devastated farm ready to head west.

Allie could not have fully understood what she was getting into. First of all, she had been content with one member of the Earp family and now she was traveling with five of them. It was about to get more complicated.

Next, the wagon train trudged into Dodge City, and almost immediately, Nicholas called out, "Hey you, Wyatt!" Wyatt's walking companion turned out to be Morgan. Soon after Virgil jumped down to greet them, Allie observed, "They looked alike as three

---

* Some accounts contend this was in 1876, but the Dodge City visit that became part of this trip makes more sense in 1877.

peas in a pod—the same height, size and mustaches. In Tombstone later men were always mistaking one for another."

Virgil and Wyatt had light brown hair and bushy mustaches and blue eyes and a similar lean but strong six-foot build. As Virgil gazed at his younger brother, to Allie it must have appeared that he was looking into a mirror. She would learn, though, that there were differences in the brothers' personalities. Virgil and the shorter yet also fair-haired Morgan were outgoing and enjoyed a laugh. Wyatt rarely expressed emotion of any kind and was a keen observer of others, determining those he could trust and those he could not. In Wyatt's world, there was very little gray area.

Nicholas and his companions camped on the outskirts of Dodge City for several weeks, perhaps hoping to persuade Wyatt and Morgan to sign on, though it is also possible that Virgil and Morgan lingered because they were earning money as deputies, either on the city force headed by Larry Deger or on the Ford County force headed by Charlie Bassett, which included Bat Masterson as undersheriff. Finally, the wagon train moved on farther west in Kansas, to a town named Peace.

This was indeed a peaceful interlude for Virgil and Allie, who rented a house there. Bill Edwards saw his strategy become successful when he and Adelia married. All of the travelers rode out the winter there, and then the following May they aimed west again. They turned onto the Santa Fe Trail, resupplying in Santa Fe and Albuquerque. In July, they arrived in Prescott.

This city had come about because an Arizona Territory governor died before he could assume office. Fifty-year-old John Gurley, who had served as an aide to General John Frémont in the Civil War and had been a congressman from Ohio, had been appointed by President Lincoln in 1863 to become the first governor of Arizona Territory. However, an attack of appendicitis proved fatal and John Noble Goodwin, originally from Maine, replaced him. When touring the territory in 1864 to select a capital, Goodwin bypassed the more populated Tucson in favor of Prescott, named after the eminent historian William H. Prescott, who had died in Boston five years earlier. Prescott the town was on the east side of Granite Creek near several newly established mining camps. The capital was moved to Tucson in November 1867, then back to Prescott a decade later.

By then, two of the newest residents of the Prescott area were Virgil and Allie, who had decided not to complete the trip to California with Nicholas, Virginia, Warren, and the Edwardses. Prescott was by no means a destination for them but a sudden decision. The wagon train stopped at a small compound for food and to take care of their horses and mules. Two brothers-in-law named Jackson and Baker operated a mail service to and from Prescott. As the Earp party was preparing to leave, Jackson asked Virgil and Allie to stay—Virgil to help with the mail route, Allie to cook and otherwise help Mrs. Jackson, who was pregnant with her fifth child. Nicholas and company pushed on without them.

The arrangement worked out fine, until the Jacksons decided to return to Missouri. Scratching out a living and feeding five young mouths was hard in Arizona Territory, and the occasional Indian uprisings were nerve-racking. Making things worse was the increasing tension between business partners Jackson and Baker. Virgil and Allie were inclined to side with the Jacksons but mostly hoped the wrestling over who was boss would end.

It did not look as if it would end well. One night, when Virgil and Baker were sitting by the fireplace, Baker gestured to the rifles in the rack above the mantel. He said, "You know Jackson and me can't settle our contract. Well, if one of them guns should fall down and kill Jackson, you'll be witness to the accident, won't you?"

Eyes fixed on the fire, Virgil replied, "Sure. But I won't be able to help it if that other gun falls right down after it and kills Ben Baker."*

The implied threat persuaded Baker to negotiate with Jackson, and a settlement was reached. He took over the mail service, the Jacksons loaded a wagon and left, and Virgil and Allie headed to Prescott proper, which Virgil had become familiar with thanks to work-related overnight stays. When he and Allie arrived at an abandoned sawmill just west of the city, they found Newton and Jennie Earp living there with their two young children (the son was named Wyatt). The six put up together, but after only a few weeks, Jennie especially found the existence too hardscrabble and the couple turned back toward Kansas.†

In Prescott, Virgil found work similar to what he had done before, driving freight wagons. Then came a life-changing event, in October 1877—a shoot-out that featured at least as much firepower as that of the O.K. Corral.

The Yavapai County sheriff at the time was Ed Bowers, and ex-

---

* According to Allie, when Virgil saw Baker in Prescott a year later and offered a greeting, the latter refused to acknowledge him. Virgil twisted him around by his nose and said, "When I speak to a low-life skunk like you, you answer." Baker managed a gruff "Hello" and hurried away.

† From this point on, Newton is not part of the Earp story in the West. He and Jennie did return to farming in Kansas (minus the grasshoppers) and had three more children, the youngest named Virgil. Later, Newton and Jennie moved to California, where he was a home builder there and in Nevada. Newton died in Sacramento in 1928, aged ninety-one.

tra lawing was provided by U.S. Marshal William Standefer. Virgil had become acquainted with both of them, and one day the three were in the street having a conversation when an excited local resident, Colonel W. H. McCall, ran up to them.

In a rush of words, McCall explained that he had observed two men riding into town and had recognized one of them as a man named Wilson, who, the colonel claimed, was wanted for a murder committed in Texas. His companion was John Tallos, who was most likely wanted for something somewhere. The alleged outlaws were busy drinking in the Jackson and Tompkins Saloon when McCall hurried to the office of Constable Frank Murray and swore out an arrest warrant. Murray went to apprehend the men, who were now entertaining themselves by shooting at a dog outside the saloon. They diverted their attention to the approaching constable, fired a few more shots, then mounted their horses and rode away.

McCall paused for breath, then he and Standefer hopped onto a carriage and took off in the direction the outlaws had gone. Bowers and Murray jumped on horses and did the same. Virgil, carrying a Winchester rifle, followed the four on foot. When he arrived at one end of Prescott, Wilson and Tallos were firing fast and furious at the lawmen. Virgil immediately entered the fray with his rifle spitting bullets.

The Weekly Arizona Miner would report in its October 19 edition that gunfire was "gallantly returned both by Bowers and Murray from one direction and Standifer [*sic*] and McCall from the other, and in the meantime Earp, who appears to have been playing a lone hand with a Winchester rifle, was doing good service between the two fires."

Tallos was killed, and with a cigarette still sticking out of his lips, Wilson lay on the dusty ground badly wounded. The same edition of *The Weekly Arizona Miner* would report that he soon died.*

Virgil's coolness and accuracy in the midst of violent chaos was immediately recognized by the lawmen and the local press. This led to him being able to supplement his income thanks to the formation of P.C. & Co. to haul freight and anything else transportable to and from Prescott. With his experience and newly enhanced reputation as a rifleman, Virgil was hired right away.

Life was good for him and Allie. They had settled into a rented home, money was coming in steadily, Prescott appeared to be thriving, and because of an increasing army and law-enforcement presence (which included Virgil), the frontier was becoming less dangerous. Their situation was to get even better: Virgil had such an appealing personality on top of being a top-notch driver that he became the favorite of some dignitaries. These included John J. Gosper, who in the spring of 1878 was the secretary of Arizona Territory. Virgil drove the stage that took Gosper on a weeklong tour of mines and mining camps surrounding Prescott. The two hit it off, which would benefit Virgil as Gosper's star rose . . . or as far as it could until it bumped into Frémont at the top of the political food chain. It was also during this time that Virgil met the new U.S. marshal, Crawley Dake, who immediately liked the handsome driver. This would turn out to be a valuable friendship for the Earp brothers.

In 1878, Dake was a forty-two-year-old transplanted Canadian.

---

* In the surprisingly small world the Earps occupied, two years earlier Wilson had been confronted by part-time deputy Wyatt in Wichita, who collected a debt Wilson owed. And as it turned out, in the fall of 1877, when he died in Prescott, Wilson was also wanted for the murders of a sheriff and his deputy in Colorado.

At nineteen, he had moved from upstate New York to Michigan, where he ran a store, married, and was defeated twice in bids for the House of Representatives. He was more successful as a recruiter. When the Civil War began, Dake raised a company of soldiers who were accepted into the Fifth Michigan Cavalry. Into 1863, Dake and his men helped to safeguard Washington, D.C.; then things got hot. That year, the Michigan troops, now members of the Army of the Potomac, participated in the Battles of Hanover, Gettysburg, Williamsport, and Mine Run. In the latter, Dake was seriously wounded, and he retired as a major in August 1864.

He and his wife and son may have never intended to live out west. In fact, Dake returned to Michigan to become a deputy U.S. marshal in Detroit and to work for the nascent Office of the Commissioner of Internal Revenue, which had come into being in July 1862. However, when informed that a fellow from Michigan was being considered for a pretty well-paying and powerful position in Arizona, Frémont's predecessor, Governor John Hoyt, objected. But the Michigan lawmakers in Washington had much more leverage, and Dake was offered the badge of U.S. marshal for the entire territory. He packed up his family and headed for a decidedly warmer climate.

Dake found an environment that was a tad too hot. Stagecoach holdups were becoming more commonplace. The freshly minted marshal set about to create a new and efficient law-and-order system. This turned out to be not as easy as he had hoped because of poor funding. Dake was able to hire eight deputy marshals, but he had barely a budget for chasing after and apprehending outlaws. If a bunch of bad guys robbed a stage and got away, in most cases they could hide out safely in the mountains or in Mexico and weeks later come back for more. The increasingly frustrated Crawley Dake kept sending telegrams to his superiors in Washington requesting funds for posses to track down and capture highway robbers. There was not a similar sense of urgency back in the East, so Dake's requests kept getting shoved under piles of paper.

After only a few months on the job in 1878, the lawman's patience ran out. That September, when there was another stagecoach robbery, Dake dug into his own pocket and posted a $500 reward. This ploy proved successful, but it was one he could not repeat without going broke. He was persistent, though, and slowly the federal purse strings began to loosen.

When the P.C. & Co. freight firm fell on hard times—an almost inevitable consequence of the boom-and-bust cycles of mining—Virgil operated a sawmill and sold lumber to the army and to Prescott landowners building new and larger homes. Also helping was that in September 1878 the Prescott government appointed Virgil as night watchman at a salary of $75 a month. Two months later he was elected constable, his second law-enforcement post. And into 1879, he continued to earn money selling lumber.

To Allie's way of thinking, their lives in Prescott could go on indefinitely. But she had not counted on what she would term the "silence, secrecy, and clannish solidarity" of the Earps. Virgil had been writing letters, to Morgan in Montana and Wyatt and James in Kansas. He reported that life was good in Prescott but speculated it might be even better to the south. He had been hearing people talk about a new destination named Tombstone, where prospectors were flooding in to stake claims, mines were being carved out of the mountainsides, and businesses were being set up to take advantage of the early and expected riches.

Virgil may not have been aware of the growing restlessness of his brothers in Dodge City and that the younger Morgan had had his fill

of Montana, especially its seemingly endless winter. More important, the letters struck a common chord among the brothers—the
opportunity to reunite in a young and apparently thriving territory that promised a bright future to enterprising young men. That
would be especially true for the Earp brothers and their "all for one
and one for all" solidarity.

Allie later claimed that she knew nothing of any such corre-
spondence until a letter arrived from Wyatt in which he suggested
a trip to Tombstone. "We got a good home right here!" she said an-
grily to Virgil. "We're too busy cutting wood to be traipsing around
the country."

It was already too late—by the time she and Virgil had this
heated discussion, the other Earps were on their way.

If they were going to uproot themselves, Virgil wanted to give
himself and Allie some financial protection. He and Crawley Dake
had gotten to know each other pretty well, and the U.S. marshal
respected Virgil. When Virgil came to see him, Dake agreed to
appoint him deputy U.S. marshal with his mission to look into the
rampant robberies in Pima County, where Tombstone was located.
Virgil would now be leaving Prescott with a badge and an opportunity to earn federal dollars.

This would be one of the two law-enforcement positions Virgil
held three years later when he and his brothers squared off against
two other sets of brothers in Tombstone.

Chapter Seven

"NOBODY MUCH LIKE HIM"

By this point in their lives, when the Earp brothers traveled somewhere, they did not do so alone. They were accompanied by their women, who considered one another sisters-in-law even though there had not been an official marriage ceremony among them.

By the time she left Dodge City, drinking laudanum may have become part of Mattie's daily routine. This bitter, reddish-brown concoction contains most of the opium alkaloids, including codeine and morphine. Its primary use was as a cough suppressant and pain medication. Today, its use is strictly controlled, but in the 1870s it could be obtained from a local doctor or apothecary.

Life on the frontier was not easy for women, and Mattie had her share of physical ailments. But she had psychological ills, too, some stemming from having to be a female survivor on the frontier at a young age. Taking up with Wyatt meant some emotional but especially financial stability. And there had to have been a mutual physical attraction. In his biography of Mattie, E. C. (Ted) Meyers writes that her first impression of Wyatt was that he was "tall, slim, with blond hair and neatly trimmed mustache, he was very handsome. She could not have helped but also notice his blue eyes and how ice cold they were."

Wyatt apparently consorted with her, but not for long. He left Mattie behind when he moved on to Peoria, where he took up with Sarah Haspel, whom some regard as his second wife. Sarah was just sixteen when she met Wyatt, who had been hired as a bouncer at her mother's brothel in Peoria, Illinois. When she and Wyatt were arrested in September 1872, a local newspaper identified her as Sarah Earp and Wyatt as "the Peoria bummer." (Obviously, he had not yet traveled very far down the path to redemption.) When he left Peoria to go to Wichita, Sarah went with him.

Wyatt came to regret this. In Wichita, Sarah kept getting arrested for various infractions, most of them for operating a brothel with Bessie Earp, James's wife. This was embarrassing for a police officer, even a part-time one, plus expensive because of fines and sometimes attorneys' fees. Sarah and Wyatt must have had a serious falling-out, because in the 1875 census conducted by the state of Kansas, James and Bessie Earp are listed as well as Wyatt, but no Sarah. In her book *Mrs. Earp*, about the women who were or believed they were married to the Earp brothers, Sherry Monahan reports that Sarah does not reappear until eight years later, when she is Sadie Haspel and living in Kansas City. She lived with a prizefighter for a decade, then married another man. Sadie Bollman, the somewhat secret second Mrs. Wyatt Earp, died in 1919 at age sixty-six in Oak Forest, Illinois.

With Sarah out of the way, it was Mattie's turn again, and this time it stuck. In May 1876, when Wyatt rode out of Wichita to head west to Dodge City, he had a third wife. With apparently more physical and emotional staying power than the last two wives, Mattie remained with Wyatt during the Dodge City days to when they ended in the fall of 1879.

Allie was probably Virgil's third wife. There was the first wife who had been misled by the story that he had died during the war and had left Kansas with a daughter Virgil knew nothing about. In May 1870, while living in Lamar, and with his father presiding, Virgil married seventeen-year-old Rozilla Draggoo. Her fate is unknown—she may have gotten tired of Virgil off hauling freight and driving stagecoaches and found someone else or she may have died. In any case, he was a single man when he met Allie—or believed himself to be—and they would stick to each other through thick and thin.

And then there was Morgan, who Allie later maintained was the "nicest of all the Earps, the most good-natured and handsomest," even though his "thick straight hair never did stay combed and his moustache was always scraggly." Nellie Spalding was his companion during the Wichita days, and most likely she, too, was a sporting girl. She did not last long in the Earp orbit, and while Morgan was in Montana working as a rancher and hunter, he met Louisa Alice Houston, who had been born in Wisconsin as the second of twelve children.

Louisa was of frail health, having been diagnosed with edema and rheumatoid arthritis. She must have had an independent spirit—or couldn't stand what had to be a crowded house—because at age fifteen she had left her family and was living in Iowa. When she met Morgan is unclear, but in the fall of 1877, when she was twenty, the two were living together in Montana, which for most of the Earp brothers was as good as being married. When the time came for Morgan to head to Tombstone, she was too ill to go along . . . but she made it there eventually.

In addition to James and Bessie, there was another couple who would find their way to Tombstone and be part of the Earp presence there. Kate Elder was not a fan of Wyatt since the days of working in Bessie Earp's brothel in Wichita.* Incredibly, as if Doc Holliday needed any provocation for belligerent behavior, Kate believed that Wyatt was a bad influence and that it was not coincidence that wherever Doc and Wyatt went, trouble followed. And there was some jealousy involved, because to Kate, Doc was a lot closer to Wyatt than to her. Their friendship was like a brotherhood.

Wyatt and Doc first met in Griffin, Texas. The latter was with Kate, and the army outpost town happened to be one of their stops in the autumn of 1877. Wyatt was moonlighting. With the cattle-drive season waning in Dodge City, he had taken a job tracking down some bandits, and the trail had led from Kansas into Texas. When Wyatt entered the saloon where Doc was playing solitaire, the bartender suggested the mysterious gambler might have information because of having recently played a few hands with one of the outlaws.

Doc was not cooperative. He did not really know anything about the men Wyatt was chasing, but even if he had, he was not eager to share it with this lawman or bounty hunter or whatever he was. Still, there must have been some connection between the two, because

---

* No doubt out of deference to Doc, Wyatt always claimed he did not know Big Nose Kate back then. A few writers have suggested that Wyatt was one of Kate's customers. If so, it was an arrangement both preferred to think had never happened.

Wyatt invited Doc to look him up in Dodge City someday, especially if he needed help. And that is what happened when Doc killed a man over a gambling dispute in Griffin and he and Kate barely escaped. Wyatt, the brother of Union soldiers, was only too happy to help a man fleeing angry Texans. He had not expected, though, that he and the Georgia dentist would become as close as brothers.

The combination of Wyatt Earp, Doc Holliday, and Bat Masterson could have been a troubled one in Dodge City. The latter was not fond of the frequently drunk dentist. Holliday, Bat would later write, "had a mean disposition and an ungovernable temper, and under the influence of liquor was a most dangerous man."

Bat was not necessarily bothered by dangerous men—he counted a few, such as Ben Thompson and Frank James, as friends—but Holliday was someone he respected even less than he liked, which was mostly not at all. "Physically, Doc Holliday was a weakling who could not have whipped a healthy fifteen-year-old boy in a go-as-you-please fist fight. He was hot-headed and impetuous and very much given to both drinking and quarreling, and, among men who did not fear him, he was very much disliked." Bat added, "Holliday had few real friends anywhere in the West. He was selfish and had a perverse nature—traits not calculated to make a man more popular in the early days on the frontier."

However, Bat, the more outgoing and generous of spirit of the three men, made it work between them in Dodge City. Though he and Wyatt professed at times to be best friends, Bat knew there was a strong bond between Wyatt and Doc, too, so he tolerated Doc with as much good cheer as he could muster, "on account of my friendship for Wyatt Earp."

When Doc left Dodge City, Kate later claimed that as a send-off, Bat presented the gambler with a nickel-plated revolver. This gift was either a courteous gesture or an indication of Bat's pleasure that he would be rid of Doc. With or without the revolver, Doc traveled to Otero, New Mexico, in the summer of 1879, where he had previously practiced dentistry. His stay there this time was short, and he moved on to Las Vegas, the New Mexico edition. There, Doc proved he did not need Wyatt around to get into trouble.

Mike Gordon was a former army scout in his late twenties who did not handle alcohol well and who did not fare well in brawls either, as evidenced by most of his nose having been bitten off during one. He was in the midst of a bender when on the night of July 19 he tried to take a girl out of one dance hall and haul her off to another one. She refused the rough invitation. Gordon, out on the street, began shouting threats that he was going to come back into the dance hall shooting. Doc appeared in the doorway and gunfire erupted. Gordon staggered away, and an hour later he was found dead.

Doc was fortunate in that the Las Vegas coroner then was Hoodoo Brown (real name: Hyman Neill), and he had known Doc in Dodge City. He let Doc slide, and no one in town was going to miss Mike Gordon anyway. But during the next few weeks there were other incidents, including Doc being arrested at least twice, once for gambling and another time for carrying a deadly weapon. It seemed the town was getting hotter than the weather for a gambling man with a suspect reputation.* However, he lingered there, apparently not motivated to return to Dodge

---

* Perhaps that reputation explains the interest shown by Frank and Jesse James. Both were in Las Vegas the last week in July, and it is believed that Doc dined with them at the Las Vegas Hotel at Montezuma Hot Springs. How nervous might that waiter have been?

City or to try for a cooler climate to the west. That changed when Wyatt Earp arrived.

Wyatt and Mattie and James Earp and his family stopped in Las Vegas on their way to Arizona. Finding Doc there and maybe enjoying the gaming tables with him, Wyatt was in no hurry to leave. He and his party had arrived in September and it was not until October that they left. When their wagons rolled out of Las Vegas, Doc and Kate were with them.

It seems that initially Doc did not have much interest in Tombstone. The Earps arrived in Prescott and were reunited with Virgil and Allie. In November, when they all set out for Tombstone, Doc and Kate did not go along. According to the Holliday biographer Gary L. Roberts, "Prescott was a nice change with attractions boom camps did not have, including a level of stability and a more settled and cosmopolitan society that must have appealed to something deep and almost forgotten in John Henry Holliday. Doc made no effort to establish a dental office there. He was a professional gambler now, and he found his place in Whiskey Row, Prescott's gambling district."

At Virgil's urging, the Earps were going to Tombstone no matter how accommodating Prescott might appear. That November, they found a very bustling and promising town.

Ed Schieffelin had filed his first claim on September 21, 1877, for what would be a silver mine called Tombstone. With almost telegraphic speed, other men arrived to explore the Dragoon Mountains and its surroundings. The first settlement of tents and wooden shacks was at Watervale, near a mine named Lucky Cuss, also owned by the Schieffelins and Richard Gird, and close to a hundred people lived in it. The Goodenough Mine strike occurred shortly after. When a former territorial governor, Anson P. K. Safford, offered financial backing for a share of the mining claims, the Schieffelins and Gird formed the Tombstone Mining and Milling Company and built a stamp mill near the San Pedro River, about eight miles away. As the mill was being constructed, a U.S. deputy mineral surveyor by the name of Solon Allis finished surveying the new town's site. His completed project was unveiled on March 5, 1879.

As a result, the tents and shacks near the Lucky Cuss were moved to the new town site on Goose Flats, a mesa above the Goodenough Mine. This site was 4,539 feet above sea level and could accommodate a growing town. Lots were immediately sold on Allen Street for $5 each. The town soon had some forty cabins and about one hundred residents. At the town's founding that same month, it took its name from Ed Schieffelin's initial mining claim. Before long, a few thousand hardy souls were living in a canvas-and-matchstick camp perched amid the richest silver strike in the Arizona Territory.

From this vantage point, in one direction, Casey Tefertiller writes, "they could look out upon the mighty rock formation called Cochise's Stronghold. Turning in the other direction, the miners could look past the miles of grassland to the Huachuca Mountains, standing like temples in the desert; far in the distance stood the taller San Joses across the border in Mexico." A little sturdier were the small buildings constructed to house shops, saloons, bordellos, stables, and other businesses looking to feed off the expected riches.

The Tombstone Townsite Company was also founded in March 1879, and with it arrived the first heated controversy of the young settlement. The original partnership consisted of five men, but almost immediately two of them, James Clark and Mike Gray, bought out the other three. Their aim was to carve up the Tombstone town site into separate and standard lots and establish a proper title for each one, to in turn be sold. The problem was that by the spring of 1879 many of the lots were already occupied, with a tent or building on them. Company representatives went to the occupants to persuade them to buy a clear title, thus making them legal residents. This made some sense, although some squatters balked at being sold property they had already claimed as their own. However, an aggravating catch was that in addition the quasi residents were being charged for "improvements," meaning whatever structure they had erected on it.

Some squatters just went along, while some objected and appealed to the new town council headed by Mayor Alder Randall. Recognizing which side their bread was buttered on, the lawmakers supported the Tombstone Town Site Company. After this, those squatters who did not purchase their lots or were unable to prove a clear title of ownership were removed from their ramshackle properties.

One of the impediments to expansion was the availability of water. Tombstone had not been founded next to a stream or any immediate source of drinking water, and southeast Arizona was and is a very dry place. Early on, water was brought to the mining camps and the young settlement in barrels hauled by wagons. A big advance was the construction of a pipeline the seven miles from Sycamore Springs in the Dragoon Mountains to Tombstone.

This alleviated some concerns about drinking water, but at least as important to a rapidly emerging town was water as a firefighting tool. Most of the businesses and dwellings in Tombstone were made of wood, tinderboxes in a dry climate. Barrels of water were suspended on the ridgepoles of buildings. However, firefighting techniques remained primitive. When flames were seen anywhere in town, residents shot holes in the barrels. This rudimentary sprinkler system proved not to be effective enough—especially in 1881, when a conflagration nearly burned Tombstone off the territorial map.

By the middle of 1879, Ed Schieffelin was a rich man. He and his brother Al had sold their interest in mines for $600,000 each—and this was in an era when that amount was truly a fortune fit for a lifetime of luxury.* There was no need to be chipping away at rocks looking for the hint of ore and ending each day covered with dust and sweat. And Ed could certainly afford to dress a lot better. With Tombstone growing and the unexplored frontier diminishing, he decided it was time to move on.

For a time Schieffelin chose to travel, but apparently being only a rich man was not as stimulating as the prospector had envisioned when he had sat in a solitary, fireless camp at night listening for approaching Indians. The desire for the next strike returned. In the spring of 1883 Ed had a boat built, collected a crew, and set off up the Yukon River. He had become convinced there was a lot of gold to be found in the Arctic region. He turned out to be right about gold but wrong about a lot of it, and he returned to the Lower 48. He took up residence in Alameda, California, with his new bride, Mary Elizabeth Brown, and in 1884 they moved to Los Angeles. Ed believed, mistakenly, that he was through with prospecting.

A clear indication that a town was earning its way onto the map of Arizona Territory was the establishment of a Wells Fargo office. In Tombstone, that happened in late spring of 1880. This connection to Wells Fargo would once more benefit the Earps—Virgil and Wyatt had worked for the company before—and a particu-

---

* Richard Gird would sell his shares in 1880 for even more money. Al Schieffelin would not have long to enjoy his windfall, dying of consumption in 1885.

lar employee, acting as a spy, would become a staunch ally of the brothers.

Often, long before railroad tracks were laid out connecting a community with the rest of the world, Wells Fargo arrived. The company's history and that of the American West are tightly entwined. As the western historian John Boessenecker, author of *Shotguns and Stagecoaches*, writes, Wells, Fargo & Co. Express—its official title—was "one of the most important business enterprises in American history. From 1852 to 1918 it reigned as the country's biggest and most reliable express delivery service. In an era when the U.S. mail was unreliable, the private company shipped gold, silver and other valuables, and unlike the federal government, it promptly paid for any items lost or stolen in transit."

Henry Wells—who had previously cofounded American Express—and William Fargo were the founders of the freight-hauling and stagecoach line. The catalyst was the gold strikes in California. The company provided shipping and banking services. This could be a dangerous business. As Boessenecker notes, "Wells Fargo followed the money, and robbers followed Wells Fargo."

Unless they might be more of a danger to the customers than the outlaws, men who had experience with guns and didn't scare easily could find a job with the company. ("Riding shotgun," by the way, is a twentieth-century term; in the 1800s, guards were called "shotgun messengers.") They rode as guards on freight wagons and stagecoaches. In the latter case, their priority was more to protect shipments than passengers. The shipments usually contained gold or silver from mining camps to the nearest bank and payrolls to those camps or other settlements and, increasingly, remote sites as railroad construction took off. Thieves knew this, and Wells Fargo vehicles were frequent targets.

Hence the danger, and there were no benefits other than what the company was willing to pay for the recovery from gunshot wounds or to widows. Some shotgun messengers and detectives, such as Mike Tovey and James Hume, became legends, though sadly for Tovey, he became one of fifty-three Wells Fargo express-men to die in the line of duty.

Another sign of a town being established was a newspaper to inform the public of everyday activities and newsworthy events. The *Tombstone Daily Nugget* had begun publishing on October 2, 1879. It would have a monopoly on local journalism for only seven months.

So this was the town that awaited the Earps. The brothers left Prescott with stars in their eyes, seeing a bright future there. Mattie and Bessie thought it would be as good a place as any for a fresh start. Allie was the only one sad. She had created a home for her and Virgil in Prescott, and it plus most of her possessions would become part of her past, not the future. As Sherry Monahan writes, "Allie's prize possession was a sewing machine Virgil had given her and the first one she ever owned. It was so big that Virgil told her she had to leave it behind. Allie being Allie said, 'All right, Virge. Leave it behind. I'll stay with it.' She recalled there being a long silence at that moment until Wyatt broke it. He came over and said, 'Oh, we can get it in someplace.'"

Finally, the short wagon train got going. The trip there was not without incident. Years later, Adelia, the youngest of the Earps, in reminiscing about her brothers, offered that "Virgil was Virgil and there wasn't nobody much like him. He was a fine man. He was the biggest and had a big booming voice and laugh and a real big heart too. You would really have to push him some to make him angry but then he really did explode."

A stage driver found this out. On the way from Prescott to Tombstone, the wagon with Virgil and Allie was in the lead. Suddenly, they heard a stage racing up behind the short column of wagons. Deferring to a vehicle carrying the U.S. Mail, all three wagons moved aside so the stage could get through on the narrow road. When the stage, at what seemed like reckless speed, got to Virgil's wagon, there was a quick collision and one of Virgil's horses was slightly injured. Instead of an apology, the driver laughed as he forged ahead.

The Earps found the stage five miles later. It had stopped so the passengers could refresh themselves and the team of horses could be changed. In his capacity not as a deputy U.S. marshal but as an angry Earp, Virgil went up to the driver and knocked him down. As Allie remembered, "Virge just thumped the pudding out of him, knocking him down as fast as he could get up." It had to be enjoyable for Wyatt and James to see their brother in action.

They arrived in Tombstone without further incident. Allie was not overjoyed at the prospect of setting up a living situation with Wyatt and James, but, even with Virgil's devotion to her, she really did not have a say in the matter. He and Wyatt and James were thinking along the same lines: the booming Tombstone offered an exciting opportunity, and if they could get Morgan and Warren to head south and east, respectively, five Earp brothers together would be an unbeatable combination. The oldest of them, James, was still in his thirties, Virgil was thirty-six, and Wyatt was thirty-one— even with the average life spans of the time, there was plenty of future ahead.

There was not much left to the year—and the decade of the 1870s—so the Earps had to get to work. However, there was an immediate disappointment for Wyatt. His plan had been to use the wagon he and Mattie had traveled in to haul freight and possibly passengers. He found there were two stage lines already established in Tombstone. Plan B was to use their savings to stake mining claims. This they did, and eventually their collection of mines would be called Rocky Ridge, Grasshopper, Mountain Maid, Mattie Blaylock, and just plain Earp. However, even if there was to be a payoff, it was not about to happen overnight. In the meantime, they had to earn an income.

Virgil began his duties as the local federal marshal, but because he was paid only when called upon to chase thieves or perform another law-enforcement duty, he took on any freight-hauling jobs he could find. By now, all Wyatt knew was lawing and gambling, and neither was in high demand in Tombstone. James had the bad shoulder thanks to a Johnny Reb bullet, meaning manual labor was out, so he tried to get a bartending job. In general, though, with all the people who had flocked into town in 1879, there was no work going begging.

As the year came to a close, the Earp brothers and their nervous "wives" were wondering if traveling to Tombstone had been a major mistake.

Chapter Eight

"A CITY UPON A HILL"

Pima County covered much of south and southeast Arizona and included Tucson. When its board of supervisors had voted to incorporate Tombstone as a village in November 1879, that was a recognition of its rapid growth and prospects for the future. Another was an action by the federal government, presenting Tombstone with its own post office. Given his role in helping to establish Tombstone, it was fitting that Richard Gird was appointed the first postmaster.

A village council began to pass laws, and a forty-year-old attorney, William Harwood, had been elected mayor. On January 6, 1880, the first official town marshal was elected; his name was Fred White. This was an odd choice by voters because of his inexperience as a lawman, but White turned out to be a good selection. Though often depicted in movies and television shows as a middle-aged (or older) nervous or incompetent man with a tin star, White was originally from New York City and only thirty-one years old. He, too, took the term "peace officer" seriously, arresting those who needed arresting while avoiding gunplay. White earned respect by existing only on the marshal's salary and not having vested interests in any of the local gambling halls or saloons. He quickly gained the reputation of being a fair and impartial lawman. Even the notorious Curly Bill Brocius (much more about him later) liked Marshal White and occasionally even helped him to defuse tense situations with drunken cowboys.

A count taken in 1879 toted up 900 residents of Tombstone. By the following June, there would be 2,100 people living there. Typical of a frontier boomtown, only 212 of them were women. That would likely change with enhanced accessibility: three months earlier, the railroad had arrived in Tucson, making the trip to Tombstone less daunting, uncomfortable, and time-consuming. An even more immediate connection to the outside world, telegraph lines, arrived in Tombstone in July.

The potential for prosperity in Tombstone was seen in the expectation that people would want to visit the new village, and obviously they would need lodgings. The previous year, Tombstone's first hotel had opened for business. It was, to say the least, a modest one—the Mohave, owned by Charley Brown, at the corner of Fourth and Allen Streets, was a large tent that could take up to twenty guests. Soon, though, thanks to a robust surge in available lumber, more permanent accommodations, including private residences, were being constructed.

It seemed as though in the blink of an eye another hotel would be erected. Still, the supply of rooms was barely keeping up with the influx of new residents and people considering becoming ones. Semantha Fallon opened the San Jose House at Fifth and Fremont Streets. On a grander scale was the Cosmopolitan Hotel on Allen Street, the most well-known thoroughfare in Tombstone, which would also feature the Occidental, Alhambra, Hafford's, and Oriental Saloons, Can Can Restaurant, Vogan's Bowling Alley, and Bird Cage Theatre.

The street was named after John Brackett Allen, a native of Maine who had moved to Tucson in 1858 to, of all things, sell pies, which cost a dollar each. He became quite successful as his activities expanded into dairy farming and beekeeping. After the Civil War, Allen was one of the proponents of making Tucson the territorial capital. He would serve in the legislature and as Arizona's treasurer and was known as General Pie when he held the office of adjutant general.

His direct connection to Tombstone was arriving there after the initial silver strikes and establishing several businesses. Allen's life took a dramatic turn in 1881 when at age sixty-three he married a teenager named Lola Tapia. Not long after the marriage ceremony, Lola repaired to a convent, where she gave birth to a daughter. After ten years of a rather unusual marriage—presumably, Lola left the convent after giving birth—the couple divorced. During an expedient fifteen minutes in the same court, Lola was fined $25 for adultery, her divorce from Allen was granted, and she married her lover. The lovelorn "Pie" Allen died penniless in Tucson in 1899, his only possession of any value a tombstone that had been gifted to him by friends that April.*

People had to be fed while they were in Tombstone. The Cadwell and Stanford grocery store opened, and it soon had competitors.

---

* This tombstone adorned his grave in the paupers' section of the Court Street Cemetery in Tucson. Years later, when that section of the cemetery was needed for a building project, Allen's tombstone was moved to the Pima County Cemetery, but his remains were not and are now considered lost.

The City Bakery was begun by two brothers from Bavaria. A German immigrant opened a butcher's shop, and an Irishman opened the City Meat Market. There were ice-cream shops and candy shops squeezed in between the saloons and dance halls. Thanks to the railroad reaching Tucson, imported goods, including fresh fruit from California, arrived there and could be shipped by wagons the seventy miles to Tombstone.

And early on, an effort was made by entrepreneurs from the East to turn Tombstone into a culinary destination. One would not think this about a frontier town that seemed to emerge overnight. However, according to Sherry Monahan's *Taste of Tombstone*, "While Tombstone is associated with gunslingers, gamblers, and cowboys, it was a mining boomtown. It had all the modern conveniences by 1880s standards, including restaurants that were beautifully decorated and often compared to the finest in San Francisco." She adds that those restaurants advertised that they were "the most elegantly appointed" and had "the best cooking and polite attentive service." And here were new eateries that "were decorated with chandeliers, Brussels carpeting, and walnut tables adorned with imported china, cut glass, and stylish cutlery."

Whereas only two or three years earlier prospectors such as Ed Schieffelin were subsisting on whatever wild game they could kill and dismember, in 1880 hotels and restaurants were offering big-city fare. On the menu at the Cosmopolitan were oyster patties and English plum pudding (with queen sauce), "fish and game a specialty" at the Elite, at the Occidental one could order "Filiet d Boeuf, aux Champignons, Chateaubriand, Aux Petite Pois," and Sunday dinner at the Grand Hotel included calf's tongue with mushrooms and venison with jelly.

Midway through the year, the mines surrounding Tombstone

were offering up large quantities of silver, delighting those who had invested in their operations. The desire for food and entertainment grew even greater. "Some of the entertainment included theater shows, grand balls, private parties, and dining out," Monahan reports. "Some of the newest restaurants in Tombstone were Delmonico's, the Golden Eagle, an Italian restaurant, the Bodie restaurant, and the Star Restaurant." Also by then, Charley Brown had replaced his tent hotel with Brown's Hotel, which in turn would be torn down to make room for a two-story establishment built of brick that could accept up to 150 guests.

One more indication of a town on the rise—people were finding it interesting enough to write about. For some, that took the form of keeping journals, with the most helpful today being the one meticulously kept by George Whitwell Parsons. This energetic young man became something of a poster boy for those who were attracted by the potential of a booming frontier town but were not miners.

Parsons had been born in 1850 in Washington, D.C. His ancestors included a soldier who had fought the British at Bunker Hill in Boston and an officer who had been a member of General George Washington's staff. He was educated to be a businessman in New York City but had a restless spirit and set sail around Cape Horn to San Francisco. He found a job in banking but lost it when that industry was gutted by the Comstock Lode becoming played out. "My future is discouraging," he fretted.

But the prospect of turning thirty spurred him into action. In February 1880, he left San Francisco bound for Arizona, drawn by headlines about new and ongoing silver strikes. After a few lackluster attempts at mining—by then, any claim worth staking had been staked—he and a partner founded a mining agency that managed claims and their owners' finances. Earning a pretty good living and surrounded by all kinds of excitements, George Parsons decided to stay for the long haul.

Others wrote about Tombstone people and events for publication. That was true of reporters and contributors to the *Tombstone Daily Nugget* and the rival newspaper that made its debut in 1880, *The Tombstone Epitaph*, with John Clum at the top of the masthead.

He had been the editor of the *Arizona Citizen* in Tucson and was doing well enough to support his wife and young son. However, when reports came in about the enticements of the new town called Tombstone, the restless Clum felt he was missing a better story. In December 1879, he rode south for a visit, and what he saw and heard confirmed his feeling. Clum sold the *Citizen*, moved his family to a new residence, and, declaring that "every Tombstone must have an Epitaph," he founded the newspaper.[*]

During the first few months of 1880, Clum had to literally build readership by first constructing a place to put the printing operation. With helpers, he created a wood-and-canvas building for his presses and office. On May 1, the first edition rolled out. Not shy about promoting the prospects of the young mining town, Clum proclaimed that Tombstone "is a city upon a hill promising to vie with ancient Rome upon her seven hills in a fame different in character but no less in importance."

This reads like hyperbole, but Clum had jumped into Tombstone with both feet and he would be one of its strongest champions. "One may think that Clum was merely employing the editorial privilege of boosting the home town to woo its support for his new paper,"

---

[*] Clum had a partner, Thomas Sorin, who managed the printing chores. After a year, he sold his share of the *Epitaph* to Clum.

writes Douglas D. Martin in *Tombstone's Epitaph*. "But succeeding editorials prove he meant what he wrote. He believed implicitly in the future of the town and he fought fearlessly for the policies he thought would advance the growth of the community."

Clum was a keen and industrious part of that growth. The same month the *Epitaph* published its first issue, Richard Gird resigned as postmaster. Soon after, Clum took the position. "The rush was on," he noted in his journal. "I removed and refitted the post office three times within a year in an endeavor to keep pace with the rapid growth of the community."

And then there was Clara Brown, who spread the word about Tombstone through her descriptions published in southern California. Clara Spalding had been born in 1855 in New Hampshire. She received a good education, first in local public schools and then at the Massachusetts State Normal School. At age twenty-three she was married to a thirty-three-year-old Maine man, Theodore Brown, and on her way cross-country. The couple settled in San Diego, where Mr. Brown found work as a teamster and ranch hand.

They did not stay there long. Brown was not immune to the siren call of ore strikes, and when news reached San Diego of the silver being found in southeast Arizona, he was one of 150 men from that city to head east. Teamsters would be needed to haul all that extracted ore, and Brown figured to be one of the first to be hired.

He was not, by a long shot, but during that optimistic spring of 1879, there was plenty of work to go around. His wife found work, too, though not in an anticipated occupation. Clara's education had given her an interest in theater, and in San Diego while her husband was away she undertook roles in amateur productions. But she also had an interest in writing. She had an acquaintance at a newspaper in Boston, which began publishing her descriptions and observations of the San Diego area. A lifelong journalism career was born.

When Theodore Brown finally asked his wife to join him, he had traded hauling freight for being a partner in the Saladin silver mine. Clara gamely undertook the journey, taking a steamer to Los Angeles, the railroad to Tucson, then a stagecoach to Tombstone. Theodore waited for her in a cabin at the corner of Fourth and Bruce Streets. Here she set up her writing table, as she had arranged to send dispatches to the *San Diego Union*. Among her first impressions of her home was that "it was not the most charming place to live." However, she allowed that it was "endurable" and possibly "enjoyable."

Her first full dispatch was dated July 7, 1880. "That I survived the journey this letter testifies," she informed her curious readers, "but that anything short of a life and death matter would induce me to go back over the road this summer, I doubt."

One had to wonder, though, if she would change her mind after reporting, "The camp is one of the dirtiest places in the world. When black garments appear to have been laid away in an ash barrel, and one is never sure of having a clean face, despite repeated ablutions, it is time to talk about dirt. The soil is loose upon the surface, and is whirled into the air everyday by a wind which almost amounts to a gale; it makes the eyes smart like the cinders from an engine; it penetrates into the houses, and covers everything with dust. I do not believe the famous Nebraska breeze can go ahead of the Tombstone zephyr."

And there was the southeast Arizona heat: "The mercury gallivants around in the nineties, with altogether too highminded ideas. One could stand two or three days of that sort of thing with tolerable grace, but it taxes one's endurance to receive no quarter at all." Clara does express gratitude that there "had been only one murder since my arrival."

The murder she alludes to demonstrated that no matter how fast Tombstone was growing, it was still a frontier town subject to disputes being settled with guns . . . especially when a woman was involved. Such was the case on June 22, 1880, when Frank Leslie killed his girlfriend's husband.

"Buckskin," as he was known, because of the fringed buckskin vests he preferred, was one of those western characters who at any given time was on one side of the law or the other, and he has a prairie dog–like way of popping up in Tombstone tales. He was born Nashville Franklyn Leslie in 1842 in San Antonio, Texas. He claimed to have served in the Confederate army during the Civil War, was a deputy when Wild Bill Hickok was marshal of Abilene in the early 1870s, and spent much of that decade as a scout for the U.S. Army. Leslie also contended that he had worked as a cowboy in Australia and piloted a ship in the Fiji Islands. He managed to return to the States in time for the Tombstone boom years, and he and a partner opened the Cosmopolitan Saloon next to the hotel of the same name.

May Evans was a chambermaid at the Cosmopolitan Hotel, and in April 1880, she married Michael Killeen. It must not have been a fulfilling honeymoon because the two soon separated. Apparently not one to regret the loss of the promise of domestic bliss, Mrs. Killeen took up with Buckskin Frank. Still smarting over the brevity of the marriage, Mr. Killeen became even more unhappy and angry. On the night of June 22, he soaked up a large quantity of whiskey and went looking for his wife and Leslie, whom he found keeping company on the Cosmopolitan Hotel's front porch.

Killeen had a gun and he fired two shots. Because of his highly intoxicated state, he may have been seeing two Buckskin Franks, and he didn't kill either one, though one bullet grazed the victim's head. Killeen jumped up onto the porch and began pounding his wife's lover with the pistol. Suddenly there was a shot, and Killeen fell, wounded, and would die the following week. While it was not clear if Leslie or another man who had intervened fired the fatal shot, self-defense was the determination. Eight days after Killeen met his Maker, May and Frank married. Being practical, the bride used the same maid of honor and parlor at the hotel as in her previous ceremony.*

Despite an incident like the Killeen killing, Tombstone strained at the bit to become a sophisticated town on the frontier that would attract more investment and families. Thus, the last thing Mayor Harwood and local lawmakers wanted was turmoil—the kind brought by those still living in the 1870s. But like most frontier towns, Tombstone could not pick and choose who passed through and who decided to live there. It attracted other kinds of "entrepreneurs," too, looking to feed off the boom times, and they brought their rough edges with them.

The Earps were just one example. Another was the Clanton brothers, who had arrived in the area in 1878. Joseph Isaac Clanton, known as Ike, had opened up a restaurant that same year at

---

* It would be strike two for May Evans Killeen Leslie. In 1887, claiming her husband had an affair with Miss Birdie Woods and that he had beaten and choked her, she was granted a divorce. Leslie took up with Mollie Edwards. When he found her chatting with another man, he shot and killed her. Sentenced to life in prison, he served six years, then was pardoned by Governor Benjamin Franklin. He went to California to marry a pen pal, Belle Stowell, and when that union failed (this time without gunshots), Leslie eventually wound up back in Tombstone. At some point he returned to California, where he died in 1927 at age eighty-five.

the original Tombstone site, but soon ranching was more time-consuming than serving steaks.

The patriarch of the family—who appropriately would be known as Old Man—was Newman Haynes Clanton. He had been born in Tennessee in 1816, and in Missouri in 1840 he married Maria Kelso. The couple had two daughters and five sons—John Wesley, Phineas Fay, Joseph Isaac, Alonzo Peter, and William Harrison (called Billy). Newman Clanton seems to have been as restless as Nicholas Earp, driving his growing herd of a family through Missouri to Illinois to Texas and California. From farming and slaveholding he attempted gold mining and ranching and more farming. When the Civil War began, he and his oldest son enlisted in the Confederate Home Guard.

After the war it was back to California. In 1873, seven years after his wife passed away, Old Man Clanton and his family quit being sharecroppers in Santa Barbara and tried the new territory of Arizona, establishing a ranch in the southeast in the San Pedro Valley, which had plenty of good grazing land. "Establishing" may be too strong a word, as it is believed that the Clantons simply found a good site and squatted on it, with no official transaction taking place. Also, it was a common practice there at the time for grazing cattle to wander off private land onto public land and no one took much notice. Solidifying his hold on the property, Clanton and his sons built a large adobe house there.

"The cheapest way for poor but aspiring ranchers to build up their herds was by rounding up mavericks—unbranded calves whose mothers had died—and putting their own brand on them," writes Andrew C. Isenberg in *Wyatt Earp: A Vigilante Life*. (The title certainly gives away the author's view of the Earps.) "In the early 1870s in most western territories, mavericks were considered part of the public domain; like unclaimed land, they were free for the taking. . . . Mavericking remained one of the best ways for the rural western poor to rise to respectability. In short, the Clantons were property-less migrants who employed two of the most common means to exploit the public domain in the nineteenth-century West: squatting and mavericking. Both were, or became, technically illegal."

Another entrepreneurial family was the McLaury brothers, represented locally by Frank and Tom. There were three brothers originally from Iowa, but on their way west through Texas, Will, an attorney, had chosen to open up a practice in Fort Worth. An office did not appeal to Frank and Tom; they wanted open spaces and hoped to establish a ranch. They did that when they reached Pima County, on the Babocomari River. There they raised sheep as well as cattle. Because of their proximity to each other and mutual business interests, the Clantons and McLaurys became friends.

As Jeff Guinn points out, "Not everyone rushing to the area settled in Tombstone itself. Previously, only a few major ranching operations could survive the Apache presence in the area. But with an exploding, hungry population creating an urgent demand for fresh beef, small ranchers began setting up along the San Pedro River and in deep, grassy arroyos."

By the end of 1879, the Clantons were doing well. Their cattle could not grow to slaughtering size fast enough, such was the growing demand for beef in Tombstone, Bisbee, and other nearby communities. No one seemed to notice that the family had never registered a brand in Pima County, a legal requirement to raise cattle. The Clantons were generally well regarded, and their supply of beef was most welcome. What also wasn't questioned—at that time, at least—was how the Clantons managed to "raise" so much cattle so quickly. Rustling was conveniently ignored, as long as it was not rampant . . . a scenario that would soon play out when the "cow-boys" took control of it.

While the Clantons and McLaurys had a regard for Tombstone because of its hungry consumers and plentiful saloons, there was some resentment, too. The ranchers saw themselves as true residents of the area who intended to stay even if, or when, the silver boom went bust. They were putting down roots and foresaw raising broods of Clantons and McLaurys there, and other nearby ranchers felt the same. But in town they encountered many people with silver in their eyes and get-rich-quick schemes in their hearts, who would abandon Tombstone at the first sign of a dip in its prospects.

As Casey Tefertiller observes, "Most of the people who came to this desolate spot were not looking for a home . . . they were coming to make money then leave. This sojourner mentality would quickly establish an antagonism between the transitory townsfolk and the cattlemen who came to Arizona to build ranches and start families that would populate the Southwest for generations."

Clara Brown had written to her San Diego readers about the festivities held in Tombstone on July 4, 1880, noting that it was "celebrated only by an increased amount of drunkenness" and, ominously, "a few rockets, which was anathematized by the cautious, who realize that the town is a tinder box, and liable any day to be swept from existence."

The reporter was obviously referring to the predominance of wooden structures and hot, dry heat combining to turn Tombstone into a conflagration waiting to happen. This would prove to be disastrously true. However, Tombstone as a tinderbox also meant the confluence of forces—squatting ranchers, increased cattle rustling with mavericking as a quaint alibi, cowboys finding work in the area as well as inadequate law enforcement, newly entitled families such as the Clantons and McLaurys, and the ambitious and clannish and perhaps mercenary Earps (soon to be joined by Doc Holliday)—that would inevitably erupt as conflagrations of a different kind and climax in the most famous gunfight in the American West.

Chapter Nine

"YOU WILL HAVE TO FIGHT ANYWAY"

The Earps' early days in Tombstone were not auspicious ones. An immediate disappointment was where they first lived, which was a humbling comedown from their Dodge City and Prescott accommodations. One can understandably imagine the Earp women wondering, "We came to Arizona for *this*?" If their situation had not improved, it is likely the brothers would have elected to move on to seek their fortune in the next boomtown, and the history of the American West would be much different.

In what must have been extremely cramped and intimate quarters, the extended family resided in a small house. It was all they could afford, and even at that, in a boomtown it did not come cheap. As Allie described it, "We happened on a one-room adobe on Allen Street that some Mexicans had just left. It didn't even have a floor—just hard packed dirt, but it cost forty dollars a month. We fixed up the roof, drove the wagons up on each side, and took the wagon sheets off the bows to stretch out for more room. We cooked in the fireplace and used boxes for chairs."

The spunky Allie was not about to sit around and wring her hands about the employment status of the menfolk. It turned out to be fortunate that she had insisted on bringing her sewing machine along. Allie was hired to make a canvas tent for a new saloon. This project turned out fine enough that others in the town began giving her jobs, and she hired Mattie to assist her. The money they brought home helped the Earps stay afloat until more revenue came in. Allie would crow, "That big canvas tent with its double rows of stitching changed our luck."

Virgil had his occasional federal pay and secured jobs as a wagon driver. And because Tombstone was a boomtown, before long James found a job dealing faro and bartending in a saloon. Wyatt began gambling, but it was more as something to pass the time until less risky employment came along. Finally, he was offered a job as a Wells Fargo stage guard. Wyatt surely had not anticipated such a position, but he had been a shotgun messenger before, while on sabbatical from Dodge City lawing, and with all the cash being transported, men with experience were welcomed. What he also could not have anticipated was how his renewed connection to Wells Fargo would benefit him in the near future.

The trickle of money coming into the Earp household became a stream, but the men weren't necessarily happy about it. As Casey Tefertiller points out, "They had arrived seeking fortune, not wages."

Still, the brothers were better able to put food on the table, and the living became easier for their women. "Within a few weeks Mattie considered herself settled, content to lead a quiet life, and she remained so throughout her entire stay," contends E. C. (Ted) Meyers. "Although she was admittingly drinking (she and Allie are known to have shared many an afternoon nip) she kept it private.

As in Dodge City, her stay in Tombstone is notable mainly for its almost total anonymity."

Some of this was by design. Although Tombstone was a relatively new frontier town, far from the social mores of society to be found east of the Missouri River, Allie and Mattie had become Earp wives without real weddings, and the only occupation Bessie had known in her adult life was as a prostitute and brothel owner. There was a strong element in town, which included the wives of prominent businessmen, who wanted Tombstone to become respectable, to be a civilized community in which to raise children, educate them, and attend churches as families. The Earp women were from the wrong side of the tracks. And that posed a problem for the brothers' financial and social aspirations.

"While a man and woman lived together as common-law husband and wife, no one questioned their standing as a couple," explains Jeff Guinn. "But in territorial towns of any consequence, there would always be a small, select upper class of investors and merchants, and these men often did bring their wives with them, women who were married in every legal sense. Formally married women might associate in a reasonably friendly fashion with common-law wives, but they would rarely invite them into their homes."

Allie tells of a day that she and Mattie broke free of their tiny box of a home to stroll through the downtown area, admiring displays in the storefronts and the menus posted outside hotels and restaurants. When Wyatt found out about their escape, he was furious. Their women were not to be representatives of the Earp brothers and risk thwarting the respectability they, particularly Wyatt, intended to acquire. As Guinn adds, "The things he wanted—money, social prominence, *importance*—were far more likely to be found within Tombstone's town limits." And the women needed to be cloistered in the claustrophobic home limits, not strutting about.

The U.S. Census figures for Pima County in 1880 listed Alvira Earp, Bessie Earp, Hattie Earp (Bessie's daughter), James Cooksey Earp, Mattie Earp, Virgil Walter Earp, and Wyatt Berry Stapp Earp. Allie's, Bessie's, and Mattie's occupations were given as "Keeping House," James was a "Saloonkeeper," and "Farmer" was the fanciful occupation given to both Virgil and Wyatt.

By the time the census was taken, the Earp family members had dispersed. With almost everyone working and earning fairly steady pay—Bessie probably did most of the "Keeping House" while caring for her daughter—they could afford their own homes. But these were the clannish Earp brothers, so they were not about to spread out too far. Virgil and Allie found a house at the southwest corner of First and Fremont Streets, Wyatt and Mattie lived on the northeast corner, and James and Bessie were only one block away.

They would soon have company. After Morgan resigned as a peace officer in Butte, he did not come directly from Montana but detoured to the Earp homestead Nicholas and Virginia had set up in San Bernardino County in California. Morgan left Louisa there, unsure if her fragile health was ready for the rigors of life in southeast Arizona. Even though Allie liked the boyish Morgan, upon his arrival in Tombstone she now had four clannish Earp brothers together, and word was that the youngest, Warren, might soon be on the way.

The only official lawman of the family, Virgil, found himself becoming busier. According to the March 26 edition of *The Weekly Arizona Miner*, one of the territorial newspapers that included Tombstone news, "Deputy U.S. Marshal V. W. Earp arrested a man by the name of C.S. Hogan at Tombstone, a few days since, for counterfeiting trade dollars. He was examined, held to bail in $5,000, but escaped from the Tombstone prison. The plates and dies were found with the prisoner." As we shall see, the porous walls of the Tombstone jail would be a persistent problem.

There were times, though, when the sturdiness of the jail did not matter . . . and that Tombstone could still be a rough-and-tumble town. A FATAL GARMENT was the headline of an article in the July 23, 1880, edition of *The Tombstone Epitaph*, and Tom Waters had the misfortune to be wearing said garment.

He and E. L. Bradshaw were both miners and friends who had the worst kind of falling-out. On the morning of July 22, while in town, Waters bought a blue-and-black plaid shirt and, quite proud of himself, wore it on what was apparently a day off from digging for silver. The colorful pattern was a tad loud, and passersby remarked on it, irritating the wearer. The peeved Waters sought shelter in Tom Corrigan's saloon on Allen Street, where he declared the next person to comment on his new shirt would get a sock in the jaw.

In walked Bradshaw, who innocently complimented his friend on the new garment. Waters's aim was off, and he hit his friend above the left eye. The effect was the same, though: Bradshaw fell unconscious to the dirt-filled floor. He remained there as Waters left. He visited other saloons, announcing his continuing displeasure at the reception his shirt received. When Waters weaved back to Corrigan's, Bradshaw was gone.

The abruptly former friend, after shaking himself awake and rising from the floor, had returned to his cabin, washed up, and found his pistol. When he arrived back at Corrigan's, he found Waters standing at the saloon's entrance. When asked, "Why did you do that?" Waters replied with a string of oaths. They were interrupted by the sound of gunshots as Bradshaw fired, altering the blue-and-black pattern to include four bullet holes. Waters was dead before he hit the wooden sidewalk. Bradshaw submitted to arrest, but a grand jury refused to charge him with murder—perhaps some of its members had gotten a gander at the dead man's shirt.

In addition to catching counterfeiters, Virgil performed other lawing duties capably; then came an event that would have far-reaching consequences. That same month as the Waters killing, six army mules were stolen. The commander at Camp Rucker, the stockade once known as Camp Supply, assigned Lieutenant J. H. Hurst to take four soldiers and go find the purloined property. The young lieutenant was smart enough to assume that the crime had been committed by cowboys and that he should have help. His party rode to Tombstone and Hurst looked up Virgil, who agreed that the deputy U.S. marshal should be in on the hunt. Virgil in turn deputized a posse to swell the number of searchers—his brothers Wyatt and Morgan and the local Wells Fargo agent, Marshall Williams.

The nine riders set off, stopping at ranches along the way. On September 25, the searchers arrived at the Babocomari ranch belonging to the McLaury brothers. It was bad enough for the owners that the six missing mules were there; worse, ranch hands were in the process of changing the brands on them. If this had been up to Virgil, there would have been immediate arrests. But this had originated as an army matter. To Virgil's disappointment, Hurst was persuaded by Frank Patterson, a Babocomari foreman, not to arrest anyone and to await the return of the mules in Tombstone.

The gullible officer may have been the only one surprised when the mules did not show up—but Patterson, the McLaurys, and their young friend Billy Clanton did, to taunt Hurst for being such a rube. Instead of immediately repairing to the ranch to seize the mules, the army officer, perhaps believing the pen was mightier than the saber, created and posted notices naming several men as the thieves and adding that they had been assisted by the McLaurys. Making the matter more farcical, Frank McLaury paid for a notice published in the *Tombstone Daily Nugget* that defended the integrity of his ranch and his own honesty and alleging that Hurst had himself stolen the mules. He further contended that the officer "is a coward, a vagabond, a rascal and a malicious liar" and the "base and unmanly action is the result of cowardice." McLaury looked forward to the matter being "ventilated" so the truth would emerge.

This incident, even with McLaury's rancor, could have been settled over a couple of drinks, but it took an extra serious turn that would later be seen as a catalyst for the gunfight thirteen months later. Not satisfied with the power of the press, Frank McLaury looked up Virgil, accompanied by his brother Tom. Hurst, they believed, was not their only enemy.

"If you ever again follow us so close as you did," Frank McLaury said, meaning Virgil and his posse visiting the ranch, "then you will have to fight anyway."

"If ever any warrant for your arrest were to be put in my hands," Virgil responded, "I will endeavor to catch you, and no compromise will be made on my part to let you go."

Frank said, "You'll have to fight, and you'll never take me alive."

The standoff could have easily escalated. But the McLaurys backed off a bit, asking Virgil if he'd had anything to do with the notices Hurst had posted around town. When Virgil honestly replied that he had not, they appeared satisfied with that and left.

Possibly the McLaury brothers bracing Virgil persuaded Wyatt to put on a badge again, or with hoped-for mining riches proving

11111111

elusive, lawing was a more respectable way to make better money. The Pima County sheriff that summer was Charlie Shibell, and that July he offered Wyatt the position of deputy, with Tombstone being part of his jurisdiction.

Shibell is often overlooked in Tombstone tales, appearing only because of a disputed election that took place later that year. But he had an especially eventful life before he set foot in the town, filled with the kinds of adventures a young man could have because of war and an expanding frontier. And the biggest impact he would have on Tombstone was not that he was elected sheriff but how he did it.

Charles Alexander Shibell had been born in St. Louis in 1841, attended Iowa College, and then relocated all the way west to Sacramento. He was another member of the California Column during the Civil War.* He was with this force of Union soldiers when it took Tucson from Confederate troops in May 1862. Finding the town to his liking, Shibell remained there for the rest of the war, working as a teamster and miner. Immediately after the war ended, he began operating his own ranch on the Sonoita Creek but was bedeviled by Apaches repeatedly stealing his cattle. Throwing in the towel, he returned to Tucson.

Shibell had another reason not to be fond of Apaches, retroactively. In March 1860, they kidnapped Mercedes Sais Quiroz and

---

* The California Column originally consisted of ten companies of the First California Infantry, all five companies of the First Regiment California Volunteer Cavalry, Company B, Second Regiment California Volunteer Cavalry, and Light Battery A of the Third U.S. Artillery. This command contained 1,500 well-drilled and disciplined men. When Lieutenant Colonel George W. Bowie's Fifth California Infantry was added, the total strength was 2,350 men. The objective of the California Column commander, Colonel (and soon-to-be General) James Henry Carleton, was to drive Confederate troops out of the New Mexico Territory.

another girl, and the two were held captive until sometime later when the army traded them for Apache prisoners. After the war, Mercedes met and married Charlie Shibell. Life was productive for a time—perhaps too much so, because after giving birth to four children, Mercedes passed away, at only twenty-six. (The following year, in 1877, Shibell remarried and the couple had two more children.) By then, he had gotten some measure of revenge against Indians for his failed ranch and traumatized wife. Shibell was a customs inspector in April 1871 when he participated in the Camp Grant massacre—144 members of the Aravaipas and Pinal tribes, most of them women and children, were killed and their bodies mutilated.

Shibell's introduction to law enforcement came in January 1875 when he was appointed a Pima County deputy sheriff. He then successfully ran for sheriff. His most notorious escapade as a peace officer was in August 1878, when he led a posse that tracked down the stagecoach robber William Whitney Brazelton, who had vowed not to be taken alive. Though otherwise of dubious moral character, Brazelton was a man of his word—he was shot to death during an encounter with Shibell's posse at the Santa Cruz River south of Tucson. His body was photographed, and copies of the image were sold to the public.

Shibell knew of Wyatt's service in Dodge City and believed selecting him as a deputy was a good idea. John Clum agreed. "The appointment of Wyatt Earp as Deputy Sheriff, by Sheriff Shibell, is an eminently proper one, and we, in common with the citizens generally, congratulate the latter on his selection," opined the editor in the July 29 edition of *The Tombstone Epitaph*. "Wyatt has filled various positions in which bravery and determination were requisites, and in every instance proved himself the right man in the right place." Clum added that Wyatt was about to resign as a Wells Fargo shotgun messenger and would be replaced by Morgan.

One of the last pieces of the puzzle to make the Tombstone picture complete was the arrival of Doc Holliday. According to "Big Nose" Kate Elder's account, in the spring of 1880, Doc received a letter from Wyatt suggesting a move to Tombstone. Kate was not keen on this at all; her dislike of Wyatt had not dwindled. If they were going to leave Prescott at all, better to give Globe a try. More in the center-east section of the territory, it was not as remote as Tombstone, and its mining operations were expanding. That meant, of course, that there were more people with money in their pockets ready to lose it at the gaming tables.

Surprisingly, Doc was intrigued. The couple even set off from Prescott for Globe. But along the way, Doc changed his mind: he was going to reunite with the Earps. Kate said no. Doc said goodbye and detoured to Las Vegas to settle whatever affairs he had to settle. One of them was shooting Charles Wright.

Wright and Holliday had crossed pistols before, during a dispute in Dodge City. Both, obviously, had survived. And they probably thought they had seen the last of each other. But some frontier people tended to get around, and when Doc returned to Las Vegas he learned that Wright was in town. In fact, he was operating his own saloon and gambling parlor named Wright's Place on the town plaza. It was exactly the wrong place for Doc to be if he wanted to avoid any further trouble before moving on to Tombstone, but Doc never was one for letting bygones be bygones.

First, to fortify himself Doc went to dinner, which no doubt included some whiskey, at a nearby eatery. When he walked into Wright's Place, he held a cocked pistol. Doc may have hesitated until he could get a clear shot, not wanting to involve customers, and this gave Wright time to recognize the visitor and crouch behind the bar. He straightened up holding a pistol of his own. Patrons threw themselves to the floor and the shooting commenced.

It quickly became clear that Wright was as equally poor a shootist as Doc because bullets whizzed both ways without effect. Suddenly Wright dropped behind the bar. Doc assumed he had successfully concluded the night's business, and he left. Wright, however, had been only stunned by a bullet grazing his head, and he was soon back to doling out drinks. Still, he did not want to take any more chances. That summer, he sold his interest in the saloon and left Las Vegas.*

Oddly, having shed Big Nose Kate, Doc was not in a hurry to head to Tombstone and his best—and possibly only—friend, Wyatt. Holliday biographer Gary L. Roberts has the former dentist going to Albuquerque, New Mexico, and there he was probably a partner with William Sanguinette in the short-lived Palace Saloon. Doc returned to Arizona, this time back in Prescott, where he spent the summer of 1880. He had roommates—a miner, Richard Elliott, who supported temperance and must have been appalled by Doc's capacity for alcohol; and John Gosper, the future would-be governor of Arizona Territory who had befriended Virgil Earp.

Doc may have gotten sick of hearing about the virtues of sobriety, because before the summer was over he was on the move again, this time to Tucson. The attraction was the San Augustin Festi-

---

* Charles Wright roamed from town to town yet could never seem to leave his Dodge City rivalries behind. While in Fort Worth in December 1890, he tried to gun down Luke Short, a friend to both Wyatt Earp and Bat Masterson who had been the catalyst of the Dodge City War seven years earlier. Wright's marksmanship had not improved, Short prevailed, and the inept Wright, fearing revenge, hit the road again.

val, a mecca for southwest gamblers. It was a sort of convention of cardsharps, faro dealers, dice tossers, and other practitioners of the gambling arts . . . and, no doubt, a fair share of grifters, too. Doc saw familiar faces, and quite possibly one of them belonged to Wyatt Earp, though as a newly minted deputy sheriff of Pima County, a gambling excursion might have been a bad idea.

In any case, Doc finally decided it was time to try Tombstone. That September, he boarded a train, rode it until the tracks ended, and then climbed aboard a stagecoach. One might never consider Doc Holliday a conscientious citizen, but it is known that he arrived in Tombstone no later than September 17, because on that day he registered to vote.

It is entirely possible that another passenger on the journey to Tombstone was a man named Behan . . . someone Doc and the Earp brothers, fairly or not, came to despise.

Chapter Ten

"AN INCREDIBLE BEAUTY"

We cannot travel any further into the Tombstone saga without paying a good amount of attention to two people who would have a strong impact on subsequent events there, and both came very much into Wyatt Earp's orbit: John Behan and Josephine Marcus.

In many books and films about Tombstone, John Harris Behan has been presented as a corrupt lawman, a coward, a good man in a very difficult position, a political operative, a doting father, a philandering husband, a lawman with shifting loyalties, and a fool whose feckless actions led to unnecessary deaths. At various times, he was all of the above. On the big and small screen he usually was played by an unrecognizable or vaguely familiar actor receiving twelfth or fifteenth billing in the cast of characters. His role was certainly bigger than that.

His father, Peter Behan, hailed from County Kildare in Ireland. When old enough, he immigrated to America, where he enlisted in the U.S. Army. He was mustered out in Missouri, worked several jobs, and sometime in 1836 he was introduced to Sarah Ann Harris. She and her family lived in Westport, Missouri, which at that time was on the edge of the frontier and was a stepping-off point for those heading west. (The town would mature into Kansas City.) It was from there, for example, that John C. Frémont's much-lauded expedition to map the Oregon Trail embarked in 1842. The courtship was a successful one, and Peter and Sarah were married the following May 1837. Not feeling any pull to migrate west, they set up living in Westport.

With rabbit-like rapidity, the Behans had fourteen children. The third one was their first son, John, born on October 24, 1844. He received a routine public education and, obviously, gained a lot of experience as an older brother. When the house became too crowded, he left, wandering west and winding up in the San Francisco area, mining and freight hauling. When the Civil War began, he became a civilian employee of the California Column, which participated in the Battle of Apache Pass in July 1862, in southeast Arizona. Behan apparently took a shine to the area, because he did not return to California but lived in Tucson, hauling freight to and from army forts.

His political career began at the tender age of nineteen when he was hired as a clerk at the First Arizona Territorial Legislative Assembly in Prescott. In this capacity, Behan encountered many of the men who would become important figures in territory politics and governments. He was an outgoing young man, possessing some of his father's Irish charm. Reasonably handsome, he learned how to dress as well as he could afford. He also listened and learned and recognized that Arizona was a very promising place for a young man with ambition.

And like many young men, he could not avoid the lure of

prospecting. This almost got him killed. In February 1866, Behan was one of six men searching for valuable ore along the Verde River, which flows west of Flagstaff until it joins the Salt River east of Phoenix. They were attacked by Indians, and while fending them off, Behan was viewed by the others as a courageous fighter. It was probably not a coincidence that later the same year he was hired as a deputy by John Bourke, the sheriff of Yavapai County. The older lawman probably had not foreseen Behan and his fourteen-year-old stepdaughter, Victoria, becoming infatuated with each other.

The ambitious Johnny set his sights on a better job and found one when, at twenty-three, he was elected the county recorder. A year later, in March 1869, he and a pregnant Victoria married. Henrietta Behan was born three months later. Their son, Albert, would be born two years after that. Behan must have maintained a good relationship with his father-in-law, because he succeeded Bourke as the Yavapai County sheriff when the latter stepped down. Two years later, in 1873, Behan was elected to the Seventh Arizona Territorial Legislative Assembly. His star was on the rise.

However, missteps began to pile up. The following year, Behan decided to be sheriff again and ran for the office but lost. And he had formed a habit of having affairs—not only with friends' wives but with his favorites at local brothels. When he wasn't there, he was in Prescott saloons. His carousing had so little discretion to it that the shamed Victoria was forced to file for divorce. To make matters worse for his nonsexual ambitions, Behan's chronic bad behavior was made public in court, this time including verbal abuse and threats of physical violence and his claim that another man had fathered Henrietta. Putting an especially painful coda on the divorce is that soon after it was granted, seven-year-old Henrietta

contracted scarlatina—later more commonly known as scarlet fever—
and died from it.

Behan led an itinerant life the next few years, perhaps trying to
escape an unsavory reputation as well as grief, or guilt. He ran for
Yavapai County sheriff and again lost. For a short time he was in
Tucson as an assembly sergeant at arms, then he was the recorder
in Mohave County in the territory's northwest region. He relocated
south a bit to the mining town of Tip Top, where he operated a
saloon. That is where the U.S. Census found him in June 1880. He
was engaged—at least in her mind—to a nineteen-year-old woman
named Josephine Marcus.

It was because of her that John Behan and Wyatt Earp became
romantic rivals. According to some accounts—mostly hers—she
first came to Tombstone perhaps within days of Wyatt's arrival.
She was a member of the Paula Markham Troupe on a tour of
Arizona performing Gilbert and Sullivan's *H.M.S. Pinafore*. In
December 1879, the company's next stop was Tombstone. At eighteen, a wide-eyed innocent, she had visions of a stage career. However, when Josephine left her home in San Francisco, her vision
had not included jostling in a wagon along the dust-choked roads
of southeast Arizona.

According to her recollections written down decades later,* she
met John Behan during what was first thought to be a holdup. After
several performances of the light opera, the troupe left Tombstone,

---

* Part of the fun of reading *I Married Wyatt Earp*, "written" by Josephine decades
later, is trying to discern fact from fiction. The book, published in 1976, contained
only the sanitized narrative of her life. Still, among the many fabrications there
are kernels of truth in the book. It became a movie in 1983, with Josephine played
by Marie Osmond.

bound for the next frontier venue on the schedule. Suddenly, their coaches were confronted by a band of riders brandishing rifles and wearing guns. This was much more theater than any of them had encountered before. Would it be their last production?

The riders turned out to be members of a posse led by Behan, a sheriff, and the scout Al Seiber. They had stopped the troupe to relay a warning about "marauding savages." (It's not clear if they meant Indians or Mexicans, as the term was sometimes applied to the latter, too.) The posse would not be successful in capturing the miscreants, but Josephine, having become immediately enamored with the dashing (or so it seemed at the time) lawman, thought things had turned out pretty well. She had to figure out how to meet him again.

Okay, that is one version of how her relationship with John Behan began. It was Josephine's story and she stuck to it to the end of her life, which lasted into the 1940s. However, there are reputable researchers who, since her death, have contended that her life was not nearly so virtuous and that by the time she landed in Tombstone she had plenty of "soiled dove" on her résumé.

Let's return to when Victoria Behan was divorcing her husband. During the proceedings, a witness for Victoria, Charles Goodman, testified that he saw John Behan at a house of ill fame, at which resided one Sada Mansfield, a woman of immoral character, and that "said defendant did at the time and at the house spoken of, stay all night and sleep with the said Sada Mansfield." It is believed by some that the prostitute cited was actually Josephine Marcus, even though at most she was fourteen at the time.

Let's journey back even further, to New York City in 1861—a necessary trip, as Josephine Marcus would become the most important woman in Wyatt Earp's long life. She was born the second of three children of immigrants Carl-Hyman Marcuse (later Henry Marcus) and Sophie Lewis. The Lewis family was Jewish and in 1850 had emigrated from the Posen region of what is now Poland. Sophie was a widow with a three-year-old daughter, Rebecca Levy, when she married Marcuse, her junior by eight years. The couple had three children together: Nathan, Josephine, and Henrietta (yes, strange but true: the same name as John Behan's ill-fated daughter).

Henry Marcus was a baker who grew disenchanted with the prospects of New York, and his radical solution was to move his family completely across the country, to San Francisco. Josephine would later claim that her father hailed from Germany and was a prosperous manufacturer. Indeed, many of the German-speaking Jews in the city were doing well, but at the lower level were Yiddish-speaking Poles, and Henry Marcus was one of them. In San Francisco, he again found himself working as a baker.

He did well enough, though, to send Josephine and Henrietta to a school that offered music and dance lessons, and apparently the older sister took to performing, envisioning the glamorous life of a musical comedy actress. However, her life became the opposite of glamorous. The Panic of 1873 had national consequences, including in San Francisco. Henry Marcus could not support his family, which had to move in with his newly married stepdaughter, Rebecca, and her husband in a poor neighborhood. Soon after, the teenage Josephine's life gets murky, and one branch of it might explain what Bat Masterson wrote about her. In addition to Josephine being "an incredible beauty," he would recall about meeting her in Tombstone in 1881 that she was the "belle of the honkytonks, the prettiest dame in three hundred or so of her kind"—the implication being that she had once been or continued to be a prostitute.

As early as age thirteen, Josephine may have assumed the name

Sadie Mansfield—Sarah was her middle name, and Sadie was a common nickname for Sarah then—and worked in a San Francisco brothel on Clay Street owned by Hattie Wells. She offered in *I Married Wyatt Earp* that she had matured physically at an early age and could have passed for being an older teenager, though she mentions nothing about such a scandalous occupation. In 1874, Wells filled a stagecoach with several of her girls, including Sadie Mansfield, and they traveled to Prescott. *The Weekly Miner Journal* noted the arrival of the party from San Francisco and that it included "Miss Saddie Mansfield."

She worked at a brothel on Granite Street in Prescott run by Josie Roland. It was near the Yavapai County Courthouse . . . where the sheriff had an office, and at that time a deputy sheriff was John Behan. He apparently patronized this brothel, and this was when he and Josephine Marcus met. (And yes, for armchair psychologists, she was the same age as Victoria when she and Behan first met.) They must have consorted with some frequency because it was Sadie/Sada Mansfield who was cited prominently during the divorce proceedings brought by Victoria Behan in 1875.

They continued to consort. When Behan ran the Tip Top, the census had Sadie Mansfield as a resident there, her occupation listed somewhat exotically as "Courtesan." But it was also around this time that Sadie, or Josephine, returned to San Francisco. She would later claim that she and her friend Dora, with whom she had joined the Paula Markham Troupe that was touring with *H.M.S. Pinafore*, had gotten homesick. The more likely explanation was that even though free to marry since the divorce, Behan refused to do so, and "Sadie" saw no promising future for herself through a continuing life of prostitution in Prescott.

It may have been an awkward and by then unwelcome reunion

with her family. In any case, it did not last long. John Behan arrived in San Francisco with a marriage proposal. Josephine would write cryptically in her memoir, "In spite of my bad experience of a few years ago the call to adventure still stirred in my blood." That call would lead her to Tombstone and probably much more adventure than she anticipated.

In March 1880, Behan and the once again Sadie Mansfield were reported to be together in Phoenix. Then it was back to Tip Top for a few months. Behan made the move to Tombstone in the late summer of 1880. His reasons were no more intriguing than those of other men on the frontier—an opportunity to get a fresh start in a boomtown. In his case, his fresh start included a familiar companion. He and Sadie—who as part of her fresh start had reverted to Josephine Marcus—set up house together. It became a tad crowded when Albert Behan showed up. Because his mother was about to remarry, the nine-year-old had been shipped to Tombstone to live with his father. Victoria may not have known her previous and younger rival was a member of the household.

This would become a combustible situation, especially as time went on and Behan refused to be dragged to the altar. Fortunately for the onetime actress, when her plans went awry, Wyatt was waiting in the wings.

As the summer of 1880 ended, Warren visited and there were five Earp brothers living in Tombstone, which continued to boom and strive to be more sophisticated. There was able law enforcement led by Fred White and Virgil Earp and Charlie Shibell, young men such as John Behan and George Parsons were looking to reinvent and make a good name for themselves, and ranchers such as the Clantons and the McLaurys were on their way to prospering thanks to the insatiable demand for beef. Tombstone could be mostly known today as a frontier success story, a place of peaceful transition from the Old West to the approaching twentieth century.

But then there were the cowboys. Men such as John Ringo and Curly Bill Brocius were much more interested in the present and lining their own pockets than the future. While neither participated in the most famous gunfight in American history, their transgressions and those of their followers set the stage for it.

ACT III

THE COWBOYS

Tombstone looking north, 1881.

Oh, beat the drum slowly and play the fife lowly
Sing the Death March as you carry me along
Take me to the valley, there lay the sod o'er me
I'm a young cowboy, I know I've done wrong.

—MARTY ROBBINS, "THE STREETS OF LAREDO"

Chapter Eleven

"GIVE UP THAT PISTOL"

For many people today, "cowboy" has a romantic resonance. Countless novels, movies, and television shows have portrayed him as an independent individual who worked hard for his wages, was chivalrous to women, was kind to children, and adhered to a code of honor. They are heroes in most tales of the Wild West, rescuing those in distress and vanquishing evildoers, often with a six-shooter spitting fire. Thanks to this image, the cowboy is one of the most popular archetypes in American culture.

No doubt there were men who rose to that high standard in the 1800s . . . but they were pretty rare in Arizona Territory, where "cowboy" had both a political and a practical connotation: "The word had a sinister meaning," writes Lynn R. Bailey in *The Valiants,* her book about the Tombstone Rangers (more about them later). "Republicans used it to label Democratic opponents whether or not they engaged in nefarious practices. 'Cowboy' also became synonymous with robber, outlaw, and rustler, particularly the latter. All were hard cases who sensed money could be made in Arizona's mining boom."

This was especially true when it came to stealing cattle in Mexico and selling them on the American side. U.S. border agents were as plentiful as icebergs there, and their poorly paid Mexican counterparts depended on bribes to feed their families. Often at night, cowboys would slip into Mexico, cut out a manageable herd of cattle, and drive them through isolated mountain passes into southeast Arizona and southwest New Mexico. On the U.S. side, the thieves had properties they had illegally claimed—or had cozy arrangements with conniving ranch owners—and on them were corrals and a supply of water for the cattle and shacks for the cowboys to sleep in. At these way stations the cattle could be fed while they were rebranded, if the rustlers bothered to perform that chore at all. These four-legged immigrants would be welcomed by ranchers, mining camp butchers, and even U.S. Army contractors. Agents for the Office of Indian Affairs were customers, too, because with Indians on reservations not allowed on or anywhere near their traditional hunting grounds, beef had to be found to feed them, and the cheaper the better.

Newman Clanton and his sons were in the thick of such shenanigans. Old Man was no stranger to legal troubles, which may have predated the time he and his son were convicted of desertion during the Civil War. (It is a mystery how they avoided execution.) Because the Clantons had not registered a brand in Pima County yet owned as many as seven hundred head of cattle, it was commonly believed that some if not many of those cows had been stolen. People might turn a blind eye if the rustling was taking place across the border in Mexico—let the Mexicans worry about that. But if the Clantons were stealing from their neighbors, that was a recipe for trouble.

The family was doing both, because the demand was growing faster than cattle did. Also, at that time the Mexican government charged high tariffs on goods crossing into the United States, including cattle, so as strong as the demand for beef was, the tariff on cattle made it unprofitable to purchase them legally from Mexico. Stealing and smuggling them across the mostly unguarded border made more sense.

However, this antagonized ranch owners in Mexico, who saw themselves as unwilling subcontractors for gringo ranchers. They complained to frustrated government officials who found that their complaints to U.S. state and federal officials were ignored. American ranch owners such as Henry Hooker resented the rustling, too, because they spent the money on land and water to raise domestic cattle and then faced lower prices for their beef because of the unnatural supply. It was a legitimate gripe that it cost a lot more to raise cattle from birth to sale, feeding them and protecting them from Indian raids, whereas thieves were overnight the owners of market-ready beef. The law-abiding ranchers' complaints were also mostly ignored by officials. This was the frontier: let things sort themselves out.

To the Clantons, business was business, and the law should keep its hands off. Their friends the McLaurys helped with the buying of rustled cattle and, after a brand change, selling them for slaughter in Tombstone and wherever else they were wanted. This was hard country, and you had to be even harder to survive.

As most ranchers did, the Clantons and McLaurys employed cowboys. The difference was that just as these ranch owners had lower ethical standards, their standards for whom they employed were practically underground. Cowboys with criminal backgrounds or who otherwise possessed poor reputations were not hired by Hooker and his colleagues but found a welcome mat waiting at the Clanton and McLaury spreads, among others.

Old Man Clanton and his sons were not necessarily disliked. Some Tombstone residents found them, especially Ike, personally engaging, and other than the rustling, which was done as discreetly as possible, the family did not look for trouble. There was the view—which extended to the McLaury brothers, too—that because ranching in general was a tough living, if no one got hurt cutting a few corners, so be it. In southeast Arizona, a man did what he had to do to stay in business and feed his family. Allowances were made.

But a big difference was the caliber of cowboys the ranchers employed. More than a few of the cowboys in southeast Arizona had been shoved or had fled there. Texas had told them to get out. Lawmakers there had passed legislation putting more teeth in their laws, and marshals and sheriffs got tougher in enforcing them. Cowboys who rustled or committed other crimes faced prison or worse.

According to Jeff Guinn, the campaign was wildly successful: "From 1874 through roughly the end of the decade as many as three thousand [cowboys] were jailed, killed, or, more frequently as word of the Rangers' lethal prowess spread, fled Texas to try their criminal fortunes somewhere else. This was exactly what the Texas legislature had intended. Its members didn't care where the rustlers and gunslingers went next. They just wanted them out of the state."

New Mexico, especially after the Lincoln County War, turned out to also have little tolerance for cowboys who rode on the wrong side of the law. Best to keep riding to more open spaces . . . which is what Arizona offered. One who arrived as Tombstone was beginning to boom was William Brocius, known as Curly Bill because of his mop of unruly black hair. Another one was Johnny Ringo.

Brocius remains one of the more mysterious characters of the American West. It is generally believed that he was born in Crawfordsville, Indiana, in 1845. There is little more than speculation about his early years and what he did during the Civil War, or if he participated at all in the conflict.

The eminent historian Robert Utley has suggested that Brocius was a member of the Jesse Evans band of outlaws in New Mexico in the mid-1870s because the cowboy Robert Martin was, and the two were known to be good friends who traveled the frontier together. Billy the Kid was an Evans follower, then he went to work for John Tunstall and became involved in the Lincoln County War. Evans and his companions—Brocius believed to be among them—joined up with the Regulators during the Lincoln County War. When it was over, many who participated were encouraged to move on.

Curly Bill's next "appearance" was as a cowboy in Texas, because several researchers have connected Brocius with a man known as William "Curly Bill" Bresnaham. He was arrested for a robbery in Texas in 1878, along with Robert Martin. The men were convicted and sentenced to five years in prison, but both escaped, winding up in Arizona Territory. Since both Robert Martin and Curly Bill became known as leaders of the rustlers in Arizona Territory, they are considered to be the same outlaws who committed the Texas crime.

Most likely, Brocius was part of the wave of cowboys and outlaws—and some could be both on the same day—who were pushed out of Texas and New Mexico and had little choice but to see if Arizona would tolerate them. He found work on the McLaury ranch, and his rustling skills were put to use. Brocius also became a leader of some of the local cowboys, because despite being a sociopath—or perhaps because of it—he had charisma, a dramatic personality, and a sense of humor that at times turned cruel. It was easy to believe stories about him of a violent past, and no one wanted to cross him. Cowboys carried guns, but that did not mean they were all gunmen, often referred to at the time as "shootists" or "man-killers." Their pistols were for killing small game, herding cattle, fending off Indians, and what they saw as harmless hurrahing while in town. Curly Bill Brocius was a different animal.

The state of Indiana has the unhappy distinction of also producing John Peters Ringo. He was born in Greens Fork in May 1850. His family moved to Missouri, and he counted among his cousins the infamous Younger brothers, who teamed up (much to their disadvantage) with Frank and Jesse James.*

When Johnny was fourteen, the family loaded a wagon and set off for California, where his father hoped the milder climate would slow down his tuberculosis. He never found out. During a stopover in Wyoming, he was cleaning his shotgun. His wife, two sons, and three daughters were nearby when he accidentally blew his head off. Not surprisingly, during his lifetime Ringo was believed to have suffered from severe depression.

Ringo's first reported connection to violent crime was in Mason

---

* There were false reports at the time that have persisted to this day that John Ringo was the college-educated scion of a privileged family who fled west to escape a scandal. He could read and write and speak like someone with good manners, but the bottom line was Ringo was a thug who was no more enlightened and gentlemanly than his rustling partner Curly Bill.

County, Texas, in 1875. He had become friends with Scott Cooley, who had been adopted by Tim Williamson, a local rancher, and his wife after Cooley's parents had been killed by Indians. The boy had grown to become a Texas Ranger and earned a reputation as a merciless pursuer of outlaws. Whatever Ringo's tendencies were by age twenty-five, being associated with Cooley was not a bad thing.

But soon, it was. Cooley had resigned as a Texas Ranger to work with his adoptive father as a rancher. On May 13, a deputy sheriff, John Worley, arrested Williamson for rustling. Whether or not the accusation had merit, enough people thought it did and were furious enough about it that while Williamson was being taken to jail, a mob of German-immigrant cattlemen took the prisoner away from Worley and shot him to death. This incident was the catalyst for what would be called the Mason County War.

When there were no arrests for the murder, Cooley enlisted the help of several men, including Ringo, to avenge Williamson's death. Their first stop was Worley's home, where Cooley shot the deputy, scalped him, and tossed him in a well. Next up was Peter Bader, one of the German ranchers believed to have pulled the trigger. After disposing of him, the outlaw band found another one of the ambushers and he, too, was dispatched. Sheriff John Clark put together a posse that found two of Cooley's men; one was killed, the other wounded and arrested. The Cooley-Ringo gang killed more Germans, then two of their men were found and hanged.

As the violent retributions continued, Sheriff Clark begged the Texas Rangers for help but was rebuffed because many of its members secretly supported their former colleague Cooley. It was a different sheriff, A. J. Strickland, who finally arrested Cooley and Ringo, in December. They were housed in a jail in Lampasas County . . . but not for long, as friends helped them escape. To better their chances of eluding the law, the two friends split up. Cooley went into hiding in Blanco County, and soon rumors alleged that he died there of brain fever. Ringo and another friend, George Gladden, were found and arrested. While awaiting trial, they shared a jail cell with John Wesley Hardin, the young man-killer who put other shootists to shame.

Though both had done their bit in the Mason County War, Gladden was convicted but Ringo was acquitted. Gladden was sentenced to ninety-nine years in prison. In what was a fox-guarding-the-henhouse scenario, Ringo returned to Mason County and was elected a constable there. For unknown reasons—perhaps it got boring, with the baddest guy in Mason County to face being himself—Ringo decided to leave that job, head west, and give Arizona a try.

He was first sighted there in 1879 in the company of a man known as Joe Hill, whose real name was Joseph Graves Olney, another pal from the Mason County War days. Ringo may have simply been passing through, but when he shot a man and got away with it, he surmised that Arizona Territory was his kind of place.

The incident occurred about a hundred miles north of Tombstone, in Safford, in a saloon. As chronicled in *The Arizona Star*, Ringo and his unpredictable temper were having a drink at the bar next to a man named Louis Hancock. Ringo offered to buy him a whiskey, but Hancock replied that he was satisfied with beer. This rejection infuriated Ringo, who whipped out his pistol and hit Hancock in the head with it. Worse for the pummeled patron, the gun went off and the bullet went through the earlobe and into Hancock's neck. Ringo was arrested, let out on bond, and told to appear before a grand jury in Tucson. He instead wrote a letter to Sheriff Charlie Shibell, claiming a foot injury prevented him from making the trip. No doubt to poor Hancock's chagrin, Pima County did not pursue the matter any further.

In another incident, an unrepentant and drunk Ringo was gambling in a saloon in Galeyville, east of Tombstone and very near the New Mexico border. When Ringo was wiped out and no one would lend him money, he stalked out. He soon returned with a rifle and robbed the other players. To rub it in, when he rode away, it was on a stolen horse. Again, local law gave him only a slap on the wrist.

Ringo came and went from Tombstone as the whims seized him, and when he was in the area, he and Curly Bill Brocius went rustling together. They found in each other kindred spirits, both having twisted minds and little regard for human life. They were the two kings of the cowboys, their reputations and actions striking fear even in their friends. Meanwhile, local lawmen such as Marshal Fred White and Sheriff Shibell and Virgil Earp, the deputy U.S. marshal, tried to keep the peace as best they could.

Coping with cowboys and their wild ways when drinking in town was work enough, so what the peace officers did not need was a wild card such as Doc Holliday in Tombstone, a man whose disposition and moods could be as volatile as any cowboy's. But he was Wyatt's good friend, and Virgil had to bite his tongue and cross his fingers. He had to go through especially painful contortions when Doc tried to kill a prominent Tombstone saloonkeeper.

Doc had taken to Tombstone and may have wished he'd reunited with Wyatt there sooner. Though still in its infancy, the town was more cosmopolitan, and the saloons and hotels, especially the newer ones, were of a higher standard than other boomtowns he had lived in or passed through. As Gary L. Roberts points out, Doc noted that there was "a public library at J. Goldtree & Company's cigar store, complete with a carpeted and well-decorated reading room, and a school under construction. There were also Masons, a brass band, a miner's union, a miner's hospital, the Home Dramatic Association, the Tombstone Social Club, a fire department, two daily newspapers, and a variety of other social and political clubs."

Such surroundings appealed to the Georgia blue blood in Doc Holliday. He could excel at the town's gaming tables, dress well, drink better whiskey, not have Big Nose Kate bothering him, at any time any one of the Earps was within shouting distance, and the dry desert air had him feeling stronger than he had in years. There could be something for him in Tombstone that Doc had not thought about since his college days—a future. He probably also recognized the mounting tension in the area, the dynamic between a growing Tombstone aspiring to be more sophisticated and progressive and an infestation of cowboys committing crimes on a daily basis. But that was not his concern. Doc wore no badge, so let the people getting paid to do the lawing look after it.

But Doc encountered Johnny Tyler and as a consequence jumped right into the middle of that dynamic.

John E. Tyler could match Doc in the bad temper department, so it did not bode well when the two men spotted each other in the Oriental Saloon. Tyler was a gambler from Missouri who was known to have shot and killed a man in California, and during the summer of 1880 he had caused some agitation in the saloons of Tombstone. He believed, with justification, that there was an entrenched gambling establishment in the town and he had not been welcomed into it—by not only other gamblers but the men who operated the saloons and gambling halls. One night in September 1880, Tyler and another gambler had squared off with guns drawn, but friends of both men prevented any shooting.

A couple of weeks later, there were not enough friends to go around. Doc and Tyler were both in the Oriental Saloon, owned by Milton Joyce, a former blacksmith capable of acting as his own bouncer. An argument began, one that looked likely to escalate. Demonstrating once again his cool head and efficiency, Marshal Fred White was soon on the scene and he disarmed both men. The gamblers were told to get out and cool off, and their pistols would be kept behind the bar.

They did leave, but they did not cool off and did not stay gone. A short time later, Doc and Tyler reappeared in the Oriental. Joyce refused to give up their pistols and told them to get out. Tyler reluctantly complied. Doc did not. He was in one of his drunk and contentious states. He drawled a few choice insults at Joyce, who came around from behind the bar, grabbed Doc, hoisted him up, and threw him out in the street. Doc got up, patted the dust off his clothes, and went back inside the Oriental, where he demanded the return of his pistol. When an exasperated Joyce began to come out from behind the bar again, Doc turned and essentially threw himself out.

That should have been enough humiliation for one night, but once again, alcohol and anger overwhelmed any good sense Doc possessed. He obtained a pistol and once more walked into the Oriental. This time, when Joyce emerged from behind the bar, Doc began firing. Joyce tugged out his own pistol and fired back. Neither man would have eclipsed Wild Bill Hickok's reputation as a marksman. Joyce batted Doc in the head with his gun, the two men kept struggling and shooting, Joyce was wounded in the hand, and then White was back with a deputy, James Bennett. The fracas ended with Doc's arrest.

The next day, a sore and achy Doc appeared before James Reilly, a judge, and pleaded guilty to assault and battery. He was fined a total of $31.25. It was not good to have Joyce as an enemy, but Doc had overachieved in doing that.

Given how good a lawman he had turned out to be, one wonders if the tensions between the gamblers within Tombstone and between the cowboys and the community would not have boiled over a year later if Fred White had still been marshal. Alas, it was not to be, thanks to Curly Bill Brocius and what was for him a routine night on the town gone very wrong.

Not long after midnight on October 28, a group of cowboys did what they had grown too accustomed to doing—drinking and, when the mood struck them, firing their six-shooters. Some did not bother to step outside the saloon first. A less conscientious lawman might have let the night run its course, but Marshal White took some pride in wearing the badge and he went out to confront the cowboys. He wore his gun, but at the same time he had a good relationship with the cowboys and he expected this to be just one more peacekeeping intervention.

And that is how it started out. White stopped in at several saloons, and where he found cowboys, he asked for their weapons. A few were not happy about it, but they all complied. Believing his duties had been successfully carried out, the marshal was back at his office depositing an armload of pistols when another burst of shooting was heard. White went out to track down the source.

So did Wyatt Earp. The deputy sheriff had heard the commotion, too, while playing cards at the Bank Exchange Saloon. Once outside, he followed the sound of the shots and found his brother Morgan and Fred Dodge, a bartender, doing the same. They spotted the marshal up ahead. Wyatt borrowed Dodge's gun, stuck it in his pants, and walked ahead. Curly Bill Brocius was, as usual, intoxicated and had decided to wander down a dark street to an empty lot. That is where White found him. He said, "I am an officer; give me your pistol."

If another lawman had confronted him, Curly Bill might not have been so cooperative; but with White, he began to comply by taking his gun out of its holster. However, he offered it to the marshal barrel first. At the same time, Wyatt came up behind Curly Bill and grabbed the cowboy's arms to search for any other weapons. Aggravated by the night's commotion by now, White growled, "Now, you goddamn son of a bitch, give up that pistol," and grabbed the gun. Curly Bill had not completely let go of it, and as it was jerked out of his hand, the pistol fired. The bullet struck White in the groin.

The lawman fell to the ground. Wyatt yanked the pistol out of his pants and buffaloed Brocius, striking him on the head with the barrel of his pistol. "What have I done?" Curly Bill complained. "I have not done anything to be arrested for." A couple more blows from Wyatt and Brocius was on the ground, too.

White was hauled to a doctor's office. The marshal's bad luck was compounded by not dying for two more days, suffering much of that time. However, this miserable delay allowed him to give a statement exonerating Curly Bill, explaining as best he could that the cowboy had no intention of killing him and that the gun going off was an accident. This was more consideration than Curly Bill deserved, but the marshal met his Maker with a clean conscience.

Some Tombstone citizens wanted Brocius to meet his Maker, too, and quicker than a jury would decide his fate. When it was learned that the marshal had expired, there was talk of lynching the cowboy. Judge Michael Gray ordered the case and the defendant immediately transferred to Tucson. Wyatt was placed in charge of the mission. Assisting him when they left town were a well-armed Virgil, Morgan, John "Shotgun" Collins, and Doc Holliday.*

Incredibly, during the trip, Curly Bill asked Wyatt where he could get a good lawyer. The deputy suggested that Hereford & Zabriskie were considered a competent firm. Brocius said that he didn't want Zabriskie, as he had prosecuted him once in Texas. Afterward, Wyatt looked into the story about Curly Bill's time in Texas and learned that the cowboy had been convicted of robbery in El Paso, during which a man had been killed. Zabriskie had prosecuted Brocius for the crime. He was tried and sentenced to the penitentiary but managed to escape shortly after being incarcerated.

For now, though, once in Tucson, Curly Bill was deposited into jail, where he would remain for the next two months.

Ironically, instead of gratitude, Curly Bill held on to a simmering anger over the buffaloing Wyatt had administered. This might not have mattered much if the resentment had been strictly personal, but Curly Bill, especially when drunk, railed against Wyatt and his brothers, further instigating tensions and the climactic gunfight.

---

* Collins is a Forrest Gump–like figure, encountering many people and situations in the American West. He was born Abraham Graham in South Carolina, where his great-grandfather had served under Francis "Swamp Fox" Marion during the Revolutionary War. A teenage friend while growing up in Texas was the notorious John Wesley Hardin, and later he served time in jail with Johnny Ringo. Graham participated in the Lincoln County War and befriended Billy the Kid. He renamed himself Collins because of past legal troubles and wives; with his fourth wife, he had six children. His nickname was bestowed when working for Wells Fargo out of Tombstone, where he became a friend of Wyatt's, even though he rediscovered there a cousin, Curly Bill Brocius. He later was a scout for the U.S. Army during one of its pursuits of Geronimo. With Wyatt, Collins was a member of the Dodge City Peace Commission in 1883. In December 1922, at age seventy-one, Collins died in a gunfight in El Paso. He was buried in the Concordia Cemetery.

White was buried at the end of one of the biggest funerals ever held in Tombstone. He had been a good man and a good peace officer, but he was gone and Tombstone needed someone similar to help prevent further bloodshed. That man turned out to be Virgil Earp. Now, with him as the top lawman in Tombstone and Wyatt as the county lawman with jurisdiction, the Earp brothers represented law enforcement in the town and its immediate surroundings. It is no wonder the cowboys and the rustling ranchers they worked for saw the Earps as their most high-profile adversaries.

Chapter Twelve

"VERY LIVELY TOWN"

The Earp brothers had not intended to get into lawing when they came to Arizona. Virgil fell into it easily enough in Prescott as a way to help make a living, and he was more of a natural at it, having both an outgoing and calm disposition coupled with a firm sense of right and wrong. He could handle guns and he could handle people. For Wyatt, too, putting on a badge and once more being a deputy had been a necessity once he realized that the road to riches—for him, at least—might not go through Tombstone.* The often cheerful and occasionally tempestuous Morgan was glad to get the piecemeal work as a deputy to supplement his Wells Fargo income and to be riding with his brothers, knowing James

---

* Contrary to what has been portrayed in countless books, movies, and television shows, Wyatt Earp was never marshal of Dodge City. This fiction was prevalent especially during the twenty-year run of the TV series *Gunsmoke*, and it was often offered (especially by CBS publicity flacks) that Marshal Matt Dillon was based on Wyatt Earp. In reality, though, the character was a composite of Dodge City lawmen Charles Bassett, Bill Tilghman, and Ham Bell.

would have a drink (or, in Wyatt's case, coffee) waiting for them when they returned.

Especially with such tenuous ties to the rough frontier justice system, the Earp brothers certainly never envisioned that in the fall of 1880, less than a year after their arrival, Virgil and Wyatt would hold the positions of deputy U.S. marshal, Tombstone marshal, and Pima County deputy sheriff. Maybe lawing was the way to go after all.

And then even those plans went awry.

By this point, having served as deputy sheriff for several months, Wyatt had his eye on a higher office. It was commonly known that with the population of Pima County growing and with the sheer geographic size of it, the territorial legislature was going to cleave the southeast section away and create Cochise County. Once that became official, the new county would need a sheriff. Wyatt, with his present deputy position and his solid law-enforcement experience, would be the logical choice. John Behan would not agree, but Wyatt did appear to have the upper hand . . . until election day that November.

For Pima County sheriff, the incumbent, Charlie Shibell, was being challenged by Bob Paul. Many believed Paul would win. First, there was the political reality that he was a Republican and the majority of voters (including the Earps) in the county were Republican. For another, Paul was a popular and experienced man. Born in Lowell, Massachusetts, in June 1830, Paul was fifty years old and an intimidating presence at six feet six and 240 pounds.

Few men could match his résumé or his size. At fourteen, Paul had gone to sea on whaling ships, and when one put in at San Francisco, he heard about the spread of gold fever and decided to give mining a try. He actually did okay but found himself drawn to lawing, first elected constable and then becoming deputy sheriff of Calaveras County and then undersheriff. He was credited with running down the Tom Bell gang.*

Paul married a young Irish immigrant, and he was home often enough that they produced ten children. After giving up the badge and not having any further success in mining, he became a shotgun messenger for Wells Fargo. He performed his duties so effectively that the company transferred him to Pima County. His instructions were to scout the area and see if it was worth expanding Wells Fargo routes. In Paul's opinion, it was worth it. As the company established more of a foothold, Paul became something like a top stage-riding security officer. The transition to elected county lawman was expected to be an easy one.

Well, not so fast. Bob Paul and his supporters were shocked when all the votes were counted on November 2 and Shibell was declared the winner by a forty-two-vote margin. Initially, the loser had to accept the will of the people. Then, however, Paul became suspicious. It was known that Shibell had the support of ranchers such as the Clantons and the McLaurys and many of the cowboys, most of whom were southerners. It wasn't so much that Shibell was a corrupt lawman and was heedless of cowboy violence, it was more that Bob Paul was viewed as having no tolerance for illegal activities, especially robbing and rustling, and he had the visible support of Republicans, many of whom were northerners and some Union

---

* Known as the Outlaw Doc, Bell was a physician who found crime more stimulating than medicine. He was the first outlaw to organize a stagecoach robbery in the United States. He should have stuck to surgery, because after a botched robbery in 1856, in which a woman was killed, Bell was caught and hanged.

army veterans such as James and Virgil. But would Paul's opponents sink so low as to rig the election?

He and his supporters did not have to look far for evidence. The ballot box for the San Simon precinct—presided over by Johnny Ringo—was opened and examined. Startling enough were the 103 votes for Shibell compared with a single vote for Paul. Decidedly disturbing was the fact that there were only ten eligible voters in that precinct. Greatly enhancing suspicions were the facts that the balloting in that district had been conducted at the home of the disreputable rancher Joe Hill and in addition to Ringo, a poll official had been Ike Clanton.

Something was very rotten in Pima County. Two weeks after the election, Bob Paul filed a lawsuit to overturn the results.

Whatever the result of the lawsuit, it would come too late for Wyatt Earp—he resigned as deputy sheriff. During the ensuing decades, there have been several explanations for this. One contends that Wyatt was so disgusted by an obviously fraudulent election and Charlie Shibell's reelection that he just wanted out. Those favorably inclined toward Wyatt claimed he resigned because it was the right thing to do. During the campaign the Earps had supported Bob Paul, and maybe if he had lost fair and square that would have been the end of it. But Wyatt believed the election was stolen, and with Paul planning to contest it, Wyatt could not fairly serve his Democrat boss.* One other likely possibility was that Shibell did not want a Bob Paul supporter as his right-hand man, and he took the initiative and ordered Wyatt to resign.

---

* Wyatt's support of Bob Paul as Charlie Shibell's replacement included donating money to help underwrite Paul's litigation, which had to drive an even bigger wedge between the sheriff and his deputy.

What Wyatt may not have counted on and what had him immediately regretting his decision—if it had been his—was Shibell appointing John Behan to replace him. This was a galling turn of events. Why Behan? The most benign reason was that he did have law-enforcement experience, and an understandable political reason was that Behan was an active Democrat. But an ominous reason was that he was favored by the ranchers and cowboys, and thus Behan's appointment was a thank-you for the election results.

Worse, there was the emerging rivalry for the affections of Josephine Marcus. Though much is suspect about Stuart Lake's *Wyatt Earp: Frontier Marshal,* one can give some credence to his statement in a letter about the book: "Johnny Behan's girl was the key to the whole yarn in Tombstone."

In the fall of 1880, Sadie and Behan and his son, Albert, were living together in Tombstone. This would be a rather scandalous situation for a proper young woman from San Francisco, but either no one considered Josephine a proper young woman or it was accepted that her marriage to Behan was imminent. She had already begun calling herself Mrs. John Behan. It is not known exactly when she and Wyatt first met. Though it had grown rapidly since Ed Schieffelin's discovery of valuable ore only three years earlier, Tombstone was still a small town and many people observed and knew one another. Both Wyatt and Behan rented office space above the Crystal Palace Saloon, and Josephine might have visited the latter there and encountered the tall, handsome deputy sheriff with the piercing blue eyes.

However they first met, Wyatt, as well as other young men, would have noticed Josephine. One of the most vivid descriptions of her was by Allie Earp in *The Earp Brothers of Tombstone.* Pointedly referring to her as Sadie and echoing Bat Masterson a bit, Allie reported that her "charms were undeniable. She had a small, trim body and a *meneo* of the hips that kept her full, flounced skirts bouncing. Sadie was an attractive woman with thick, dark hair, vivid black eyes, and was well-endowed."

It is unlikely that so soon after her arrival in Tombstone and with the cover story of marriage that Wyatt and Josephine had anything more than a nodding acquaintance. But there had to have been at least a spark between them. If so, it might have stayed in its proper place . . . except that her "fiancé" replaced Wyatt as undersheriff around the time it appeared that Josephine might be available.

Week after week went by and there was no wedding ceremony. Josephine felt she had been hoodwinked. Behan was free to pursue his business and other interests (which probably still included visits to brothels) while she kept house and looked after his son. Worse, the house they were living in had been constructed when they arrived in Tombstone with her money, possibly a wedding gift from her father or the proceeds from her years as a sporting girl.

"Josephine Marcus Behan's social status was even murkier than that of the Earp wives," writes Ann Kirschner in *Lady at the O.K. Corral.* "She was caught in the netherworld between wife and mistress, stepmother and governess. Johnny continued to escort her to social affairs, where she mixed with couples who were legally married. After all, she argued to Johnny, couples did marry, even in Tombstone. Even James Earp's stepdaughter had married a local businessman in a legal ceremony, despite the fact that her mother," Bessie Earp, was a former madam and her "aunts" were in common-law relationships.

Exasperated, Josephine returned to San Francisco, where she

would remain for the rest of the year. One account has her bringing Albert along to be evaluated by doctors for a hearing impairment. Behan may not have missed her . . . but perhaps Wyatt did.

With Wyatt returning to Wells Fargo as a shotgun messenger, at least Virgil was still upholding the law as marshal and deputy U.S. marshal. However, only days after Wyatt removed his badge, Virgil lost one of those positions.

It was generally agreed that Virgil had done a good job in the wake of Fred White's death. In the special election set for November 12, he had every right to expect that he would defeat challenger Ben Sippy and remain as town marshal. Sippy had on his résumé being indicted for theft in Parker County, Texas, and vanishing before the trial. However, when the votes were tallied, Sippy had won 311 to 259. This shocking outcome could also be attributed to voter fraud, just one not as clumsily handled as the sheriff vote, but Virgil did not file a lawsuit or in any other way contest it. He turned his badge over to Sippy and, while he was at it, resigned as assistant marshal, too. Virgil would retain his federal post, but it did seem overall that the law-enforcement faction was losing its grip on Tombstone.

Not that Curly Bill Brocius had much to do with it. Any political persuasions he may have had were on hold while he languished in a Tucson jail for two months waiting for his trial to begin. Once it did, however, his fate was settled quickly: by the end of December, he was a free man.

There was no disputing, including by the defendant, that it was a bullet from his gun that killed Fred White. But the deathbed statement the marshal had made convinced the jury that Curly Bill had no intention to cause harm and that in the heat of the moment things had gotten out of control. Clearly, White should not have grabbed and tugged the barrel of the pistol; that was a dumb thing to do. Further aiding the defense was Wyatt making the trip up from Tombstone to testify to the events of that night in October, including how he had grabbed Curly Bill's arms from behind. The jury might consider Brocius a crazy cowboy, but they determined that in this case, at least, he was not a murderer.

As the end of 1880 approached, Morgan Earp, perhaps feeling Louisa's absence more than usual, wrote to her care of his family in California. If she was well enough, it was time to come to Tombstone. She was fit for the trip, and in January she moved in with her "husband." With excitement, Louisa wrote family members that letters to her should be addressed to "Mrs. Louisa Earp."

In Tombstone, Louisa and her neighbors found a new administration taking office. John Clum had been an especially active newspaper editor, using the editorial page as a pulpit. One cantankerous position he took was against Mayor Alder Randall, who he alleged (correctly) was in cahoots with the Gray and Clark's Tombstone Townsite Company to carve out more lots and sell them at reduced prices to favored friends—just one way they could control most of the town's real estate. Clum could not dislodge the company, but maybe he could do something about sending the mayor into retirement.

However, his primary concern was law and order—or, as he feared, the insufficient amount of it, allowing the cowboys to run riot. Clum supported the contention that rustling ranchers and their cowboy employees had stuffed the ballot boxes in Charlie Shibell's favor in the November election. He saw the election of Ben Sippy over Virgil Earp as another indication of the ascension of the crooked cowboys, and Shibell appointing Johnny Behan to replace Wyatt would lead to further erosion of law and order.

On Friday, December 10, George Parsons had recorded in his diary, "Shooting now about every night. Very lively town. Strange no one is killed. Another great racket tonight." Clum's editorials represented the fears of many Tombstone residents that if there continued to be shootings regularly and a "great racket" became the norm, inevitably people would be killed. Even the most cautious citizens might not be safe in their beds with bullets flying about indiscriminately.

Indeed, only twelve days later Parsons reported, "Shootists again on the rampage. 'Red Mike' shot last night and another man reported killed tonight. Heard shots. Things lively." What the diarist viewed with some sardonic pleasure as "lively" many others considered dangerous. Given the shady tabulation of votes for Charlie Shibell in the previous month's election, there was less faith in local lawmen to confront the violence, let alone stop it.

The Earp brothers had not necessarily presented themselves as the guardians of law and order, they just had jobs to do and paychecks to collect, but *The Tombstone Epitaph* portrayed them that way. Some citizens accepted that perception. And in an ominous portent of future events, so did the ranchers and cowboys. Now, when cowboys were in town, they eyed the Earps warily. Even without wearing badges, Wyatt and Morgan were easily recognizable, and Virgil, of course, still had some jurisdiction. The risk of a confrontation over something, anything, was growing and bull's-eyes were beginning to form on the Earps' backs.

They did have some support: according to Gary L. Roberts, "Perhaps unnoticed at the time was that the relatively unknown John Henry Holliday was playing a backup role whenever the Earp brothers needed men they could depend on in a fight."

Partly to help avoid any fights between the forming factions,

Clum took his editorial agitation one step further—he announced he was running for mayor. He did so out of sincere belief in the peaceful future of Tombstone, which would take another step forward by being officially incorporated as a city in February 1881. Yet it was not a good time in his life. As Clum later recorded, "With the approach of the Yuletide season, there was unfeigned joy in our little home when a daughter was born. And then, only a week later, I encountered the major tragedy of my life when, on December 18, my wife passed away."

He was left to raise the baby and his young son—Elizabeth and Woodward Clum—plus run a newspaper, and now he was running for mayor. Parsons, a friend of the family, attended the funeral and wrote, "Poor Clum felt his loss severely."*

The grieving editor received the endorsement of the recently formed Law and Order League. Its leaders had tapped into a reservoir of concern that the progress Tombstone was making toward a sophisticated and safe city was being hampered by giving the cowboys a free pass to rob and rustle and hurrah the town with guns blazing.

"By late 1880, the character of the area was changing," writes Casey Tefertiller. "[Newcomers] came knowing of the dangers of the Apaches and snakes; they did not expect or easily accept the presence of a group of backcountry toughs endangering travel and even their very lives. The early boomers had more or less accepted the cowboys" because they kept the Indians at bay and freely spent their wages. "But tolerance began running thin with more and more robberies, and gradually even the term *cowboy* became a slur."

---

* John Clum had more to grieve about that following summer when his daughter, who had been sickly since birth, died.

The campaign was short and, for John Clum, successful. On January 4, 1881, he defeated Mark Shaffer easily, 532 to 165. The 367-vote difference reflected the law-and-order desire of the vast majority of the populace. Perhaps 1881 would be a turning point, a year when Tombstone would enjoy peace as well as prosperity.

And then W. P. Schneider was killed, with the immediate aftermath placing the Earps unavoidably in the forefront of those defending a fragile justice system.

Well, if there seemed little choice in becoming targets, at least the brothers, particularly Wyatt, had help coming to town—Bat Masterson was soon to arrive. However, that would not be until February, and between John Clum's promising election and then, there would be a huge heap of trouble.

Chapter Thirteen

"STRIKE UP A TUNE"

As is true of many communities, the new year in Tombstone brought new hopes and a rosy view of one's surroundings and prospects for the future. In her January 4 missive that would be published two weeks later in *The San Diego Union*, Clara Brown noted the beauty of the area in winter and that "patches of snow are visible on the mountains." She reported, "Three churches and a school house are now ready for occupancy. Miss McFarland will know how to appreciate the latter, for she has been laboring at great disadvantage, having charge of nearly one hundred pupils, cooped up in a shanty of two little rooms, and standing the classes outdoors to recite."

Churches, a school, and crisp fresh air—perhaps Tombstone had turned a corner from its roughneck past. But things were about to go wrong, and quickly.

For Wyatt Earp, the early months of 1881 would bring him old friends and new enemies and an opportunity to make money now that he seemingly was through with lawing. One friend was Luke

Short, who in what was a short life even for that time packed in a lot of living between his birth in Polk County, Arkansas, in January 1854, and his death, at not yet forty, in Geuda Springs, Kansas, in September 1893.

Short grew up in Texas and was only eight years old when he helped his father fight off an attack by Comanches. By age fifteen, he was already working as a cowboy, and not long after that he also served as a scout for the U.S. Army. Several accounts claim that during those scouting years he was in thirty engagements against Plains Indian tribes. His toughest scrape came in 1876, while attached to units commanded by General George Crook. Short was scouting solo when he was ambushed by at least a dozen hostiles. Short jerked his pistols out and killed three of the attackers right away, and in the ensuing mad dash to the nearest army camp, Short shot two more Indians off their horses.

This incident did not persuade him to try a different line of work . . . but being arrested did. To supplement his scout salary of about $40 a month, Short bought barrels of whiskey and made the rounds of Indian camps, selling the firewater, which was sometimes fatal to Indians. The army arrested him and had an escort take him by train to Omaha. When the train arrived, Short was not on it. He had given the accompanying soldiers the slip and gone in the opposite direction, winding up in Denver. There he turned his talents to gambling. And he hadn't lost any speed on his draw, reportedly killing two men there and wounding another in Leadville, Colorado.

It has been reported that Luke Short and Wyatt Earp did not meet until Tombstone, but this makes no sense. Short was known to have done some gambling and even owned a piece of a saloon in Dodge City when Wyatt was a peace officer there. Also, Bat

Masterson considered Short a good friend, and with Bat and Wyatt being best friends, all three would have spent some time together, with gambling as a mutual interest. And chances were that Wyatt would not have hired Short at the Oriental Saloon without previously knowing he could trust him.

Why was Wyatt hiring anyone there? Because by early 1881, he had a piece of the action at the saloon. One of Milton Joyce's partners was William Harris, a Long Branch, New Jersey, native who had operated a saloon in Dodge City bearing the name of his hometown. Harris was one of many businessmen who had seen Tombstone as fertile ground for a watering hole and had purchased an interest in the Oriental. It was much more than a place for Doc Holliday to shoot old and new antagonists. To her readers in San Diego, Clara Brown declared that the Oriental was "simply gorgeous and is pronounced the finest place of its kind this side of San Francisco."

The Oriental was nothing like the standard-issue saloon often seen on screens, where cowboys push through the doors, clap dust off their clothes, knock back shots of cheap whiskey, intimidate the nervous and barely competent piano player, and during fights break cheap wooden chairs over each other's heads as the bartender ducks down. Here, fine music was offered every night by good piano and violin players, patrons dressed well, and the menu was one of the finest in town. The gambling room was plush and was run by men from San Francisco. Joyce took care of the bar and restaurant.

Harris offered Wyatt an interest in the Oriental in exchange for dealing faro and sort of being head of security. The success of the saloon had caused a decrease in business for some other saloons, and the possibility existed that their resentful owners would cause trouble. The offer came at a good time. Wyatt was no longer collecting a deputy sheriff's paycheck and the Earp brothers' mining interests were not producing profits. If generating revenue at the Oriental Saloon—an establishment Clara Brown also described as "respectable"—meant not bouncing around on a stagecoach or wagon the rest of winter as a Wells Fargo shotgun messenger, it was a welcome position. Having Luke Short back him up would be all the better.

And Wyatt had a new friend in town by the name of Fred Dodge, whose gun he had used to buffalo Curly Bill Brocius after Marshal White was shot. Dodge was a gambler as well as a bartender. He had roomed with Morgan before Louisa had arrived. But what no one, including the Earps, knew then was that Dodge was employed by Wells Fargo and was in the area as an undercover detective. The company had become alarmed by recent robberies and general lawlessness, and they wanted eyes at ground level. The man from Sacramento, then twenty-six years old, befriended the Earps, partly because he and the gregarious Morgan had hit it off and partly because he saw the brothers as supporters—and probably more than that—of law and order. Dodge would become an essential ally of the Earps, before and after the O.K. Corral gunfight.*

Cheerful visions of Tombstone's immediate future indicated by Clara Brown's words were soon dashed by a new outbreak of violence. Curly Bill was on the warpath. Apparently not giving much

---

* Fred Dodge would have a long and distinguished career with Wells Fargo, not retiring until 1917. Among his most famous cases as a detective were the investigation into the Bisbee massacre in 1883 and in the 1890s teaming up with the federal marshal Heck Thomas in pursuit of the Doolin-Dalton gang. Dodge was a disciplined diarist, and by the time of his death in 1938, he had written twenty-seven journals about his activities and travels.

thought that it was his drunken escapade that had led to the death of Fred White the previous October, he was instead dwelling on his mistreatment by Wyatt and subsequently the prison guards and court in Tucson. He had lost two months of valuable rustling and carousing time, and somebody had to pay for that. Curly Bill, alcohol, firearms, and innocent victims were a bad combination.

The first venue where he "celebrated" his release was a social hall in Charleston, nine miles southwest of Tombstone. A dance was under way, with most or all of the revelers being Mexican. Brocius and another man leaned against the wall for a time, then they took out their six-shooters and shouted, "Stop the music!"

The band quit and the dancers stared at the armed intruders. Some may have recognized Curly Bill and understood how volatile he could be, especially when drunk, which he obviously was. Their eyes widened and their jaws dropped when Brocius ordered them to remove their clothes. Threatening gestures with the pistols persuaded them to start stripping. Curly Bill then told the musicians, "Strike up a tune."

The band played, and encouraged by the guns aimed at them, the revelers resumed dancing, though all feelings of fun had gone out of the room. For close to a half hour, Brocius enjoyed the dancers' humiliation. It could have continued all night, except a local peace officer on his rounds glanced in the window. At first, he must have thought he was dreaming, seeing dozens of naked bodies cavorting, then he spotted the armed cowboys. He quietly retreated and recruited several men to hide out in the corral next to the hall and make sure that Curly Bill's cruelty would come to an end.

The trap was set, and when Curly Bill and his companion left the social hall they weaved toward the corral. The gun of one of the ambushers accidentally fired. Alerted, the two cowboys began firing into the corral. Terrified, the men inside escaped out the back way. As they got on their horses inside the corral, Brocius noticed that a few of the horses had been hit by bullets. The next day, he sent a messenger to Charleston to pay for the horses' care.

Contention City, fourteen miles west of Tombstone, was the next town to experience Brocius's peculiar sense of humor. First, though, on their way there, Curly Bill and his companion stopped at a church three miles out. Did they want to atone for the previous night's debauchery with a Sunday-morning service? Not likely. With guns drawn, the two men interrupted the sermon being given by the Reverend Joseph McCann. They told him not to move, then started shooting, each man trying to see how close he could come to the minister without striking him. McCann remained stock-still, gazing upward and praying.

Next, the poor preacher was told to step down from the pulpit. As the appalled congregation watched, he was forced to dance a jig. Whenever he tried to stop, the guns were trained on him. Finally, Brocius had enough. "Now go right on with your gospel chin music," he said, "and proceed with your Bible lessons to the kids."

Little seemed to escape the notice of George Parsons, who now had more free time after serving as John Clum's campaign manager. After commenting on the "bright, clear, grand weather," his January 10 diary entry continued: "Some bullying by the cowboys. 'Curly Bill' and others captured Charleston the other night and played the devil generally, breaking up a religious meeting by chasing the minister out of the house, putting out the lights with pistol balls and going through the town. I think it was tonight they captured the Alhambra Saloon here and raced through the town firing pistols."

It had been a full weekend for Curly Bill. Not full enough,

though, that he was through terrorizing the area. On January 18, he and another the cowboy named George began bothering citizens in Contention City, firing their pistols and pulling cash out of their pockets. Local law was more vigorous than they had been outside the social hall the week before, with T. B. Ludwig, a deputy sheriff, approaching the cowboys to make an arrest. He was met by bullets spitting from the duo's Henry rifles. Ludwig took cover, and when Curly Bill and George rode out, a hastily organized citizens' posse gave chase. There was another exchange of gunfire, but the cowboys made good their escape.

Charlie Shibell, as the top peace officer in Pima County, began to feel the heat for what appeared to be an expansion of lawlessness, with Curly Bill as its poster boy. "It is disgraceful that this 'Curly Bill' should occupy the gate to Tombstone . . . after such an outrage as that of the 18th," groused a letter writer in the *Arizona Daily Star*. "The time has come to make this community too hot to hold them. The terror these men have caused the traveling public, as well as the residents along the San Pedro, is having a serious influence, and this scab on the body politic needs a fearless operation to remove it. Let the Sheriff and his deputies see to it." That meant Johnny Behan, too.

Instead of getting tough on crime, Behan appeared to embrace it: after Cochise County became a reality, he hired Brocius as a tax collector. A man who belonged in jail would instead have an official county position. The sheriff sent his deputy Billy Breakenridge to find the king cowboy and offer him the job. "The idea of my asking the chief of all cattle rustlers in that part of the country to help me collect taxes from them struck him as a good joke," Breakenridge recalled in his memoir, *Helldorado*.

But after Curly Bill stopped laughing, he accepted the job. Most startling, Brocius took to the work, and after making the rounds, the deputy and the cowboy rode into Tombstone with more than $1,000 in collected taxes. However, this one foray as a Cochise County official did not turn Curly Bill into an altar boy. He was soon back to his rowdy ways.

For the Earps, the killing of W. P. Schneider and its aftermath could not have come at a worse time—in the midst of Curly Bill's depredations. They may not have cared for the cowboys and their antics and dangerous illegal activities, but the Earp brothers had their own business to attend to. Virgil was a federal lawman, not the first line of defense as the town and county authorities were supposed to be. Then a violent death in Charleston put the Earps in the thick of the Tombstone tensions.

On January 14, Michael O'Rourke, known as Johnny-Behind-the-Deuce, had a dispute over cards with Schneider, a local miner. The dispute ended with Schneider suffering a fatal bullet wound. He was well-known in Charleston, and immediately after the shooting a crowd formed, intent on administering swift justice. But before O'Rourke could be strung up, the constable, George McKelvey, pushed him into a buggy and took off for Tombstone.

On the way, there was a handoff. Virgil had been out riding, and after he halted the racing buggy and heard the story, he pulled O'Rourke up behind him on the horse. McKelvey was only too happy to turn the prisoner over to a deputy U.S. marshal. In Tombstone, Virgil stopped in at the Wells Fargo office and was glad to find Wyatt there. The younger brother grabbed a shotgun and rode the rest of the way into town with Virgil. Not trusting the local law, they brought O'Rourke to Vogan's Bowling Alley, where James Earp worked. The prisoner was stashed there, with James, in one of the few times he used a gun, helping to provide protection.

Expecting that angry citizens from Charleston were on their way, Virgil set off to find help.

He returned with Marshal Ben Sippy, Morgan and Warren Earp, Doc Holliday, Fred Dodge, and several other men.* Soon after, the Charleston crowd rode in. They demanded the guards turn O'Rourke over to them. Sippy, flanked by the other guards, refused. Instead, when O'Rourke was brought out, he was placed on a horse, the others mounted their horses, and the party began the sixty-five-mile trip to Tucson. Behan was a Johnny-come-lately, but he did show up in time to join the group as it left Tombstone.

By protecting Johnny-Behind-the-Deuce and making sure he would arrive safely at the Tucson jail, Virgil was simply doing his job as a federal peace officer. In the newspaper accounts, Ben Sippy received most of the credit for the guardians standing up to the vengeful Charleston mob. However, many residents of Tombstone, most of whom had wagging tongues, had witnessed the standoff, with all five Earp brothers and Doc Holliday at the center of it. Surely these men offered a clear example of championing law and order by facing down a crowd bent on hanging a killer and getting that man to where he would be given a fair trial.

So, the first few weeks of 1881 had seen cowboy mayhem, most of it led by Curly Bill, and an unequivocal statement that the rule of law trumps anarchy. If indeed Tombstone was the last American frontier, as some recognized, then like the previous edges of the

---

* The restless Warren, twenty-five years old at the time, did odd jobs in the Tombstone saloons and Virgil gave him some guard duties, but otherwise he stayed in the background. Like the much older James and Newton, he had no interest in wearing a badge.

frontier it, too, would be tamed and civilized, becoming a place to raise children and prosper.

The Clantons and McLaurys and their rancher allies and Johnny Ringo and Curly Bill Brocius and their cowboy cronies took no pleasure in this rosy view, one that endangered their freewheeling way of life. It sure looked to them as though the Earps and their ilk stood in the way of running the new Cochise County.

Wyatt was determined to be the first sheriff of that county. With Virgil still the deputy U.S. marshal overseeing the Tombstone area, the brothers would once again have the upper hand in law enforcement. Presumably, that would mean the cowboys could face their stiffest opposition so far. Wyatt had not come west to be a lawman, but if he was going to be sheriff—the highest office he had held to date—and with the backing of his brothers, he was going to do it right.

But Johnny Behan made it known he wanted the job, too. It would be a step up from being a Pima County deputy, more money and prestige. And maybe he wanted it because Wyatt did. Josephine was back from San Francisco, and one way to best his romantic rival was to beat him out for an important position.

Wyatt would seem to have the upper hand, and not just because of his Dodge City reputation and his previous and lauded service under Shibell. The Earps were staunch Republicans, as were Governor John C. Frémont and John Gosper, the territorial secretary, and, for that matter, U.S. Marshal Crawley Dake. Behan was a registered Democrat. And at first glance, it would seem to help Wyatt's chances that Gosper had become favorably acquainted with both Virgil and Doc Holliday.

Then the politics of it became more complicated. Frémont and Gosper despised each other, and the latter was actively agitating to get the former's job. The influential *Weekly Arizona Miner*, published in Prescott, took a dislike to Gosper and began editorializing against him. Frémont began to figure that by appointing Behan as the new sheriff, he could stick it to Gosper, gain the praise of the popular newspaper, and have an IOU from the Democrats.

Wyatt became aware that the wind across the desert had shifted direction. In what had to be a stomach-churning move, he met with Johnny Behan. Ordinarily, Behan might have wilted under the gaze of the taller Wyatt's cold blue eyes, but he knew he had the advantage politically, if not domestically. Wyatt offered to remove his name for consideration and to be Behan's deputy after he was made the new sheriff. They would both earn a salary and share in tax collection fees, license costs, and other steady revenue. What to do about the cowboys could be hacked out later. If at some point Behan found another position—say, moving up to a federal one by replacing Dake—Wyatt would become sheriff.

Behan agreed. On February 3, the Arizona Territorial Legislature passed the required bills and Frémont signed them, creating Cochise County. Behan was appointed the new sheriff, and Wyatt waited to hear news about his own appointment. The news that arrived, though, was that Behan had tapped Harry Woods, editor of Tombstone's Democrat-leaning *Tombstone Daily Nugget*, as deputy sheriff. The soon-to-be tax collector Curly Bill and his cowboy colleagues laughed out of both sides of their mouths in the saloons that night.

Wyatt still had his gambling interest in the Oriental Saloon, but with law enforcement, he was once more out in the cold. It had to be some comfort, though, that he could turn to a trusted friend: Bat Masterson had come to Tombstone.

Chapter Fourteen

"DEAD WHEN HE HIT THE GROUND"

While in the process of creating Cochise County, the Arizona Territorial Legislature had also designated the thriving Tombstone as the county seat. Wyatt Earp returned to it without the county job he coveted. With the family's mining interests stuck on mediocre results, and with five brothers and four wives to support, for any of the Earps whatever paid the bills was a position to keep. Wyatt continued to deal faro and provide security at the Oriental Saloon. It was a good thing he could count on Luke Short and now Bat Masterson, because Tombstone was being drawn into what became known as a gamblers' war.

How was it that the Canadian-born Bertholomiew Masterson wound up in Tombstone? A simple explanation: he believed Wyatt and the other Earps needed him and his white-handled six-shooters.

When Wyatt left Dodge City in the fall of 1879, Bat's intention was to stay on there and in law enforcement, but the voters had decided otherwise. He had received a ringing endorsement from

The Dodge City Times: "Bat is acknowledged as the best Sheriff in Kansas. He is the most successful officer in the State. He is immensely popular and generally well-liked. Horse thieves have a terror for the name of Masterson." However, Bat was not as well liked as the editor, Nick Klaine, thought, or there was an unusually high turnout among horse thieves that November, because the incumbent lost his bid to remain the Ford County sheriff. From now on, gambling would be his game.

Bat did not quit Dodge City entirely, though. His brother Jim was a peace officer there, his brother Ed's grave was in Dodge City,* he had good friends there, and he kept a hand in Ford County Republican politics. But he spent more time on the road in towns where the gambling was good, such as Leadville and other mining towns in Colorado. Bat managed to squeeze in a couple of adventures, one being doing a favor for his friend Ben Thompson the gambler and gunman, by springing his brother Billy from custody in Ogallala, Nebraska, with the assistance of Buffalo Bill Cody. Bat returned regularly to Kansas to visit his parents, who lived in Sedgwick, and to enjoy the gambling in Kansas City.

It was while he was once again visiting Dodge City, in February 1881, that a message from Wyatt caught up with him. Bat was informed that there was increasing friction in Tombstone and his help would be appreciated. Bat repacked his bag and boarded a train bound for Trinidad, Colorado. There he changed to a southbound train that took him into New Mexico. There was a stage-

---

* As detailed in the book *Dodge City*, Ed Masterson was the marshal in April 1878 when he was gunned down by drunken cowboys. Sheriff Bat Masterson arrived on the scene seconds too late to save his brother, but he shot two of the cowboys (both died) and arrested the others.

coach ride through Apache territory, then another train, this one landing him in Benson, Arizona. From there, he took a stagecoach to Tombstone. As it happened, the Wells Fargo shotgun messenger on the coach was Bob Paul, whose election litigation had yet to be resolved. Along the way, Paul gave Bat an earful.

He brought Bat up-to-date on events in Tombstone—the nasty competition among gamblers and how the Earps were seen as standing in the way of the ranchers and the cowboys, who wanted less legal oversight of their activities, which even extended to robbing stages and stealing horses. What law there was didn't care for the Earps either. Virgil was the only one of them now who wore a badge, yet the cowboys thought the brothers acted as if they wanted to run the town. The newspapers were divided—*The Tombstone Epitaph* and John Clum, also the mayor, supported law and order, while the *Tombstone Daily Nugget* and Harry Woods supported the rights of the ranchers.

Bob Paul cautioned that this was more than a Democrat versus Republican feud that could be settled at the ballot box—he was sure of that—but a real battle that was brewing. The Clantons and McLaurys were backed by Curly Bill Brocius and Johnny Ringo and a bunch of others Paul could name. That faction easily outnumbered the Earps. There were five of them in Tombstone, but the oldest and youngest brothers, James and Warren, had not done any real lawing. Wyatt could always count on Doc Holliday, but sometimes he could be more trouble than he was worth. The Earps were in a tight spot all right.

This report made Bat especially impatient to get to Tombstone. The situation could be Dodge City all over again. There, Bat had initially been hired to back Wyatt up when the cowboys became rambunctious, and here was a similar scenario. And indeed, when

Bat arrived in Tombstone, Wyatt greeted his old friend warmly, which for Wyatt meant a handshake and the rare cracking of a smile. The very next day, the newcomer was at work at the Oriental Saloon. Officially he was a faro dealer at a handsome $25 a day, but more important was Bat's fists and guns being available should there be trouble.

No doubt by then Wyatt had explained to him why there could be trouble, elaborating on the dusty dissertation Bob Paul had provided during the stagecoach journey. There was indeed a "gamblers' war" percolating in Tombstone. On one side in this conflict were men who had operated gambling halls in and around San Francisco and in Sierra Nevada mining camps: they were nicknamed "Slopers." On the other side were "Easterners," men who had run similar operations in Kansas and Texas. Each side had their own territory and exploited it as best they could. However, the boomtown of Tombstone had attracted both factions, who sort of met in the middle, and it became a battleground.

As had been seen since Ed Schieffelin's discoveries, gambling parlors sprang up first in tent saloons, then in adobe structures, then in board-and-brick buildings of several stories. One of these became the Oriental Saloon. The entrepreneurs Jim Vizina and Ben Cook, who had made money mining, owned the substantial structure at the corner of Fifth and Allen Streets and agreed to lease the premises to the aforementioned Milton Joyce, a West Coast man. While he ran the bar and restaurant, a consortium that included the San Franciscan Lou Rickabaugh and the onetime partner in Dodge City's Long Branch Saloon, William Harris, took possession of the adjoining gambling parlor. As noted previously, Harris hired Wyatt to work in and provide security for the gambling parlor precisely because of rising tensions among gambling operators.

Months earlier, when the Oriental Saloon first opened for business, *The Tombstone Epitaph* extolled the "most elegantly furnished saloon this side of the Golden Gate. Twenty-eight burners suspended in neat chandeliers afforded an illumination of ample brilliancy and the bright rays reflected from the many colored crystals in the bar sparkled like a December icing in the sunshine. To the right of the main entrance is the bar, beautifully carved, finished in white and gilt and capped with a handsomely polished top. In the rear of this stand a brace of sideboards made for the Baldwin Hotel, of San Francisco. The back apartment is covered with a brilliant body Brussels carpet and suitably furnished after the style of a grand club room, with conveniences for the wily dealers in polished ivory." The account concluded by offering "our congratulations."

The Slopers were quick to size up the opportunities in Tombstone. Their leader was John Tyler, a forty-year-old from Texas—yes, the enemy of Doc Holliday. Before deciding to exploit the silver boom in Arizona Territory, Tyler had spent time in San Francisco, and a killing blotted his record there. However, the gamblers who owned the lucrative concession at the Oriental had thrown in their lot with the Easterners, even though Rickabaugh had come to Tombstone from San Francisco. Tyler was running a faro game at Danner & Owens Hall, across the street from the Oriental, and the owners, Charlie Smith and Robert J. "Uncle Bob" Winders, were certainly in competition with Rickabaugh. Smith and Winders were also friends of the Earps and Holliday. James Earp had tended bar for Uncle Bob in Fort Worth during the late 1870s, and Winders himself was a partner with the Earp brothers in several mining ventures.

Yes, all quite confusing. On any given day, some of the participants in the so-called gamblers' war may not have understood what side they were on. In any case, tangling with Doc Holliday had not been enough for Tyler. Next on his list was Wyatt Earp.

Rickabaugh and Harris had believed that Wyatt was the man to stand up to a group trying to cut into the take at the Oriental Saloon. That belief was soon to be tested. The showdown occurred when Tyler marched into the Oriental and aimed a six-shooter at Lou Rickabaugh as he sat behind a pile of chips. Wyatt was on the spot in a flash and, clamping down on Tyler's ear, dragged the surprised gunman out the front door of the saloon and deposited him in the busy street. Doc Holliday came through as backup, keeping Tyler's men, who had drifted in a few minutes earlier, lined up at the bar, staring down the barrel of the dentist's nickel-plated Colt revolver, his gift from Bat Masterson.

That one act did not end the war, but it served notice that with Wyatt, Doc, Bat, and Luke Short in the house, anyone seeking to interfere with the operations of the Oriental Saloon had better bring a lot more, and better, muscle.

Ostensibly, Luke Short was in Tombstone to help Wyatt Earp— but he certainly did not help matters much when he killed Charlie Storms.*

It is possible that Storms had been brought to Tombstone to cause trouble at the Oriental Saloon and Luke Short just happened to be in the way. Or, Short was the target. After all, he and Bat were there to protect the Earp/Rickabaugh gambling operation,

---

* Readers of *Wild Bill* might recall that Charlie Storms was in Deadwood in the summer of 1876 and refused an offer to challenge Wild Bill Hickok. Al Swearengen and other businessmen there feared that Hickok was about to be made marshal to clean up the violence-ridden boomtown in what is now South Dakota. Alas, Storms did not have the same fear of Luke Short as he did for Wild Bill.

and the plan may have been to get rid of Short first and Bat next. However, the outcome for Storms was surely not part of his plan.

On the night of February 25, Storms was on a steady diet of drinking and gambling. He probably would have gotten drunk anyway, but there was some speculation later—including in an account of the incident in the *National Police Gazette*—that the whiskey was liquid courage for confronting Short and his reputation for being quick with a gun. Bat kept an eye on him that night, not only because it was part of his job to look for a situation that could go south, but because he had encountered Storms before. Yes, there was that unsavory reputation, but Bat considered Charlie a friend and did not want him to get into trouble.

But there was trouble, and it was between Storms and Luke Short. An argument quickly escalated. "Both were about to pull their pistols when I jumped between them and grabbed Storms," Bat recalled, "at the same time requesting Luke not to shoot, a request I knew he would respect if it was possible without endangering his own life too much."

The burly Bat was able to muscle Storms out of the saloon. "When Storms and I reached the street I advised him to go to his room and take a sleep," Bat later wrote. He escorted Storms to his room and left him there. On his way back to the Oriental Saloon, Bat found Short at the Allen Street entrance. Bat was in the midst of giving him a similar peace talk "when, lo and behold! There [Storms] stood before us, without saying a word, he took hold of Luke's arm and pulled him off the sidewalk, where he had been standing, at the same time pulling his pistol."

This lends support to the possibility that Storms was a hired gun. True, he may have approached Luke Short a second time because he was drunk and angry. But Bat was a persuasive man and

Storms should have slept it off and seen if the next day was a better one. Instead, though, he remembered that he had a job to do, and it wasn't finished until Short was, too.

Storms had only moments left to live. While his pistol was barely clearing its holster, Short had his gun out. He pressed the muzzle against his adversary's chest. As Bat reported, "The bullet tore the heart asunder and, as he was falling, Luke shot him again. Storms was dead when he hit the ground."

The corpse was carted off to the undertaker. In the morning a coroner's hearing was held, testimony was given, including by Bat, who was in the uncomfortable position of siding with one friend against another, with the one still alive given priority. The verdict was that Short had acted in self-defense. He was released and returned to his gambling ways.

According to Robert DeArment in his biography of Masterson, "The gambling rooms of the Oriental were noticeably quieter after Storms's sudden demise. Rival gamblers apparently were satisfied that the reputations of the Dodge City gunfighters were authentic, and talk of a gamblers' war subsided."

This was good news for Wyatt Earp. It is believed that Milton Joyce took full control of the gambling rooms after Storms was killed. And then, on March 1, Joyce had to shut down the gambling at the Oriental Saloon altogether following another shooting.

This event does not appear to have been connected to the gamblers' war, which, as DeArment noted, was on the wane anyway. One-Arm Kelly, nicknamed for an obvious reason, was one of the combatants and Alfred McAllister the other. Kelly was said to be connected to a gang led by Big Ed Burns. A known hell-raiser, Burns had fled Leadville, Colorado, in April 1880 just one jump ahead of a lynch mob after instigating an election eve fracas in that mining town. He then gathered up a gang of thieves, thugs, and other riffraff and took over the railway depot of Benson, north of Tombstone. He and his cohorts appear to have been out solely for themselves, which included cheating at cards and accusing others of doing the same.

Kelly and McAllister were a bad combination at a gaming table and probably anywhere. Before moving on to Benson with the Burns gang, Kelly had been in Las Vegas, New Mexico, and had been run out of there after shooting out the window of a restaurant. His visit to Tombstone was probably to raise more hell, but instead he wound up residing there. McAllister was a butcher from Galeyville not known to have a benign demeanor. It was not long before the two men got into a dispute, and before Wyatt or any of his security people could intervene, guns were drawn. Kelly was killed, and McAllister would be given the benefit of acting in self-defense. Soon after, a Las Vegas newspaper commented that the not-missed One-Arm Kelly "was handed down for the worms of that consecrated soil" in Tombstone.

Calling the saloon "a regular slaughter house now," Milton Joyce would give up his lease on the Oriental in July. From that point on, Lou Rickabaugh was in complete control, and Wyatt continued to collect his quarter interest in the games free of any interference. Just as helpful, John Tyler by then had left Tombstone. When he next appears in any records, it is almost a year later in Leadville, still gambling and nursing a grudge against Doc Holliday.

With luck, the Kelly killing would be the last of the serious violence in Tombstone, at least for a while. A court had ruled in February that the county sheriff's balloting the previous November had been bogus and ordered Bob Paul to replace Charlie Shibell. The latter had appealed, but there was now more hope for law-and-order advocates. At the Oriental Saloon, Wyatt had the ongoing support of Bat Masterson and Luke Short and that of Doc Holliday in the background. Things were looking up.

But then, only two weeks after the shooting in that saloon, the Benson stage was robbed and there was more death. Complicating matters—Doc would be implicated in the crime.

Chapter Fifteen

"I HOLD FOR NOBODY!"

Wyatt Earp hadn't had much choice but to trust John Behan and his promise that he would be appointed deputy sheriff once the ink was dry on the legislation signed by Governor Frémont creating Cochise County. Wyatt was not a naïve man necessarily but probably not the most politically astute. He had underestimated how politically savvy Behan was, including stocking the sheriff's office with his people to complement Harry Woods.

One of them was Billy Breakenridge. His legacy would mostly be as a lifelong critic of the Earp family and as the author of *Helldorado,* one of the first books to popularize the truths and myths of Tombstone. He was a Wisconsin native, born in December 1846. He was only fifteen when he left home, to work in the Pikes Peak mining area. Two years later, Breakenridge enlisted in the Third Colorado Cavalry. His commanding officer was the infamous colonel John Chivington, the former Methodist pastor who can be considered one of the most despicable mass murderers in American history because of the attack by his soldiers at Sand Creek in

Colorado in 1864. The Cheyenne village was inhabited by mostly women and children, and as many as two hundred were slaughtered.

After the Civil War, Breakenridge worked various jobs in various places, winding up in Arizona in 1876 as a Maricopa County deputy sheriff. In Tombstone four years later, where he was hired as a deputy sheriff, he also received an appointment as a deputy U.S. marshal, with his jurisdiction to include the new Cochise County. That Breakenridge became aligned with Behan should have been a red flag for Wyatt, an indication that the sheriff would surround himself with those who agreed with him and sided with the ranchers and cowboys.* Even so, Wyatt surmised, a promise was a promise, and Behan had broken his. Ironically, Wyatt soon had an opportunity to display some of his lawing skills that Behan had chosen to do without.

A stagecoach operated by Kinnear & Company departed in the late afternoon of March 15 from Tombstone bound for Benson thirty miles to the north. The driver was Eli Philpot, known as Bud, and the Wells Fargo shotgun messenger was Bob Paul. Only two miles out of Tombstone the stage stopped. It picked up two additional passengers, one of whom, Peter Roerig, had to sit up top because there was not enough room in the coach. It was a clear, late winter night with a shining moon illuminating the desert, and everyone in and on the stagecoach settled in for a routine ride.

As John Clum would somewhat fancifully describe the scene,

---

* Breakenridge's life, which did not end until he was eighty-four, included several notable achievements, one being discovering the site near the confluence of Tonto Creek and the Salt River that, when completed in 1911, featured the Roosevelt Dam.

"Fifteen miles out . . . cloudless sky . . . Bud Philpot crooning a desert lullaby from the driver's seat . . . everybody happy . . . sun casting long shadows from the sujuaros . . ." And then the ride was anything but routine. Just past Contention City, as the stagecoach was slowly going up a hill, a man stepped into view and called, "Hold!"

Without hesitation, Bob Paul retorted, "By God, I hold for nobody!" and brought his shotgun to bear as more men appeared.

There was an exchange of fire. One of the robbers was hit, as was Bud Philpot. He was already dead as he fell off the stage. With the reins free, the panicking horses surged ahead. Somehow, Paul gained control of the stagecoach and stamped his foot down to apply the brake. The would-be robbers had disappeared.

Paul found Roerig to be seriously wounded. He got the horses going, hurrying to Benson. Moments after Paul arrived, he had Roerig being attended to by a doctor, and he then telegraphed Tombstone. Borrowing a horse, Paul rode back to the scene of the crime, where he found several men from Drew's Station who had heard the shots standing around Philpot's body in the road.

In Tombstone, a posse was collected. The two lawmen in charge were Virgil Earp, as deputy U.S. marshal, and John Behan, as Cochise County sheriff. They deputized Wyatt and Morgan Earp and Bat Masterson. Also along was Marshall Williams, the Tombstone-based Wells Fargo agent.* They all rode off into the night and rendezvoused with Bob Paul, who had also found at the scene rope masks and fifteen shell casings. Tracks indicated there had been four robbers, and blood confirmed one of them had been hit.

---

* It would later be revealed that the Wells Fargo box on that particular stage carried $26,000—a handsome haul indeed if the thieves had gotten away with it.

Edward Schieffelin was told that the only thing he would find during his prospecting journeys would be his tombstone. In a way, that turned out to be correct. *(Courtesy of Arizona Historical Society)*

Richard Gird's appraisal of the value of Schieffelin's ore discovery set off a chain of events leading to the founding of Tombstone. Gird became the town's first postmaster. *(Courtesy of Arizona Historical Society)*

Virgil Earp, the second-oldest Earp brother, was the chief of police of Tombstone when the October 26, 1881 gunfight took place. *(Courtesy of Arizona Historical Society)*

Nicholas Earp sired ten children, eight with his second wife, Virginia. Virgil and Wyatt in particular shared their father's restless spirit. *(Courtesy of Kansas Historical Society)*

Wyatt Earp, still only in his early thirties, hoped to find success as a businessman in Tombstone and leave his lawman days behind. *(Courtesy of Kansas Historical Society)*

Morgan Earp was the youngest Earp brother to participate in the October 1881 shoot-out, and the only one to die in Tombstone. *(Courtesy of Boot Hill Museum)*

The volatile Doc Holliday insisted on being by the Earp brothers' side when they confronted the Clantons and McLaurys. *(Courtesy of Kansas Historical Society)*

It is likely that if Bat Masterson had not returned to Dodge City to save his own brother's life, he would have been a steadfast ally of the Earp brothers in Tombstone. *(Courtesy of Kansas Historical Society)*

Allie Earp, Virgil's wife and fiercely loyal to him, could sometimes have her fill of the Earp family. *(Courtesy of Arizona Historical Society)*

Kate Elder not only had to contend with the nickname "Big Nose" but being the companion of the cantankerous Doc Holliday. *(Courtesy of Arizona Historical Society)*

Mattie Earp's days as Wyatt's wife were numbered once he laid eyes on Josephine Marcus in Tombstone. *(Courtesy of Boot Hill Museum)*

John Clum, the future newspaper editor and mayor of Tombstone, is seen here *(center)* when he was the supervising agent at the San Carlos Reservation in Arizona. *(Courtesy of Arizona Historical Society)*

The journals of the tireless and seemingly omnipresent George Parsons offer many details about the early days of Tombstone. *(Courtesy of Arizona Historical Society)*

Johnny Behan gained the office he sought, of sheriff of Cochise County, but lost the affections of his fiancé to Wyatt Earp. *(Courtesy of Arizona Historical Society)*

Josephine Marcus exchanged Johnny Behan for the more alluring and ultimately more famous Wyatt Earp. They would be together for forty-eight years. *(Courtesy of Tombstone Western Heritage Museum)*

The residents of Tombstone lived in fear that the Apache warrior Geronimo would break free from the reservation and lead another series of violent raids in southeast Arizona. *(Courtesy of Library of Congress)*

At first cheated out of the office of sheriff of Pima County, Bob Paul would go on to have a distinguished lawman career. *(Courtesy of Arizona Historical Society.)*

Newman "Old Man" Clanton was the patriarch of a family that focused on ranching and rustling in Arizona and New Mexico. *(Courtesy of Arizona Historical Society)*

The drunken antics of Joseph Isaac "Ike" Clanton forced Virgil Earp's hand and led to the October 1881 shoot-out in a vacant Tombstone lot. *(Courtesy of Arizona Historical Society)*

During the gunfight, Billy Clanton, the youngest brother, stood his ground while his brother Ike fled. *(Courtesy of Arizona Historical Society)*

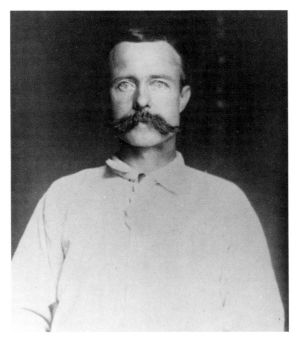

"Buckskin" Frank Leslie was one of those frontier figures who could be found on either side of the law. *(Courtesy of Arizona Historical Society)*

Tom McLaury's confrontation with Wyatt Earp was one of the pivotal events leading up to the gunfight. *(Courtesy of Arizona Historical Society)*

Frank McLaury was the older of the two brothers who operated a ranch in Cochise County. *(Courtesy of Arizona Historical Society)*

The testimony provided by his wife doomed Pete Spence as one of the conspirators in the murder of Morgan Earp. *(Courtesy of Arizona Historical Society)*

Johnny Ringo was one of the more vicious and eccentric outlaws of the American West. *(Courtesy of Arizona Historical Society)*

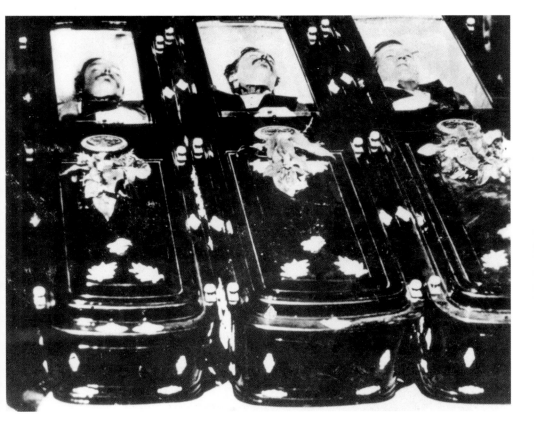

The bodies of *(left to right)* Tom and Frank McLaury and Billy Clanton were put on display by the anti-Earp faction in Tombstone. *(Courtesy of Arizona Historical Society)*

The silver-tongued orator Thomas Fitch led the defense team representing the Earp brothers and Doc Holliday, who were facing charges of murder. *(Courtesy of Arizona Historical Society)*

Judge Wells Spicer delivered the ruling that freed the Earps and Doc from criminal prosecution for the gunfight deaths. *(Courtesy of Utah Historical Society)*

Now, every extra minute spent there was a minute farther away for the fleeing outlaws. Unfortunately for the pursuers, there was not to be a quick confrontation. For three days the posse pursued the unknown thieves. Finally, they arrived at a ranch owned by Len Redfield, one of the owners believed to be in cahoots with rustling cowboys. The tracks had led them there, so the posse was suspicious anyway. Morgan noticed a man trying to hide himself and arrested him. Luther King was his name, and he was brought to Behan, who was advised by Wyatt not to let King talk to anyone at the ranch. But sure enough, after Wyatt had a conversation with Bob Paul, he turned to see King chatting with the brothers Len and Hank Redfield.

Wyatt pulled King aside and began to question him. Right away, King confessed to being one of the robbers. He insisted, however, that he had not fired a weapon and that his only role had been to hold the reins of the gang's horses. King identified the others as Harry Head, Jimmy Crane, and Billy Leonard and revealed where they were hiding out. Overhearing this, Hank Redfield quietly got on a horse and rode out. Especially with this new information, the posse had to be back on the move. Behan offered to take the prisoner to Tombstone. The Earp brothers, Bat, Paul, and Williams resumed the pursuit.

This turned out to be an even longer and more circuitous journey than before. Every so often the posse saw signs of their prey, but the outlaws stayed a few steps ahead. After six days, the lawmen came to a town where Virgil telegraphed Sheriff Behan that their horses were worn out and their supplies were exhausted and to request a fresh supply of both. But when the posse arrived at the rendezvous—a ranch eighteen miles from Tombstone—they found Behan but no fresh mounts or supplies. With a perfunctory apology, Behan wheeled his horse around and headed back, even though this was as much his jurisdiction as Virgil's.

The posse camped at the ranch, and during the night Bob Paul's horse died. In the morning it was determined that the horses belonging to Wyatt and Bat were in too bad a shape for farther travel. They were left at the ranch while the two old friends set off on a long walk. With the three fresh horses the ranch could offer, Virgil and Morgan and Bob Paul pushed on. Virgil had also telegraphed his boss, U.S. Marshal Crawley Dake, to inform him, "Have not lost a foot print. Will follow as long as I can find a track." Virgil was one to keep his word.

When the two weary walkers got to Tombstone, Behan told Wyatt that Harry Woods was in charge of the prisoner, which did not sit well at all. Swallowing his anger, Wyatt, now accompanied by Jim Hume, a Wells Fargo detective, went to Woods at the jail and asked him to put Luther King in irons because they expected that at any time cowboys would form their own posse to free the outlaw. Woods said he would do so. However, his word was as worthless as Behan's—that very afternoon, King strolled out the back door of the jail, got onto a horse conveniently tied up there, and rode away, into the mists of history.

An outraged George Parsons recorded in his diary, "Some of our officials should be hanged. They're a bad lot."

Even Behan realized that this was a colossal gaffe. Best to be out of town for a while, and a perfect excuse was that there were still outlaws on the loose. The sheriff formed another posse, this one including Billy Breakenridge and "Buckskin" Frank Leslie. They rendezvoused with the relentless trio of Virgil, Morgan, and Bob Paul. They soon split up, though, when Virgil was told that at least one of the suspects owned a ranch fifty miles away.

The dedication of Virgil and the others almost proved fatal. They made it to the ranch, which was in Grant County in New Mexico, but found it deserted. The posse was now out of food and water. Virgil's horse had lasted seventeen days on the trail, but two days after Virgil found the ranch and then pushed on, it could go no more, dying under him. He put his gear on Morgan's horse and the brothers walked. Another day of this might have been one too many, but that night the lawmen found a spring and at least could quench a mighty thirst. Virgil suggested that he and Morgan and Paul, with two horses between them, make their way west as best they could and that Behan, Breakenridge, and Leslie ride ahead to find food and water.

The three men left behind were without food, and with only the water their two weary mounts could carry, they had to put one foot in front of the other and hope that this time Behan could be trusted. It was four days of staggering through the desert, which by now, the first week in April, was plenty hot and dry. They had to wonder if they had been left stranded to die. However, riders, first seeming to be a mirage, appeared. They turned out to be ranch hands sent by Behan with water and supplies.

The search was over without the outlaws being caught. The posse had to console itself with praise offered by the *Arizona Daily Star*: "The persistent pursuit of the murderers of poor 'Budd' is a credit to each individual member of the party, and will pass into our frontier annals—more especially to Bob Paul and the Earp boys."

Less welcome attention from the *Star* was an implication that one of the would-be robbers was Doc Holliday: "The fourth is at Tombstone and is well known and has been shadowed ever since his return." It was true that Doc was not only a friend of Billy Leonard but on the afternoon of the attempted holdup had ridden out of

Tombstone with a Henry rifle. Between ten and eleven o'clock he had returned with "his horse fagged out." Such activities "look very bad indeed."

Wyatt questioned his friend about that night. Doc explained that he had ridden to Charleston after hearing of a high-stakes poker game there, but it had broken up by the time he arrived. Doc turned around, encountered an acquaintance driving a water wagon, they ambled along together, then he was back in Tombstone, where he returned the horse and went to the Alhambra Saloon to play faro. Wyatt believed what was, indeed, the truth. But the rumors that circulated were to some people further proof that Doc and his Earp pals were law-and-order hypocrites.

And if the Benson stage incident and its painful aftermath were not enough aggravation for the Earp brothers, John Behan submitted a bill of almost $800 to the Cochise County Board of Supervisors for expenses incurred during the posse's search for the outlaws. Behan did not include the Earps on the list of those to be reimbursed. (Behan had listed himself first.) As Virgil later reported, "Everybody but myself and my brothers were paid, and we did not get a cent until Wells Fargo found out and paid us for our time."

He added, "From that time our troubles commenced."

Soon after the footsore Wyatt and Bat had returned to Tombstone, the duo had to split up, and rather abruptly, too: Bat had to hurry back to Kansas to save his brother's life. Upon arriving there, he would be met by a hail of bullets in what would be called the Battle of the Plaza.

The telegram Bat had received, from an anonymous sender, read simply, "Come at once. Updegraff and Peacock are going to kill Jim." He'd had a quarrel with Jim, who had become the marshal of Dodge City, and they had not communicated for some time.

However, as Robert DeArment points out, "Quarrel or no quarrel, Jim was still Bat's brother, and that was sufficient reason for Bat to undertake a journey of almost a thousand miles to help. He had lost one brother to [a bullet] in Dodge just three years earlier to the very month; he did not intend to lose another if it lay within his power to prevent it."

He was further urged to go by Wyatt, after the latter was shown the telegram. As Wyatt well knew, aiding a brother in danger topped other considerations. "That was the old frontier's brand of loyalty," he commented.

In truth, Jim Masterson was no longer marshal of Dodge City, a job he'd held for almost eighteen months. In the April 4 election, James "Dog" Kelley and his administration were voted out and the new mayor wanted his own marshal, so Jim had to turn in his badge. But he still had some income, thanks to a partnership with A. J. Peacock in the Lady Gay Saloon and Dance Hall. Lately, though, that hadn't been going too well. Al Updegraff was the bartender who was drinking up most of the proceeds, but he retained his job because he was Peacock's brother-in-law. This unprofitable alliance had been festering between Peacock and Jim Masterson for quite a while, but it became more of an issue when the Lady Gay became the ex-marshal's sole source of income.

As Updegraff continued to imbibe behind the bar, the two partners fought—first with words, then it was reported that guns were drawn. The man who sent the telegram was privy enough to the angry dispute to glean that the next escalation was the brothers-in-law removing Jim Masterson from the partnership permanently.

Bat feared that no matter how fast he traveled he would not arrive soon enough, yet he gamely pushed on, reversing the course he had taken that past February through Arizona, New Mexico,

Colorado, and back to Kansas. It was high noon on April 16 when he stepped off the Atchison, Topeka, and Santa Fe train. It turned out that Peacock and Updegraff were gunning for a Masterson—not Jim, but him. Bat saw them approaching the tracks. However, when Bat called out to them, his right hand on the white handle of one of his holstered pistols, the two men turned and ran. The sight of the stocky former sheriff evaporated whatever mutual courage they had, and they hid behind the city jail.

It has never been determined how the Battle of the Plaza began—all of a sudden, bullets were flying. Several went whizzing past Bat before he realized he was dangerously exposed. He dropped behind the three-foot-high railroad embankment and returned fire with both pistols. Meanwhile, some of the bullets that missed Bat hit shops behind him on Front Street and sent pedestrians and horses fleeing for their lives. Even the interior of saloons was not safe, with customers diving behind bars and under tables.

The battle got even hotter. As Robert DeArment reports: "As the combatants sniped at each other, certain members of Dodge's sporting fraternity joined in the fray. Behind his rail-capped earthen parapet, Bat was receiving fire from several south-side saloons. At his rear, friendly guns opened up on Front Street. The three principals in the action suddenly found themselves in the middle of a general war raging back and forth across the tracks."

The shooting stopped when Al Updegraff staggered out from behind the jail, a bullet lodged in his chest.* As he was dragged off to a doctor, the new mayor, Al Webster, ran up to Bat holding a shotgun. Bat was greatly relieved when told that his brother was

---

* Updegraff's wound was not as serious as first believed, and he recovered from it . . . only to die from smallpox two years later.

fine, and he turned over his now empty six-shooters to Webster. That afternoon, Bat appeared in court, pleaded guilty to discharging a weapon within the city limits, and paid the $8 fine. Jim ended his partnership with Peacock, and the brothers, their differences all forgotten after Bat's rescue mission, left Dodge City together.

Bat would not be returning to Tombstone, which meant one man less on the law-and-order side of the ledger. However, on that front there was finally some good news that same April—Bob Paul became Pima County sheriff. The court had rejected Charlie Shibell's appeal, agreeing that his win in the previous election was a sham perpetrated by Curly Bill Brocius, Johnny Ringo, and the other cowboys. Paul was sworn in. Tombstone was in Cochise County now, but it still helped to have an ally in a nearby important position. Shibell took a job he had become more suited for, managing the Palace (later Occidental) Hotel.*

Even though the shooting deaths of Philpot and Roerig had taken place outside the city limits, Mayor Clum and the council passed legislation banning weapons within Tombstone. Nevertheless, with the murderers still at large and almost certainly being aided and abetted by cowboys and crooked ranchers, tensions in Tombstone continued to rise. Helping them to simmer was a spring heat wave that just would not break.

And then, in June, the city came close to being wiped off the map entirely.

---

* Several years later, Shibell would return to lawing as a Pima County deputy sheriff. During the pursuit of a man suspected of robbing a Southern Pacific train, Shibell himself was arrested, for entering Mexico illegally.

Chapter Sixteen

———

"THE FURY OF THE FLAMES"

The air in southeast Arizona can turn hot in spring anyway, but the torrid temperatures of the spring of 1881 were downright brutal. As George Parsons reported, "Thermometer 104 in shade." Every day grew longer, and with the arc of the sun's daily journey nearing its peak, there was less shade to offer any solace. It was a tad more tolerable for those who had lived in hot climates before, but Tombstone was a relatively new town and many of its residents and visitors were experiencing extreme dry desert heat for the first time.

The Earps, John Clum, and others identified with the law-and-order faction in Tombstone did not care for persistent heat any more than most other citizens did, but they had to be cheered by recent events. Bob Paul was settling in as sheriff of adjacent Pima County, so there would be no haven for outlaws there. Virgil continued as a local federal marshal. And Curly Bill Brocius was having a tough time of it.

During the late winter and spring he had continued his rustling and rampaging ways, sometimes in concert with Johnny Ringo. Even their fellow cowboys were not safe. Back in March, Brocius and Ringo and a few companions had ridden to Maxey, near Fort Thomas in Arizona. One of the cowboys took to playing cards and drinking in a saloon. Fueled by too much whiskey, the cowboy, Dick Lloyd, got into a dispute and shot and wounded a man in the saloon. He was tossed out.

That shooting, however, was not his biggest mistake that day. Lloyd got on his horse, and either out of drunken confusion or thinking it would be amusing, he rode into another saloon. It happened to be the one where Curly Bill and Ringo were doing their drinking. Objecting to the interruption, they pulled their pistols out and killed Lloyd. The saloon owner took the blame for Lloyd's death, but in a brief trial he was acquitted.

Toward the end of May, things went the other way for Brocius. He was in more familiar surroundings in Galeyville, drinking with a group of cowboys who included locals Pony Deal and Jim Wallace, a friend from the good old Lincoln County War days. Another member of the convivial gang was Billy Breakenridge, a clear indication of what side of the fence the Cochise County Sheriff's Office was on. Sometime during the bacchanal, Wallace said something that was insulting to Breakenridge. The deputy sheriff ignored it. Curly Bill did not.

He told Wallace to apologize. The request was refused. Brocius became more insistent, threatening to kill his old acquaintance. That caught Wallace's blurry attention, and he complied. However, Curly Bill was by this point in one of his rages. "You damned Lincoln County son of a bitch," he snarled, "I'll kill you anyhow." Suddenly sober and not liking the odds, Wallace got up and left the saloon. When Brocius followed him out in the street, Wallace wheeled around with his gun out and shot Curly Bill, hitting him in the cheek and neck.

It was not a fatal wound, but Curly Bill was out of commission for a while—months, in fact. This was welcome news to those hoping to curb cowboy atrocities.

And Wyatt was not seething quite as much from John Behan's betrayal. He had to realize, especially after the sheriff's disappointing performance in the aftermath of the Benson stage killings, that serving under Behan would have been intolerable. It rankled that he had lost out on both the Cochise County sheriff and deputy sheriff jobs, but he had come to Tombstone not to be a lawman but to be a successful businessman. That was happening at a slower pace than he'd anticipated, but Wyatt still had a piece of the action of the gaming activity at the Oriental Saloon.

It may also have prompted one of his rare smiles that Josephine Marcus had tossed Behan out. On her way back from San Francisco with his son, Albert, she had telegraphed Behan the day they expected to arrive. They showed up at their house in Tombstone the evening before, to find the randy sheriff in bed with a friend's wife. When the startled lady rushed out, Behan was not far behind, stuffing clothes into a suitcase. Not wanting to stay in the house that felt soiled even to a former "soiled dove," Josephine rented it to one of the city's physicians, Dr. George Goodfellow.

She was living in an apartment alone now, and many people knew this, Wyatt included. "Josephine was still calling herself Mrs. Johnny Behan," writes Ann Kirschner in *Lady at the O.K. Corral,* "but the title had long turned sour."

By itself, the dumping of Behan did not mean the door was open for Wyatt. There was, of course, the fact that he was still living with Mattie, who to anyone she discreetly encountered was known as Mrs. Wyatt Earp. But Tombstone was a particularly tough town for a single woman. Either she was married to a man, legally or not, or she was a prostitute. A third category was performer at one of the city's dance halls, but with most women the line was thin and blurry between singer and hooker.

What Josephine did during the months after Behan got the boot is not known, but Kirschner offers that she "conserved her meager store of capital and pondered her next step. She was a prisoner of Tombstone. She could find a job. Or she could find a new lover. There were nine men for every woman in Tombstone."

Wyatt must have been feeling good enough about things that he decided to strike a deal with Ike Clanton. The reason why has been debated for well over a century. First, the proposed deal: On June 7, Wyatt met behind the Oriental Saloon with Clanton, Frank McLaury, and Joe Hill. By then, it was well-known that Wells Fargo had put up a generous reward of $1,200 each for the capture of Billy Leonard, Harry Head, and Jim Crane, the men who had escaped the posse after the attempted robbery of the Benson stage in March. Wyatt suggested that if he was given information that led to the capture of the outlaws, he would give Clanton the reward money. A windfall of $3,600 was enough that Ike tentatively agreed. However, he had to know if the reward would still be paid if the three outlaws were killed, because he expected them to not go peacefully. Wyatt said he would find out.

Earp detractors have seen this offer as Wyatt throwing in with the cowboy faction. He was, as far as he could stand it, but this was not about becoming cozy with the cowboys. Whether or not Wyatt had designs on Behan's former fiancée, he did want to take the sheriff's job. After Behan's ineptitude in the Benson robbery pursuit and a prisoner escaping, if Wyatt could arrest—or, if necessary, kill—the roaming robbers, voters would remember that in the next election. Perhaps Johnny Behan would be so embarrassed that he would resign and leave town before the year was out.

And to be more fair to the Earps, and Wyatt in particular, it was a burr under their saddle that Leonard, Head, and Crane had killed two men—and tried to do the same for the respected Bob Paul—and gotten away with it. Add to that, in the process of escaping capture, the posse had almost perished. Letting the outlaws remain free and probably plotting more mischief was too much to bear. The Clanton family and the cowboys were close, and even if it was a bit of a devil's bargain, Wyatt would team up with Ike if it meant bringing the killers to justice.

As Wyatt himself later spelled it out, when he met with Clanton, McLaury, and Hill, "I told them I wanted the glory of capturing Leonard, Head, and Crane, and if I could do it, it would help me make the race for sheriff in the next election. I told them if they would put me on the track of Leonard, Head, and Crane, and tell me where the men were hid, I would give them all the reward." Wyatt further promised never to reveal the source of the information.

And there was one other reason to undertake this strategy, which Ike wound up telling Virgil instead of Wyatt: with the outlaws in jail or dead, the Clantons could claim ownership of Billy Leonard's ranch outside Cloverdale, New Mexico. After hearing that the Leonard ranch was deserted, the Clantons began grazing cattle on it, especially stolen ones that would better avoid detection. But one day, apparently thinking the coast was clear, the three outlaws rode onto the ranch. Ike Clanton had recently been given an ultimatum of buy the ranch or stop squatting his cattle on it. "I want these men captured or killed," he told Virgil, adding, "But I had rather they would be killed."

Wyatt soon had Ike's full support. He went to Marshall Williams, who telegraphed his superiors at Wells Fargo about the reward money. They responded that it would be paid dead or alive. When Wyatt showed Clanton the telegram, he was in. The oddly matched collaborators hatched a plan: Joe Hill would swing by the New Mexico ranch and somehow entice the outlaws to the McLaury ranch. Ike would happen to be visiting, which was not at all unusual. He would tell Leonard, Head, and Crane about an easy payday—money intended to pay miners would be on a certain stage going from Tombstone to Bisbee. This would be easy pickings, and the robbers would collect enough that they could go live wherever they wanted, maybe California.

This would, of course, be a trap. Virgil was brought in on the scheme so that any capturing or killing done would be under the supervision of a federal marshal.

Everyone's plans, nefarious or otherwise, were interrupted on June 22. That was the day Tombstone almost ceased to exist. There was a fire, and most of the structures in that early summer heat were made of wood and perfect kindling for a conflagration.

The blaze began when a discarded barrel of whiskey was being carried out of the Arcade Saloon on Allen Street. The bung was removed to measure how much whiskey was left inside. The laborers never quite found out because the fumes that burst out of the opening were ignited by the burning cigar clamped in the mouth of one of them. There was an explosion that spewed burning debris around the street, which in turn was carried by the wind.

Suddenly, it was like a prairie fire in the middle of the city. Wooden structures caught and the flames spread rapidly. Though there was a fire department, there really was no formal firefighting equipment in Tombstone, and barrels of water were few and far between. According to *The Tombstone Epitaph*, after three minutes dozens of buildings were engulfed by flames. One of them was the Oriental Saloon. Acting quickly and with some desperation, Milton Joyce rushed through his burning building to get to the $1,200 in paper money hidden in a desk, but he was too late, barely escaping the saloon before he, too, was consumed.

Wagons raced here and there to find barrels or even just pots of water to toss at the raging fires, and men with shovels dug where they could to throw dirt and sand to try to smother the flames. To Clara Brown, "it certainly looked at one time as if the best part of Tombstone was doomed to destruction. A fire under any circumstances is serious enough, but particularly fearful to contemplate when there is almost nothing to fight it with. People did the best they could, pulling down buildings and wetting others in an attempt to confine the limits of the conflagration, and by arduous efforts, the flames were prevented from spreading across Fremont street to the northern part of town."

The fire almost claimed Parsons. With an ax, he had run up to the top floor of the San Jose House to "cut through several posts holding the balcony roof." He was in the midst of doing that as the flames neared, and then, "I remember no more." He woke up sometime later while being put in a buggy, which took him to a friend's house where his bloody clothes were removed and he was put to bed. "It seems the roof fell in on me either by the pulling [of ropes] by the excited crowd or by the small support giving way which was left. I was thought to be killed, or at least had my legs both broken." The silver lining to all this is that when he was rescued from the collapsed building and brought into a saloon, "some dame rushed in and took charge of me, washing my face and giving me stimulants all of the time."

Such exhausting efforts by the townsfolk, including the Earps, did help the fire burn itself out. "By 6 P.M. the fury of the flames had spent itself and nothing remained but the charred and ghastly skeletons of the adobe buildings while here and there thirsty tongues of flame would break forth as if the greedy element, not satisfied with having consumed everything in its course, still craved for more," intoned the *Epitaph*.

The newspaper listed sixty-six stores, including saloons and restaurants, that had been damaged or destroyed and estimated that of the $175,000 cost, only $25,000 was covered by insurance. Ironically, as the fire had raged, Mayor John Clum was returning from a trip during which he had purchased a fire engine for the city. "On the train returning, just east of Benson, we saw a great column of smoke rising over the hills to the south," he wrote. "I tried to make my fellow passengers believe we had a live volcano over there, but when I arrived at Benson I learned that Tombstone was burning."

Though the event was surely a setback to Tombstone's boisterous growth, the hardy residents got right to work rebuilding. Relying less on wood and more on adobe bricks, they replaced all the burned buildings in three months.*

After such a brush with extinction, what Tombstone very much needed at this time was strong leadership, including its marshal. It did not have the latter. Ben Sippy "must have needed the money," writes Virgil Earp biographer Don Chaput, "because he certainly

---

* Still, Tombstone had enough wooden structures remaining to be like a match waiting to be lit. That occurred the following May, when a fire that began at the Tivoli Saloon on the south side of Allen Street quickly spread. Many familiar businesses were destroyed, including the building housing the *Tombstone Daily Nugget*, and it was estimated that this greater disaster caused half a million dollars in damages.

didn't want and couldn't handle the position. He was a nice fellow who liked to gab with the guys in the saloons, but hated violence and confrontation."

Allie Earp would recall him as a "coward." This could be attributed to Sippy having defeated her husband in the election for marshal, but in this case, there could be a reasonable doubt about Sippy's courage. As violent acts became more frequent and the cowboys and law-and-order advocates circled each other, Sippy left town.*

Officially, on June 6, the marshal had requested from the city council a two-week leave of absence, which was granted. Two weeks later, council members awaited his return. They waited in vain. There were to be no more Sippy sightings in Cochise County or in the state, for that matter. It was later reported that the runaway marshal had been seen on an eastbound train and was probably headed back to his native Pennsylvania. Correcting the voters' previous wrong, on June 28, the city council appointed Virgil to be marshal.

His first major task was to address the aftermath of the fire that had threatened to turn Tombstone into little more than a footnote in Arizona history. Even days after the disaster, no one knew how many lives had been claimed by the conflagration. Conceivably, many of the smoldering lots now were ownerless because of death, or because of lack of insurance and sufficient savings some owners simply walked away. The Tombstone Townsite Company saw this

---

* The marshal's abrupt departure also confirmed rumors that he had piled up debts he could not repay. As the *Tombstone Daily Nugget* reported, "One of the late Marshal Sippy's creditors has a large picture of him hanging in his office, and underneath the inscription: 'Though lost to sight, to memory dear. Two hundred dollars worth.'"

as an opportunity to reassert itself. The proprietors, James Clark and Mike Gray, hired men to erect tents on now vacant properties. What was called "lot jumping" was a blatant wrong to many citizens, but the company believed the gambit would not be challenged.

Clark and Gray were wrong. With the support of the city council, the new marshal deputized Wyatt, Morgan, Warren, friends such as Texas Jack Vermillion and Fred Dodge, and at least a dozen others. Their instructions were to ride through the streets affected by the fire and use their ropes to pull down the tents. This they did with gusto, calling out, "Lot jumper, you git!" as they yanked their ropes.

A few of the rousted men thought about going for their guns, but what they saw was described by Don Chaput: As the tents were being tugged down, "Marshal Earp [strolled] down the smoke-filled streets. He walked slowly, all six-feet-one of him, with pistol at his side, and Winchester cradled in his arms, carrying the double authority of a deputy U.S. marshal and a city marshal. He had to do a little buffaloing along the way, but the people on the streets of Tombstone knew what the official attitude towards lot-jumping was."

Virgil did not stop there. Though not exactly a crusade, his efforts were aimed squarely at restoring law and order. There were forty-eight arrests in the city in June, and that jumped to sixty in July. Even the mayor received no favors—Virgil arrested John Clum for riding a horse too fast.

Though he was making Tombstone too hot for outlaws, the marshal could do nothing about the chronic high temperatures, which continued to put most of Tombstone's residents on edge, and anything could happen. "I am beginning to entertain fears of there being anything left to go to San Diego with. Should the hot weather continue much longer," wrote Clara Brown about the condition of her clothes after having to hand-wring the perspiration out of them so often. "This is pronounced the hottest and driest summer in the annals of Tombstone."

Even in perfect weather, Doc Holliday had more bad moods than good ones. The potential for a really bad one arrived when Big Nose Kate turned up again in Tombstone, full of grievances. And on the larger stage of the cowboys and ranchers and rustling, making things worse was Old Man Clanton went and got himself killed.

Chapter Seventeen

"REVENGE SEEMS THE ORDER OF THE DAY"

Only four years after their discovery in the mountains that led to the creation of Tombstone, Ed and Al Schieffelin were immortalized in the city. On June 8, 1881, Schieffelin Hall had opened on the corner of Fremont and Fourth Streets. It was for a time the largest standing adobe structure in the Southwest. Ed was not there for the ceremony—he had already left town.

It was Al, who had also realized great wealth from their mines, who had underwritten the construction of the forty-foot-tall Schieffelin Hall. Upstairs was a Masonic lodge, with the first Master Mason being Wells Spicer, a justice of the peace who would later play a crucial role in the lives of the Earp brothers. The rest of the building housed a theater and meeting rooms. The main floor of the auditorium/theater could seat 450, and there were an additional 125 seats in the gallery. Schieffelin Hall immediately became the center of culture and entertainment in the city. Its first full-scale production, staged on September 5, was *The Ticket-of-Leave Man*, a four act drama that played to packed houses.

Despite this huge advance in the cosmopolitan aspirations of Tombstone, that June and into the peak of summer city lawmakers and lawmen were still grappling with lawlessness and outlaws yet to be found. Suddenly, though, it appeared one of them had been found—Doc Holliday, who was arrested for the attempted robbery of the Benson stage and the murders of Bud Philpot and Peter Roerig back in March.

Kate Elder had returned to Tombstone. She had missed Doc and may have convinced herself that Doc missed her. In any case, one day she climbed down out of the stagecoach from Globe and moved back in with her gambler boyfriend. It seems more likely that Doc had not put out a welcome mat, because they immediately resumed fighting.

Kate later claimed that she had come to Tombstone on something of a rescue mission. She had never been fond of Wyatt and Doc's strong bond of friendship, and several years after it began, she hoped to end it for good. "I became desperate and in a vain hope of breaking up their association with Doc, whom I loved, I swore out a warrant," she explained. She also referred to "Wyatt Earp and others of his gang of legalized outlaws."

If that was indeed the true motivation for Kate's action, it backfired. She was angry, she got drunk, and the longer she stayed drunk the more angry she got. Thinking it was about time to fix Doc for good, she staggered over to the Cochise County Sheriff's Office. Her slurred statement resulted in a warrant for Holliday's arrest for being a participant in the deadly Benson stage robbery.

Johnny Behan was only too happy to toss Doc into jail—maybe where he went, the Earps would soon follow. In fact, Wyatt was at the jail that same day, July 5, but it was to hand over money he had collected to bail his friend out. Doc did not encounter Kate back at his hotel room because she had chosen to continue her bender. The outcome of that was being arrested herself the next day for being drunk and disorderly. Wyatt wasn't about to show up to help her, so Kate ponied up the $12.50 and bailed herself out. The *Tombstone Daily Nugget* referred to her as "an enraged and intoxicated woman." The day after that, Kate was arrested again. A dour Behan could see the case against Holliday and by extension the Earps weakening with every shot of whiskey.

As well it should. "Doc lived on the edge," writes Gary L. Roberts. "He was guilty of many things. He was quick-tempered when he drank and had a penchant for getting himself into trouble. He did not always choose his friends well, but nothing in his life before or after the Benson stage robbery attempt indicated that he was the type of man who would participate in the kind of affair that happened on the Benson road."

Then the case against Doc fell apart entirely. The district attorney handling the Benson stage investigation was Lyttleton Price. All it took was a conversation with a disoriented Kate to realize there was not a kernel of truth in the accusation. He recommended to Spicer that the case be dropped, and it was. However, some damage had been done. According to Casey Tefertiller, "While the court completely disregarded Kate's claims, the charge would be enough to begin gossip in a community where Holliday had already made more than his share of enemies ready to believe the worst of him." Tarred with the same brush were his only friends, the Earp brothers.

Just as well that Doc was not one of the outlaws, because there had suddenly been a high mortality rate among them, which would have an impact on Wyatt's political plans. In the Animas Valley on the New Mexico side of the border was a ranch owned by the brothers Bill and Ike Haslett. The cowboys and their rancher colleagues on the Arizona side coveted it. The Haslett ranch was close to the Mexican border and would be a good way station for cattle stolen from Sonora. Thus far, the brothers had rebuffed requests and then threats to relinquish the ranch. A decision was made to simply kill them. Among the cowboys given the job were Billy Leonard and Harry Head.

However, the Hasletts got wind of the plot. They then learned that the two men chosen to carry out the mission had stopped at a nearby store to eat and drink. Ike and Bill Haslett, well armed, rode there, planning a preemptive strike. Behind the store was a corral, and the brothers positioned themselves in it. Soon, Leonard, on a horse, and Head, on foot, came along.

Bill Haslett was the first to step out and open fire, then his brother did the same. Leonard was hit in the chest. Because he fell on the other side of the horse and was out of sight, Ike Haslett shot the horse, too, which landed on Leonard. Head jerked his gun out of his holster, but before he could fire Bill Haslett shot him in the stomach. When he tried to run away, both brothers took aim, and with six bullets in him, Head was finally finished.

It was cold-blooded murder, but the men killed had been wanted outlaws, so the Hasletts not only had rid themselves of assassins but planned to collect the $2,400 in reward money, too. They had not counted on the revenge of Jim Crane, another of the Benson stage robbers. He put a posse together of eighteen or so cowboys and went searching for the Hasletts. They were found in a saloon owned by West McFadden. The brothers were sitting at a table with an acquaintance named Sigman Biertzhorff, who had the misfortune to share their fate.

Guns blazed. Bill Haslett was hit six times, Ike Haslett at least twice, with one bullet getting him in the head, and Biertzhoff was shot seven times. All three were left to die on the dirty saloon floor.

This outburst of gunfire was bad news for the surrounding community, because not only did it mean an escalation of violence, but if cowboys were turning on one another, no one was safe. What was to prevent them from settling disputes with shoot-outs in the middle of Tombstone, and doing it daily? The city's sophisticated aspirations would shatter with each bullet-broken window.

The event at McFadden's saloon was also not good news for Wyatt. The reward deal with Ike Clanton and his ilk was now $2,400 less sweet. And with Jim Crane suspected in leading the revenge killing, Ike, never the most courageous of men, was less likely to provide Wyatt with any information on him. It appeared that Wyatt's gambit for glory had failed, and if word got out about it, he and his brothers would be reviled even more by the cowboys.

And word was getting around. There were six men who knew about Wyatt's scheme—Wyatt, of course, and Virgil, and Ike Clanton, Joe Hill, and Frank McLaury, and probably Marshall Williams, the Wells Fargo agent who had telegraphed his higher-ups about the reward money. The Earp brothers could be trusted. Ike certainly could not be trusted, but trumping that was his being terrified that Curly Bill or Ringo would learn that he'd even had a conversation with Wyatt about giving up any of the cowboys. McLaury, too, did not want people thinking he was in league with the Earps. That left Williams, and one night when drunk he pulled Ike Clanton aside.

The Wells Fargo agent did not know particulars, but when he'd seen Wyatt's message and the response, he had assayed what Wyatt was up to and he wouldn't mind learning more. It is not clear why

Williams cornered Ike specifically and connected him with Wyatt, but the effect was electric on the rustling rancher. He made a beeline to Wyatt and accused him of having loose lips about the reward scheme. "I've told him nothing," Wyatt insisted. Most likely this was the truth—if Williams had been informed, he could have cut Wyatt out and dealt directly with Ike. But Ike was too petrified to care by now. He wanted nothing further to do with the Earps.

Maybe cooler heads would prevail if the air ever cooled off. And it did, with a splash. The intense heat wave finally broke, and writing on July 17, Clara Brown reported, "We were awakened last night by a good pouring rain, accompanied for a wonder with but little thunder. The fall was considerable, and the town is much cleaner and cooler for it today."

And then, as if to compensate, the precipitation sometimes went to almost punishing extremes. Poor George Parsons, not yet fully recovered from the injuries suffered in the June 22 fire, was in a buggy driving back to Tombstone from an accounting job at a mill. "After getting well down the canyon, the threatening storm burst upon us," he recorded. "The rain came down as though the bottom had dropped out. The lightning was blinding and things were not very comfortable. When we reached the mesa we traveled through miles of water, the whole country seeming to be overflowed." He managed to make it to Charleston in the storm-filled darkness, fed the horses, continued on, and finally fell into his bed at 3 A.M.

In her next missive to her San Diego readers, Brown wrote that there was a washout on the Atchison, Topeka, and Santa Fe line on the New Mexico side that extended twenty-five miles. "A passenger on one of the delayed trains says that they crossed a dry river bed, and directly after beheld a wall of water rushing toward them, from the bursting of a cloud, which struck the railroad bridge and carried it away. This flood extended for miles, up and down the country, and it was impassable for days."

There was a silver lining to all the water: "We are unspeakably grateful to be rid of that disagreeable dust, which has tormented us so much of the time."

Alas, the torrents of rain did not cool off tensions with the cowboys. In fact, they were suddenly about to become much more intense and threatened to instigate an international incident.

For the past couple of years, Old Man Clanton had operated his own ranch. He had given the San Pedro River ranch to his sons and established his own in the Animas Valley, near the one owned by the late Haslett brothers. There he had offered his ranch as both a place of employment and a sanctuary for the cowboys. At night, a group of them—sometimes including Clanton himself—would cross into the Sonora area of Mexico, round up strays or steal cattle outright from the fringes of a Mexican owner's herd, and hurry them back across the border. At the Clanton ranch, the cattle would be rebranded or at least have their original brands disguised, then they would be driven to army posts or to Tombstone or other Arizona towns with a constant demand for beef.

Occasionally, the easy border crossings of the cowboys led to stealing more than cattle. Some accounts suggest that Curly Bill Brocius—mostly recovered from being shot in the face, though still not happy about it—always had one of his cowboy minions on the Mexican side to glean information on smugglers transporting gold, silver, or other valuable items to the American side. One alluring tidbit in July was that $2,500 in silver was about to be smuggled in on the night of the twenty-seventh.

Curly Bill brought this information to the Clantons and the McLaurys. A haul of $2,500 in silver proved irresistible. A batch of hardened raiders—among them Johnny Ringo, Old Man Clanton and his sons Ike and Billy, and the McLaury brothers—was collected. They concocted a plan to ambush the Mexican smugglers in Skeleton Canyon.

This would not be the first time some members of this party saw action in Skeleton Canyon. Exactly two years earlier, rustlers had launched a raid into Sonora, and this time in addition to stealing cattle they had shot and killed several people. An officer of the Mexican Rurales, Francisco Neri, determined that the killers would not get away, damn the U.S. border. He led a posse into Arizona.

Before long, in Skeleton Valley, there was a hail of bullets directed at the Rurales. The posse was surrounded and surrendered, hoping they would be allowed to return to Mexico. They were . . . after their commandant, Neri, was executed. The rustlers wanted the survivors to return with the message that the healthiest action for Mexican authorities to take after a raid into their territory was no action at all. If he can be believed, Johnny Ringo later recollected that the 1879 raiding party consisted of Old Man Clanton and Ike and Billy, Tom and Frank McLaury, Indian Charlie, Jim Hughes, Rattlesnake Bill, Joe Hill, Charley Snow, Jake Guage, Charlie Thomas, and Curly Bill Brocius.

The night of July 27, 1881, also turned out to be a bloody one in Skeleton Valley. The bushwhackers secreted themselves in the rocks above the trail that cut through the valley. When the smugglers came into view, the ambushers had plenty of guns trained on them. Clanton and company opened up when the smugglers were most vulnerable. Some of them fell dead from the first volley, more died trying to escape.*

Losing $2,500 was bad, but worse was being killed in the process. The survivors were glad to be left with their lives. Hearing about the massacre, the governor of Sonora was outraged—even though the victims were smugglers—and demanded that the Arizona governor find the fiendish murderers and punish them. John C. Frémont ignored his counterpart across the border.

The following month, the gun was in the other hand. Curly Bill had led another raid into Mexico. He recrossed the border with stolen cattle and sold them over to Old Man Clanton, who would rebrand and sell them. On their way through Guadalupe Canyon, which straddles the border between Arizona and New Mexico, Clanton and the six cowboys with him bedded down for the night . . . unaware that Mexican troops had been stalking them. They were patient, setting up and waiting until the first light of dawn to attack.

This contingent of Mexican Rurales was led by Alfredo Carrillo, an officer who had managed to survive the Skeleton Canyon attack. Finally, he would avenge his fallen commander and comrades.

Clanton had probably risen first, because he had begun cooking breakfast when he was shot and fell into the fire. The cowboy Charley Snow was probably up out of his bedroll, too, as he was hit by a fusillade of bullets when he turned to investigate a noise. Dick Gray and Jim Crane were still sleeping when they died—the latter being

---

* Estimates range from twenty to fifty men being in on the raid, with the higher figure being the least likely. It has also been reported that as many as twenty-five smugglers were murdered, but this, too, is an unlikely number.

the same Jim Crane who had tried to rob the Benson stage back in March. Billy Lang had grabbed hold of his gun and was returning fire when he was cut down. One of the flying bullets grazed the nose of Harry Ernshaw, who managed to find shelter behind rocks and then ran off, away from the attackers. The seventh man, Billy Byers, pretended to have been shot and killed. When the shooting stopped, he quietly and cautiously dragged himself away from the clearing, then he, too, began running.

Ernshaw still had his wits about him enough to know that he could reach the ranch of John Gray, the brother of one of the victims. When he did, Gray sent word to a mining camp twenty miles away to ask for armed men to join him on the journey to Gauda-lupe Canyon. He could not know how many killers there were and if they had remained there. When they arrived, they found that the five dead men had been stripped naked. They buried Snow right away in the canyon because of advanced decomposition and being partially eaten by animals. The other four bodies were carted away and buried on the New Mexico side of the canyon.*

Billy Byers was found alive, staggering through the desert in a daze. Byers reported that the killers were Mexican soldiers, pre-sumably because he caught a glimpse of uniforms and/or heard them speaking. William McLaury, brother of Frank and Tom, later insisted that the killers were Wyatt, Virgil, and Morgan Earp. This assertion did not gain any traction in Tombstone.

If anyone other than Mexican Rurales were to be a suspect, it would be Curly Bill Brocius. His reputation was nasty enough that some believed he had double-crossed Old Man and stolen and sold

* Old Man Clanton's body would be exhumed in 1882 by his sons Ike and Phin and reburied next to the body of his youngest son, Billy, in the Boot Hill Cemetery.

the herd he had already just stolen and sold. Plus, with the patriarch of the Clanton gang gone, Brocius and Johnny Ringo had even fewer constraints on their illegal and sometimes outrageous behavior. Given that they already had firm lawmen allies at the Cochise County level in Johnny Behan, Billy Breakenridge, and Harry Woods, and with the territorial government in Tucson not interested, all cowboys and corrupt ranchers had to do was get rid of those pesky Tombstone law-and-order sticklers—the Earps especially, now that Wyatt was more involved, being regularly deputized by Virgil. Kill or chase them out and Curly Bill, Johnny, and their crowd of cowboys could do whatever they wanted.

However, a war with Mexico could get in the way of such an appealing scenario. Breathless newspaper accounts published as far away as San Francisco reported that the Clanton family had raised a force of two hundred men "as desperate a gang as could not be imagined" to invade Mexico and find the killers of their patriarch. The pro-cowboy *Tombstone Daily Nugget* declared that war was unavoidable and probably not a bad idea. After all, the last war with Mexico had resulted in the acquisition of valuable territory, including southeast Arizona and its since-revealed riches.

"The massacre of Americans near Guadalupe Canyon occasioned great excitement in Tombstone, particularly among the more lawless element of the camp," wrote Clara Brown in her next report to *The San Diego Union*. She referred to the vigilante posse that had been formed and "any Mexicans so unfortunate as to cross their pathway will be summarily shot down. The proceeding is not supported by the authorities. It is likely to lead to very serious trouble, and a war with Mexico would be a calamity greatly to be deplored, in more ways than one."

"Bad trouble on the border and this time looks more serious

than anything yet," commented George Parsons. "Revenge seems the order of the day, a gang having started out to make trouble. This killing business by the Mexicans, in my mind, was perfectly justifiable as it was in retaliation for killing of several of them."

However, Mexican officials had memories, too, and they did not want to risk a new war three decades after the last one, and especially in the 1880s when the United States was even more powerful. During the third week in August, General Adolfo Dominguez arrived in Tombstone to reveal a crackdown by his government on smuggling. Forts and camps with troops would be established just south of the border. He explained the financial losses Mexican businesses had suffered because of such porous borders and the deaths of innocent citizens as well as smugglers. It was time for strict border control to ease tensions.

Mexico was good on its word. Even remote and unobtrusive passageways between the countries were guarded. Passes were needed to cross the border into the United States, and American citizens had to prove legitimate business or personal reasons to enter Mexico. Talk of war receded. But tensions remained. In Cochise County, writes Casey Tefertiller, "the mounting bands of rustlers found themselves without the easy pickings across the border and intensified their activities on the American side."

Such activities would no doubt widen the divide between the restless cowboys and those supporting law and order. And if something was going to happen, the law might not be able or willing to stop it. As John Clum editorialized in the August 19 issue of *The Tombstone Epitaph*, "There is altogether too much good feeling between the Sheriff's office and the outlaws infesting this county."

In just two months, that good feeling would help provoke a gunfight.

ACT IV
THE GUNFIGHT

Oriental Saloon
(COURTESY OF ARIZONA HISTORICAL SOCIETY)

Some few of us pioneers are entitled to credit for what we have done.
We have been the fore-runners of government. If it hadn't been
for me and a few like me there never would have been
any government in some of these towns.
—DOC HOLLIDAY

Chapter Eighteen

"RATHER DIE FIGHTING"

It is never a good sign for law-abiding citizens to see Johnny Ringo rush into town, both him and his horse all in a lather. So it had to raise eyebrows in Tombstone on September 9 when the cowboy leader made such a dramatic entrance. He was looking for Sherman McMasters (more about him later) and obviously had to find him right away. Virgil Earp was informed that Ringo was in the city. As it happened, the marshal also was looking for McMasters.

Earlier that year, a stagecoach had been robbed near Globe to the north. It was believed that McMasters and another cowboy, Pony Deal, were the thieves. Since then, Bob Paul, having settled in as the Pima County sheriff, had been keeping an eye out for Deal, who wisely had made himself scarce. But not for long enough—that second week in September, Paul finally got his man. He relayed this information to Virgil, who telegraphed back that he had spotted McMasters in Tombstone and could arrest him.

He was waiting for Paul's response when Johnny Ringo blew

into town. Another reason he was in a hurry was that he hoped to get in, warn McMasters about Deal's apprehension, and get out before he, too, was arrested. There was an existing warrant for that August poker game in Galeyville when Ringo had stolen everyone else's winnings. Virgil knew of it, and suddenly this was turning into a busy day when Paul replied that McMasters should be picked up.

Virgil grabbed a gun and recruited James Earp. The bartender could not have been pleased at the prospect of going up against Johnny Ringo, but he was the only Earp brother available: Wyatt and Morgan had already been recruited, by Marshall Williams of Wells Fargo, to investigate the holdup of the Bisbee stagecoach the night before. Virgil knew that McMasters kept his horse at the O.K. Corral, so after poking their heads into a few saloons McMasters usually frequented, Virgil and James went there.

They were too late. Ringo had found the other cowboy, told him about Pony Deal being behind bars, and the two had stolen fresh horses and left Tombstone in as much of a hurry as Ringo had entered it. The anticipated busy and possibly dangerous day for the police chief had turned into a bad one.

The increasing turmoil in Tombstone and its surroundings was too much for any one lawman. What was needed was strong leadership at the top of the territorial government. Arizona did not have that. Governor John C. Frémont was often not in Tucson or even the territory, and sometimes not in the western half of the United States at all when he was back east attending to business and political interests. The lower third of the territory was a boiling cauldron of competitors for cattle and power and money, and the governor simply did not care.

John Gosper, the de facto governor and ongoing territorial secretary, had some skin in the game, having connections to both Virgil Earp and Doc Holliday and supporting the law-and-order faction. But his position as acting chief executive afforded him very little authority. Still, reacting to reports of increasing cowboy crime, that September Gosper visited Tucson to discuss the myriad depredations with Virgil Earp, Johnny Behan, and of course Mayor John Clum. Mostly, though, Gosper learned how much his hands were tied because of his temporary and quasi-official status. He freed up one of his hands enough to write to James G. Blaine, secretary of state in the James Garfield administration.*

In his missive, the acting governor tried to explain the futility of his uncertain status, the enmity between the city and county lawmen, how flames were being fanned by Tombstone's two competing newspapers, and how the cowboys and their rancher allies were virtually unchecked in that part of the territory. Tombstone was supposed to be an example of American growth, prosperity, and the civilizing of the western frontier. Instead, it threatened to explode.

"I am sorry to say he gave me little hope of being able in his department to cope with the power of the cow-boys," Gosper wrote Blaine, referring to the Cochise County sheriff, omitting that Behan was not inclined to do so even if he could. He continued that "many of the very best law-abiding and peace-loving citizens have no confidence in the willingness of the civil officers to pursue and

---

* The administration in Washington itself was somewhat in limbo because of violence and a power vacuum. In July, President Garfield had been shot. Primitive medical practices prevented his recovery, and he lingered near death for months, not passing away until September 19. He was succeeded as president by Chester A. Arthur of New York.

bring to justice that element of outlawry so largely disturbing the sense of security, and so often committing highway robbery and smaller thefts."

Wells Fargo was getting pretty fed up, too, by this time as its drivers and shotgun messengers faced greater risks and its vault greater losses. As one of its detectives, James Hume, would soon characterize Tombstone: "Six thousand population. Five thousand are bad. One thousand of these are known outlaws."

As if to put an exclamation point on such sentiments, there was the Bisbee stagecoach robbery on September 8. At about 10 P.M., a stage was on its way from Tombstone—on what was known as the Sandy Bob Line—when several masked men stepped out onto the road, forcing it to stop. There was no Bob Paul as the shotgun messenger on this trip and thus no resistance. The thieves grabbed hold of the Wells Fargo box containing about $2,500, a sack of mail, and the cash, watches, and jewelry of the passengers. They got away without a shot being fired.

As soon as Tombstone learned of the robbery, a posse was formed. Curiously—or tellingly—it was not organized by Johnny Behan, who as county sheriff had the jurisdiction to track down the outlaws. Marshall Williams, not waiting around, put one together, and in addition to Wyatt and Morgan he enlisted Fred Dodge, still secretly a Wells Fargo operative. Behan allowed his deputies Billy Breakenridge and David Neagle to go along.

At the scene of the stage robbery, Dodge noted that one set of footprints was different from the others. At a Bisbee boot shop, the posse learned that Frank Stilwell had recently had the heels of his boots replaced. It would not be a shock if he was involved. And over the next few months, he would become more of a prominent participant in the chaos caused by the cowboys.

Frank Stilwell had been born twenty-five years earlier in Iowa, and then his family moved to Kansas. During the Civil War, his father joined the Union army. As a member of the Eighteenth Missouri Volunteer Infantry, he had marched with General William Tecumseh Sherman through Georgia. When Frank was old enough, he accompanied an older brother through Indian Territory to Arizona. Simpson Stilwell, known as Comanche Jack, was a scout for the U.S. Cavalry who saw action against Indians on the Plains and also served as a deputy U.S. marshal and later a judge.

Frank's career path was a typical one for a young man on the frontier until it veered off in a violent way. He went to work as a ranch hand in the Prescott area. In October 1877, there was a dispute with the ranch cook about what Frank was being served and he drew his pistol and shot him. The verdict was self-defense. It was probably a factor that the cook, Jesus Bega, was a new hire and Mexican. Next, Frank went to work as a miner. In November 1879, there was a new dispute, this one with a Colonel John Van Houten. After Frank rearranged his face with a rock, the former military officer died. Incredibly, a grand jury ruled there was not enough evidence for a murder charge and Stilwell was sent on his way, eventually turning up in Tombstone.

These experiences made him eligible to be a deputy sheriff, according to Johnny Behan, who hired Stilwell in the spring of 1881—which had to further irritate the eminently more qualified Wyatt Earp. Stilwell's tenure lasted only a few months. Citing accounting irregularities, Behan fired him. The following month, in September, the Bisbee stage was held up. When Stilwell, who now worked at a Bisbee livery stable, arrived the next morning with fellow employee Pete Spence, the posse was waiting and both men were arrested.

Spence also went by the name of Peter M. Spencer, although his real name was Elliot Larkin Ferguson. He had been born in 1852 in Texas and at twenty-two he joined the Texas Rangers. That apparently did not work out well, and four years later he fled the state because he was wanted for a robbery in Goliad County. Now known as Pete Spence, he became one of the hundreds of young men from Texas and New Mexico working as cowboys and at various odd jobs in southeast Arizona. Somewhat inconveniently, he lived on the same street as the Earps in Tombstone, with his new wife, Marietta Duarte, and her mother. Wyatt and Morgan had just helped to put handcuffs on their neighbor, adding insult to injury for Spence.

But he and Stilwell were not in custody long. Their bail of $7,000 was posted by Ike Clanton and two other men. At the preliminary hearing a week after their arrest, several men appeared before Judge Wells Spicer in Tombstone to claim they were with Stilwell and Spence at the time the Bisbee stage was being robbed. Spicer may not have completely believed the duo's cowboy friends, but he dropped the territorial charges because of insufficient evidence.

Accepting the statements of the cowboys and dismissing the evidence of the boot heels—and also testimony from one of the stagecoach riders that a robber had referred to money as "sugar," which Stilwell was known to do—could indicate that Spicer was in league with them. However, he had also dropped charges against Doc Holliday that summer. He was an experienced man of the law not easily intimidated, as earlier events had demonstrated.

Spicer, originally from upstate New York, had grown up in Iowa, where he would become a lawyer and publisher of the *Cedar County Advertiser*. He was elected a county judge in 1856. He was thirty when the Civil War began, but being married with a son, he remained in Iowa. After the war the Spicer family moved to Utah. Apparently a man of boundless energy, there he had a law practice, operated a hotel, began a tunneling company, did some prospecting, and wrote for two newspapers. It was as an attorney in 1875 that Spicer became involved in the Mountain Meadows massacre.

The infamous event had occurred in September 1857. A wagon train full of families, around 120 people in all, from Arkansas was making its way through Utah, bound for California. The emigrants paused to rest outside Salt Lake City, at a place known as Mountain Meadows. This would turn out to be the wrong place at the wrong time. The so-called Utah War (or Mormon Rebellion) was under way, pitting the Mormon settlers of Utah against U.S. Army units sent by the administration of President James Buchanan. It was believed by the Mormons that the federal government aimed to take their land, and militia units had been formed to resist. One of them was called the Nauvoo Legion. Its two leaders, Isaac Haight and John Lee, concocted a twisted plan that evidence of Indian hostilities would keep the army too occupied to take Mormon territory. What better evidence than an attack on a wagon train?

On September 7, the attack was launched by a coalition of Southern Paiute Indians and members of the Nauvoo Legion disguised as Indians. The original plan may have been to spend a few hours harassing the petrified families and provide the army with panicky reports of Indian hostilities. But the emigrants had the temerity to fight back, with some of the attackers killed. What followed was a siege that lasted for five days. With each day, fear grew among the Mormons that the emigrants had seen through their hastily applied disguises and now knew that white men as well as real Indians were the hostiles, which would cause even more problems with the army. The solution? Eliminate potential witnesses.

On the fifth day of the siege, the Nauvoo Legion sent several men under a white flag to the wagon train. Its inhabitants were almost out of food and water, and especially the younger children were suffering. They were assured the attacks were finished because a truce had been worked out with the "Indians." With the siege over, the families could travel under Mormon protection to Cedar City, where water and food would be provided. The emigrants allowed themselves to be escorted out of their camp of circled wagons. Once all of them were exposed, the militia and their Paiute allies attacked. With the exception of seventeen children younger than age seven, all the men, women, and children were slaughtered—shot and hacked to death with swords.* The bodies were so quickly and haphazardly buried that many were soon eaten by wild animals.

What does all this have to do with Wells Spicer, who was still living in Iowa when the Mountain Meadows massacre took place? It was not until seventeen years after the heinous murders that arrest warrants were issued. Of the eight men jailed, one was John Lee. He hired Spicer, who urged him to confess and ask for leniency. Lee refused, and his trial began in July 1875. Spicer found himself in an extremely difficult position—despised by Mormons for basing his defense on religious fanaticism and being a non-Mormon to boot and hated by others for defending an unrepentant mass murderer. The vilification of the attorney worsened when there was a hung jury. When the trial resumed, Mormon leaders worked out a deal with federal prosecutors that essentially allowed Lee to take the fall if no blame was assigned to the church. That did the trick—John Lee was found guilty.

---

* It took a couple of years, but ultimately the surviving children were taken by the U.S. Army to Arkansas and delivered to relatives.

Spicer appealed the conviction up to the U.S. Supreme Court, to no avail. He attended Lee's execution in March 1877. Whatever was thought about Spicer—and much of it was not complimentary—for defending a ringleader of such an egregious crime, he had shown that he would not break under pressure and would not bail out of very difficult cases.

But that did not mean he had to keep taking it on the chin. The following year, considering himself the "unkilled of Mountain Meadows" because of the emotional violence he had endured, Spicer heard of a silver strike in southeast Arizona and made his way there. In Tombstone, he tried his hand at mining, established a law practice, was a correspondent for the *Arizona Daily Star*, and in June 1880 became a justice of the First District Court.

Judge Spicer's ruling in the Bisbee stagecoach case was good enough for Sheriff Johnny Behan, but not for the Earps. The cuffs were not off for long—Virgil arrested Stilwell and Spence again, not for stealing the Wells Fargo box but for taking the U.S. Mail. Because these were federal charges, and recalling how leaky the Tombstone jail could be when cowboys were in it, Virgil took the two men to Tucson, where they were housed in the territorial jail until there could be a trial. In Virgil's absence, Wyatt was appointed the temporary marshal of Tombstone.

The Clantons and McLaurys and other ranchers, along with Curly Bill Brocius and Johnny Ringo and the cowboys, were angered by the new arrest. It did not matter to them if Stilwell and Spence had actually robbed the Bisbee stage; more important was this obvious harassment of their friends and a tougher stance against the cowboys. Virgil should simply mind his own business, the way the Cochise County Sheriff's Office did. However, if the Earps kept this up, there would have to be some kind of retaliation.

Virgil, especially, would be the target. Not leaving well enough alone after Wells Spicer had released Stilwell and Spence, and now allowing them to enjoy the hospitality of a Tucson jail, was something like an act of war. Clearly, Frank McLaury saw it that way, and he wondered what Virgil would do next. No doubt he recalled what Virgil had said to him after the stolen mules episode—that he would not hesitate to come after the McLaurys if necessary. What if Virgil had a loose definition of "necessary"?

Several days after the chief of police returned from Tucson, McLaury confronted him. He insisted that Virgil was quietly pulling together a vigilance committee, and when it was ready, it would target the McLaury brothers. In fact, maybe all ranchers were vulnerable to persecution by out-of-control law enforcement.

Virgil truthfully denied that any such plan was afoot. McLaury pressed on: "I'll tell you, it makes no difference what I do, I will never surrender my arms to you. I'd rather die fighting than be strangled."

Virgil preferred to let the matter drop, seeing as how McLaury could not be persuaded otherwise. Unwisely, the rancher chose to threaten another Earp brother, and to do it with numbers. When Frank McLaury confronted Morgan outside the Alhambra Saloon, with him were Ike Clanton, Johnny Ringo, and Bill and Milt Hicks, who often rode with Curly Bill Brocius. He reiterated his allegation: "If you ever come after me, you will never take me."

Referring to Spence being wrong to allow the Earps to arrest him, McLaury added, "I have threatened you boys' lives and a few days later I had taken it back, but since this arrest it now goes."

The rancher's language could have been more explicit, but it was clear enough, especially backed by his friends, that it might soon be open season on the Earp brothers. While it appears that Wyatt was not similarly accosted at this time, he was hearing on the streets of Tombstone that the local law was coming closer to a confrontation with the cowboys. It was a good idea to never leave their houses without being fully armed.

With the Earps being mentioned more in news accounts in the *Nugget* and *Epitaph* and in saloon and dining room conversations as establishing a line between the lawlessness of the present and past and the hopes for a civilized Tombstone in the future, it was obvious that residents and the business community were relying on the brothers to maintain that line and perhaps strengthen it. County law enforcement would be of little or no help because it was openly acknowledged that Sheriff Behan was in league with the cowboys and corrupt ranchers or, at best, just wanted to stay safely out of the path of the approaching storm. The torrential rains of the summer were something like a harbinger of the bullets that could soon be flying in Tombstone.

But why had the Earps in particular become the focus of the law-and-order faction in the city? One reason was Virgil, who had taken his job seriously and thus far acted fearlessly after replacing that frightened rabbit Ben Sippy. And his "clannish" brothers were at Virgil's side. Another reason was that Wyatt had brought west with him a reputation as an effective lawman, so naturally many people thought that if pressed, he would act accordingly in his new hometown (and with the backing of his Dodge City friend Doc Holliday). And third, the Earps allowed themselves to be in this position. At any time, the brothers—Warren continued to come and go with an über-Earp restlessness—could have loaded up wagons and left town. They had been drawn to Tombstone for business reasons, not to take on any lawing crusade.

But there they were, and especially after being challenged by

McLaury and Ringo and Clanton, the Earps were not about to turn tail and travel toward the next horizon. If they had to do what others could not or would not, so be it, whether it was appreciated or not, respected or not, accepted or not.

"The four blond-haired brothers had become part of the fabric of Tombstone, with Jim tending bar, Wyatt and Virgil in law enforcement, and Morgan riding shotgun, filling in as deputy," observes Casey Tefertiller. "Still, the Earps never quite fit in with the best element in town. Tombstone's upper class respected the Earps and needed them. They did not necessarily want to be lodge brothers with them."*

Only in a high-stress atmosphere like this one in Tombstone would people feel relief when Geronimo went on the warpath. The uprising derailed the showdown an increasing number of citizens expected . . . but only for a little while.

---

* It had rankled Virgil that his request to be made a member of the Masonic lodge in the brand-new Schieffelin Hall had been rejected that summer.

Chapter Nineteen

"GERONIMO IS COMING!"

With all his responsibilities as both mayor of Tombstone and editor of *The Tombstone Epitaph*, coupled with being a single parent, John Clum had not kept track of what was happening on the San Carlos Reservation. In the early fall of 1881, that no longer mattered because the Apaches came to him.

All the attention paid to the progress of Tombstone and the emerging conflict between the city and the cowboys did not mean that the threat of Apache attacks had simply vanished. It was true that the three-hundred-year-old war between Europeans and the native inhabitants of the Southwest was in its end stage. No longer did tribes roam freely on land they called theirs to hunt and camp. The Apaches had once claimed thousands of square miles—though "ownership" was still a murky concept, something that obsessed the white man—yet now, with such great leaders as Mangas Coloradas and Cochise dead and their numbers much reduced thanks to disease and war, reservations were all that was left to them. And such areas designated by the U.S. government rarely had any mineral or agricultural value . . . or they would not have been given away so freely.

The Apaches had been subdued, but that did not mean they had to like it or choose not to resist it. There were a few leaders left with loyal followers. Every so often, they tried to break free of the chains the reservations represented.

One rebellion still fresh in the minds of southeast Arizona residents had taken place two years earlier. The Chiricahua chief Victorio refused his tribe's forcible removal from their homeland at Ojo Caliente in New Mexico to the San Carlos Reservation. He had been a protégé of Mangas Coloradas and had a sister, Lozen, who was also a fierce warrior and a prophet. In August 1879, Victorio and eighty followers left the reservation intent on war. When he was joined by other Apaches, suddenly his army numbered two hundred warriors.

Victorio's campaign of terror got off to an encouraging start. In September, his force won a battle in Las Animas Canyon. During the next few months he led a series of other actions against U.S. Cavalry units near the Percha River, in the San Mateo Mountains, in the Caballo Mountains near Animas Creek, near Aleman's Wells, in the San Andres Mountains west of White Sands, and once again in the San Andres Mountains, routing the cavalrymen and chasing them to the Rio Grande.

In April 1880, Victorio led a raid on settlers' homes around Alma, New Mexico, where forty-one men and women were killed. His warriors were finally driven off by the arrival of American soldiers from Fort Bayard. However, Victorio continued his campaign with an attack on Fort Tularosa, where his warriors had to face a detachment of the Ninth Cavalry and were repulsed by the "Buffalo Soldiers" of the Tenth Cavalry. Victorio's camp near the Rio Palomas, in the Black Range, was surprised and attacked that same year, but the Apaches succeeded in fending off the soldiers. Victorio led several raids into Mexico, repeatedly fording the Rio Grande. Back on the American side, he was pursued from one place to another by a total of four thousand armed troops, including Texas Rangers.

The end of the campaign, and of Victorio, finally came in October 1880 on the Mexico side of the Rio Grande. He sent two lieutenants, Mangus (Mangas Coloradas's surviving son) and Nana, with warriors to raid for ammunition and food. What remained at camp was discovered and surrounded by the Mexican army. In what became known as the Battle of Tres Castillos, Victorio and his followers were killed.

The death of Victorio did not reassure residents on the U.S. side of the border, because Geronimo was still alive. Victorio's bloody raids of 1879 and 1880 had not directly affected Tombstone, but a fresh outbreak could. The San Carlos Reservation, where not just Geronimo but other feared Apache leaders lived, was 170 miles away. This might appear to be a safe distance, but if there was a Victorio-like breakout and the Apache warriors wanted to seek shelter in the Chiricahua Mountains or flee into Mexico, Tombstone was especially vulnerable.

And in early autumn 1881, that is what happened. Suddenly, cattle-rustling cowboys and law-enforcing marshals were sideshows. On the night of September 30, a band of between three hundred and four hundred Apaches slipped out of the San Carlos Reservation. Only about a hundred were warriors, the remainder were women and children. Their destination was the Sierra Madre

Occidental range in Mexico. Once there, with enough water and wild game, they could hide out for months, if not years. To get to those mountains, the renegades would have to pass near Tombstone and go through the Guadalupe Canyon.

On October 5, word reached Tombstone that Geronimo and his confederates Juh and Naiche had led their warriors off the San Carlos Reservation. Tombstone citizens went to sleep terrified they would be murdered in their beds. Or as Clum put it, "A pall of terror spread over the White population of Arizona. The courier had spread his news as he galloped down Tombstone's main street. 'Indians are coming!' had been an American frontier call-to-arms for two hundred years; in Arizona, 'Geronimo is coming!' sent women to dark corners and brought vigilantes running, guns in hand, ready to go."

Juh, now in his mid-fifties, had ridden with Mangas Coloradas and then Cochise and had grown up with Geronimo, reportedly marrying his sister. He was over six feet tall and 225 pounds, particularly imposing for an Apache. He was a natural leader whose warriors would follow him anywhere. Naiche was only in his mid-twenties but had the loyalty of Apaches because he was the youngest son of Cochise. He, too, was over six feet tall. Physically, Geronimo was dwarfed by his two lieutenants, but he was an ambitious and experienced fighter with undeniable charisma.

It was also learned that the Apaches had followed the Gila River and ridden past the east side of the Santa Teresa and Galiuro Mountains. Three days earlier, on October 2, they had ambushed a wagon train hauling freight near Cedar Springs and killed six teamsters. Their next stop was a freight way station in Cedar Springs itself, where they killed the station agent and four army telegraph linemen, making sure to mutilate their bodies while they were at it to send a message. A U.S. Cavalry unit then found them, but Geronimo and his soldiers fought off the Bluebellies and fled down the west side of Sulphur Springs Valley. October 3 found the fugitives on land owned by the rancher Henry Hooker, where 133 horses were stolen and 12 other horses were slaughtered for food. On October 4 there was another skirmish with cavalry, this one north of the Middle Pass in the Dragoon Mountains. The renegades were getting closer to Tombstone, and they were murdering people along the way.

Several groups in southeast and central Arizona sort of modeled after the early Texas Rangers suddenly came into being. The Phoenix Rangers was composed of seventy men headed by Captain C. H. Vail. To help them be successful, Acting Governor Gosper requisitioned sixty carbines and rifles and four thousand cartridges. The Globe Rangers consisted of sixty men under D. B. Lacy. T. H. Cochran led the Pinal Guards. Also mounting up were the Florence Volunteers, San Pedro Rangers, and the Galeyville Rangers.

While these communities were mobilizing, a report was received that Apaches had raided the ranch of Major Edwin Frink in Sulphur Springs Valley, close enough to Tombstone that local lawmen put together a raiding party of their own. As the chief law officer of Cochise County, Johnny Behan was at the head of it, with Virgil Earp next in command. The group of forty or so men who rode out included Wyatt and Morgan Earp, John Clum, Billy Breakenridge, George Parsons, and Marshall Williams.

This was the debut of the Tombstone Rangers, a military force that had first been proposed at a town meeting at Schieffelin Hall in September when there were initial reports of Apache agitation on the reservation.* In case the mission turned into a long one, separating the Rangers from the culinary delights of Tombstone, this ad hoc militia even had its own cook come along.

In his October 5 entry, Parsons recorded that he was informed that "Indians and soldiers were fighting in Dragoon Pass, north of town, and having a regular battle." In an understatement, he added, "The Indian scare spread in town." And: "About noon a large party formed meaning business."

Meaning business and finding hostiles turned out to be two different things. There was a reminder of the odd summer weather when a rainstorm pounded down on the Tombstone raiding party. "Arizona is renowned as an arid country," Clum noted, but its downpours "are unexcelled anywhere in the world. It was our luck to encounter such a storm in Antelope Pass. Heavy thunder was continuous, and vivid lightning was sporting among the rocks all about us."

The Tombstone Rangers had to bed down at Frink's ranch. The next morning they trailed the stolen stock to Horseshoe Canyon, where not a horse or cow or Apache was to be found.

Parsons was consoling himself with thoughts of dying a hero's death, if it came to that: "I deemed it foolishness for our party to attempt a fight, but of course, being in it for now, I determined to stand by them to the last man. We were positive of a fight from what had been told us." As they rode along, with horse hooves splashing in puddles of rain yet to be absorbed by the ground, "the

---

* According to Lynn R. Bailey in her book *The Valiants: The Tombstone Rangers and Apache War Frivolities*, there would be several more editions of Tombstone Rangers during the decade.

whole situation with its possibilities came before my mind, and I saw anguish in my family over what they might be pleased to deem the rashness of the son and brother, if this expedition proved disastrous."

It was proving to be more ineffective than disastrous, not the most auspicious beginning for the Tombstone Rangers. Disgruntled and hungry, despite the presence of their cook, the troop was led by Captain Johnny Behan to the ranch of Frank and Tom McLaury.

This could have been an awkward get-together, but the McLaury brothers welcomed the well-meaning but somewhat red-faced militia. The rule of hospitality to travelers overrode the resentful feelings between the lawmen and the ranchers—even with Curly Bill Brocius and a couple of cowboy pals also in attendance. The Tombstone Rangers were given plenty of breakfast and coffee.

Parsons's tone seems a tad disapproving when he observed that "to show how we do things in Arizona, I will say our present Marshal and said 'Curly Bill' shook each other warmly by the hand and hobnobbed together some time." However, pressing the flesh with Virgil apparently did not curb Curly Bill's criminal inclinations, because, as Parsons reported, soon after the cowboy and two acolytes left, they were thought to have stolen "a pair of spurs belonging to one of our party, as they couldn't be found after their departure."

It was not until years later that Parsons revealed another observation from that October day at the McLaury ranch. It may have been Virgil's way to put differences aside and be friendly, but that was not the way of the taciturn Wyatt. "The best of feeling did not exist between Wyatt Earp and Curly Bill," Parsons recalled, "and their recognition of each other was very hasty and at some distance." As if sensing a confrontation was inevitable, the two men had been sizing each other up.

Fortunately for the abruptly thrown together Tombstone militia, the professionals arrived, in the person of Tenth Cavalry Buffalo Soldiers guided by their Indian scouts. John Clum knew several of them from his San Carlos days, and according to Parsons, "Their confab was quite extended in Indian talk, Apache."

He and Clum decided to spend the night with the scouts before returning to Tombstone. A few shots fired in the distance were heard that night, and before sleep "things were lively while the whiskey flowed." The next morning, with no new reports of Apache depredations, it was time for the untested Tombstone Rangers to ride home and disband.

Although, as Clum reported, "our strenuous march had not been rewarded by a single stirring adventure," the group led by Behan and Virgil Earp were in "fine fettle. This exuberance of spirits manifested itself in various stunts, which included cowboy tricks, fancy riding, and target shooting. Expert riders in our party demonstrated the proper method of fighting Indians on the plains."

As someone with the duly elected office of mayor, Clum added, "I maintained the dignity of the party and contented myself with witnessing the successive feats and heartily applauding the actors."

Read today, this is a poignant account by John Clum. One can picture the Earp brothers, Behan and his deputies, the impressionable George Parsons, and the other mostly young men frolicking and grinning on open ground as they rode home to Tombstone. What awaited them there was a return to the tensions that ever since the beginning of the year had threatened to engulf them in violence. Certainly Virgil, Wyatt, and Morgan Earp would never be this carefree again.

Though the immediate risk to Tombstone and its surroundings was reduced and the citizens could return to normal life, by no means were Geronimo's activities finished. He and his gradually dwindling band would elude their pursuers until January 1884, when they surrendered to General George Crook. There were subsequent escapes from the San Carlos Reservation until September 1886, when Geronimo gave up for good, this time surrendering to General Nelson Miles.

It was decided by the federal government that the best way to lower the risk of further breakouts was to remove the Apache leader from the territory altogether. He was kept in an internment camp in Florida, then shipped to Fort Sill in Oklahoma. He lived out the rest of his days there, dying of pneumonia in February 1909, four months before his eightieth birthday.

The intervention of Apache raiders and the camaraderie of the Tombstone Rangers plus the hospitality shown to them could have had the unintended but pleasurable consequence of being a cooling-off period for Tombstone and its competing factions. But that did not happen. Some of the men at the McLaury ranch that October morning did not have long to live.

Chapter Twenty

"KILL US OR BE KILLED"

Another stage robbery would disrupt any harmony that uniting against a common enemy had inspired among lawmen and cowboys. And that is what happened on October 8. But at least the thieves had a sense of humor.

That evening, five men attempted to hold up the stagecoach outside Charleston. After the driver jumped from his seat, the team of horses bolted and hurtled down the road. The robbers pursued the stage and stopped it, then held up the frightened passengers, getting away with about $800. Before leaving the scene, though, they returned $5 to each victim for "expenses."

What might rein in the increasingly chaotic situation in southeast Arizona was finally having a full-time governor. John Gosper had been angling for the position for much of 1881. John C. Frémont had continued to be not just a hands-off governor but a mostly absent one. Gosper had been a solid secretary of Arizona Territory, and his background suggested he would be a capable leader of the state.

Born in Ohio in 1842 and raised in Illinois, Gosper had enlisted in the Eighth Illinois Cavalry when the Civil War began. He somehow managed to survive thirty engagements with that unit and as quartermaster of the Twenty-ninth Regiment, U.S. Colored Infantry. However, his luck ran out during the Siege of Petersburg when he was severely wounded in the left leg and it had to be amputated. He was mustered out of the army in March 1865 and married a widow who had served as a nurse.

Back in Illinois, Gosper attended college and tried his hand at farming, but being one-legged was an impediment. He moved on to Nebraska, becoming a member of the city council in Lincoln, then president of that body in 1872. The following year he became Nebraska's secretary of state. But after visiting Arizona in 1876, Gosper determined to live there. His connections got him appointed the territorial secretary in April 1877. His aspirations for higher office were thwarted by Frémont.

Maybe that could be fixed. By March 1881, when Frémont had not had the decency to resign to pursue his other interests, Gosper wrote to James Garfield. The new president had also served honorably in the Union army during the war. The letter cited Gosper's battlefield experiences, and of course the loss of a leg, and mentioned that a former president, Ulysses Grant, would vouch for him. Garfield, besieged by job seekers crowding into the White House, did not find time to answer letters from distant Arizona. A few weeks after Garfield died, Gosper tried again, this time writing to the secretary of the interior, Samuel Kirkwood, suggesting that Frémont either return to Arizona "or be asked to step aside and permit some other gentleman to take his place and feel at liberty to act without restraint." The implication, of course, was that Gosper was ready, willing, and able to step in, even if just on one leg.

When it appeared that his suggestion was being ignored, Gosper wrote directly to the new president, Chester A. Arthur. He included in his arguments that for the past several years he had been acting governor three-quarters of the time, so why not just make it official. This finally did the trick—given an ultimatum by Arthur to return or resign, Frémont chose the latter and formally quit being governor of Arizona Territory on October 11.

It was a source of great frustration to Gosper that he was not immediately appointed to replace Frémont, but he had already proved to be a patient man. As it turned out, Gosper had to wait until the following March for Washington, D.C., to act . . . and it was to appoint not him but Frederick Augustus Tritle as governor.* He was a mining magnate who had spent most of the previous decade in Nevada. Until that happened, though, the territory continued to have only an "acting" governor, which was not the show of strength Tombstone badly needed.

One might wonder why Doc Holliday had not been a part of any posse or ad hoc Indian-chasing militia. He was fit enough. He has sometimes been portrayed as quite sickly at this time in Tombstone. However, that was not the case. In fact, the dry air of the Southwest did have the desired effect of reducing the more severe symptoms of the lung disease that plagued Doc. He could get on a horse and travel if need be, even for days at a time.

And traveling was why he was not in Tombstone the first half of October 1881. Most startling about his absence was that he was

---

* Life did not get much better for the unfortunate former acting governor. When Gosper died in poverty in Los Angeles in 1913, the Arizona State Legislature voted to put $200 toward funeral expenses. Gosper County is named after him— not in Arizona, but in Nebraska.

visiting Big Nose Kate, only three months after she had had him jailed for murder.

After her acrimonious and ultimately very embarrassing visit to Tombstone that summer, Kate Elder had headed back north to Globe and the boardinghouse where she lived there. Sometime later in July or in August, the boardinghouse burned down. She would later contend that Doc heard about the event and went to see her, suggesting they get back together. Kate may have resisted if that meant returning to Tombstone, but Doc was not aiming to return there right away. They traveled to Tucson to try his luck at its gambling parlors.

His luck must have been good, because one week at the tables led to another. It is not clear if they traveled elsewhere during early autumn, but Doc was still in a Tucson gambling hall on October 21 when Morgan Earp walked in and tapped him on the shoulder: Wyatt wanted him back in Tombstone.

While he could not have known that a gunfight was only five days away, Wyatt must have sensed that something was about to happen, and soon. Ike Clanton continued to be upset that Wyatt—as Ike believed—had blabbed about the reward arrangement for the capture of the robbers of the Benson stage. Even though three of them were dead and the fourth long gone, Clanton had spent sleepless nights fearing that Curly Bill Brocius or Johnny Ringo or both would learn about him being in cahoots with Wyatt about anything, let alone betraying cowboys. Ike had just returned from Tucson, and he claimed he had met Doc, who had brought up the deal Ike and Wyatt had made. Wyatt denied this and said he would question Doc when his friend was back in town.

Apparently, though, Wyatt did not want to wait. Clanton being even more agitated could be the match that set off an explosion.

And if there was to be a confrontation, he needed Doc back in Tombstone.

So, with Virgil preferring that Wyatt not leave town, Morgan was dispatched. Without much trouble he found the saloon Holliday was in. After Doc turned to him, Morgan said, "We want you in Tombstone tomorrow. Better come up this evening."

Doc had to know this was not what Kate wanted and that he could be walking into trouble in Tombstone when he was safe and counting his winnings in Tucson. And it would have been understandable if Doc had at least asked what the urgency was about. Instead, he simply said, "All right."

Kate could not be talked out of accompanying him, so all three left as soon as bags could be packed. They got on what could not have been a comfortable freight train that brought them to Benson, and from there Morgan steered an open buckboard toward Tombstone. They arrived in the early evening of October 22. By then, Ike Clanton had returned to his ranch. When Doc, after renting a room at the hotel owned by the photographer C. S. Fly, and Morgan found Wyatt, the latter asked about any discussion with Clanton. Doc truthfully denied there had ever been one.

The three men probably did not learn until later that night or the following morning that there was another reason to worry about the cowboys. Johnny Behan's deputy Billy Breakenridge, displaying more initiative than most people credited the sheriff's department with, arrested Milt Hicks for being in possession of stolen cattle. At almost any time there could be a cowboy stealing cattle or caring for those already stolen until they could be sold. For whatever reason, that night Breakenridge had chosen to put Hicks in the calaboose.

He should not have bothered, given that the Tombstone jail was anything but airtight. Two days later, Hicks was gone.

This time, it was not a matter of a prisoner simply strolling out the back door. Hicks had help. Late on the afternoon of October 24, Billy Soule, the jailer, left to attend to other business, leaving behind the assistant jailer, Charles Mason. When he unlocked the cell to deliver dinner to Hicks, Charles "Yank" Thompson and Jim Sharp, two cowboy friends, suddenly subdued Mason. The assistant jailer, at least, was lucky to still be alive, given that Sharp had been imprisoned on a murder charge and Thompson, no angel himself, was serving a sentence for grand larceny. Not pausing to sample the supper, the three cowboys closed the cell door. According to Mason, Sharp said to him, "We've been here for quite some time. Come in and try it yourself a while."

That "while" did not turn out to be too long because Mason's cries for help were heard and Soule was located to unlock the cell. Sheriff Behan formed a posse to find the fleeing outlaws. It consisted of his deputies Breakenridge and David Neagle and Virgil, Wyatt, and Morgan Earp. They rode off into the approaching night.

It was especially important that the jail-breaker cowboys be found, and right away. As Casey Tefertiller observes, "With the public already jarred by stage robberies and problems with the Apaches and the cowboys, the escape of three dangerous criminals exacerbated a tense situation. Between dances, sing-alongs, and fancy dinners, the new breed of Tombstoner had grown to believe that criminals could rarely be captured and even more rarely held for justice."

But it was a big territory out there, seeming to be even bigger in the dark, and the outlaws knew it well. The night swallowed up

Yank Thompson and Milt Hicks and Jim Sharp. The cowboys had brazenly gotten away with springing one of their own from the sheriff's custody. Behan was insulted as well as embarrassed, and this led to a poor decision. He ordered Breakenridge and Neagle to continue the search for as long as it took to catch the outlaws, while he and the Earp brothers returned to Tombstone. The sheriff did not comprehend that he was allowing himself to run low on peace officers at a volatile time.

It was about to get more volatile. On the night of Tuesday, October 25, Ike Clanton and Doc Holliday went at it in the Alhambra Saloon.

Earlier that day, the wheels had been set in motion that would lead to a gunfight. On ranching (and probably rustling) business, Ike had traveled to Sulphur Springs Valley. On the morning of October 25, he was in a wagon heading home from there. On the way he met up with his brother Billy and Frank and Tom McLaury. They continued on together to the Milk Ranch, owned by Jack Chandler, nine miles east of Tombstone. After breakfast the quartet split up, with Billy heading home to the Clanton ranch, Frank McLaury going on to his ranch, and Ike and Tom McLaury deciding to go into Tombstone to take care of business matters. They arrived a little before 11 A.M. and left the wagon and horses at the West End Corral. Also, as per city regulations, they checked their guns there.

The "business matters" turned out to be for Tom McLaury a few ranch-related tasks before he and his brother left for Iowa, where a sister was to be married; and for Ike, it was to see if the whiskey tasted any better than the last time he was in Tombstone.

It is understandable, then, that what Ike later reported happening that evening strayed from reality. As he would recall, in a rather bizarre way, that night he had gone into the Occidental Lunch Room—when actually it was the Alhambra—for a bite. While there, "Doc Holliday came in and commenced abusing me. He had his hand on his pistol and called me a damn son-of-a-bitch, and told me to get my gun out. I told him I did not have a gun. I looked around and I see Morg Earp sitting at the bar, behind me, with his hand on his gun. Doc Holliday kept abusing me. I then went out the door."

Ike portrayed himself as the innocent victim of mean old Doc Holliday. It was true, though, that Doc was less than gentle when he encountered Clanton. "I understand that you say the Earp brothers have given you away to me, and that you have been talking about me," Doc said. He stressed that Wyatt had not revealed to him whatever scheme he and Wyatt had cooked up and to leave him out of it.

Ike was not smart or sober enough to leave it at that. He repeated the accusation that Doc was somehow involved in the Benson stage reward plot and, in the process, pretty much spilled the beans that Clanton had agreed to betray the cowboys involved. As Wyatt would later put it, "Fear and whiskey robbed Clanton of his discretion and he let out his secret to Holliday, who had known nothing about it. Doc Holliday, who was the soul of honor, berated him vigorously for his treachery, and the conversation was heard by several people. That was enough for Clanton. He knew that his only alternative was to kill us or be killed by his own people."

Wyatt was seated, having some food. He was relaxing until he would make the rounds of gaming parlors and collect the winnings from faro and poker dealers who worked for him and benefited from his protection. This was Wyatt's kind of atmosphere, rather than idling at home with Mattie—a crowded Alhambra Saloon, male chatter and laughter, the air filled with cigar and cigarette smoke and the mingled scents of beer and whiskey and, just as familiar, men who did not bathe regularly.

Morgan, who was doing one of his periodic stints as a deputy, was there, too, engaged in conversation with the bartender. With Doc and Ike continuing to exchange angry words, Wyatt suggested to his brother that he act like a peace officer before the confrontation became more heated. Morgan took hold of Doc's arm and escorted him out of the Alhambra. However, Ike followed, and the argument resumed outside.

Virgil happened to be at the Occidental Saloon next door on Allen Street, and when he heard the commotion, he emerged onto the street. Sizing up the situation, the chief of police told Doc and Ike to go home or they would spend the night in jail. By then Wyatt had left the Alhambra and he persuaded Doc to go with him. Ike stalked off in a different direction. Morgan said he was heading home. Virgil, his peacemaking achieved, returned to the saloon, satisfied a crisis had been averted.

Alas, it had only been postponed a day.

Chapter Twenty-One

"RIGHT HERE, RIGHT NOW"

The way Allie Earp put it, when Virgil finally crawled into bed on the morning of October 26, she asked him if "anything was up."

He replied, "Oh, I been trying to keep Ike Clanton and Doc Holliday from killing each other."

"Why didn't you let them go ahead?" Allie wondered. "Neither one amounts to much." Then she went back to sleep.

There was much more to the night of October 25 into the next morning than Virgil's terse summary. But if readers will indulge their humble author, let's pause for a couple of pages. Before the end of the day that Virgil began by climbing into bed, there will take place what became known as the Gunfight at the O.K. Corral. Many books and screen versions of these events in Tombstone make it seem that the shoot-out that killed three men and wounded three others was inevitable. For one thing, shoot-outs were happening all the time on the frontier.

However, that was not necessarily true. By the autumn of 1881, most of the frontier—meaning the edge of "civilized" America, with there always being more to discover over the next horizon— was gone. The railroads had connected the East and West Coasts twelve years earlier, which had helped to speed up the process of discovering and settling the land in between. There had been significant progress in the spread west of law and order and a basic justice system. Keeping the peace by constables, deputies, sheriffs, marshals, and police departments had changed dramatically from over a decade earlier when the prototype of the frontier lawman was Wild Bill Hickok displaying his Colt pistols and cradling a shotgun as he patrolled the streets of Abilene.*

So, no, there were not gunfights all the time. Men settling their disputes with six-shooters was an increasingly rare occurrence. Gunslingers were literally a dying breed. The citizens of Tombstone, pampering themselves with dreams of being San Francisco in the desert, wanted nothing to do with unruly cowboys and their disputes and gunplay, and to some that included the Earps. Maybe those boys were pushing too hard and too fast for law and order. Others, impatient with the ongoing cowboy presence and stagecoach holdups, grumbled that the Earps and the authorities behind them were not pushing hard enough. The brothers were in a peculiar position, and that kept them on edge along with the city they had come to call home.

Another factor was ranchers such as the Clantons and McLaurys. If they kept their cowboy rustlers under control, and with Mexico

* Like other frontier cities wanting to be progressive about their law-and-order system, Tombstone within the last few months had folded its peacekeeping activities into a police department. Officially, Virgil Earp was no longer the marshal but the chief of police.

bolstering its border, a certain amount of stealing and smuggling might have been tolerated. But now the cowboys, emboldened by lax county law enforcement and getting away with stage robberies and jailbreaks, paid fealty to Johnny Ringo and a recovered Curly Bill Brocius, not the ranchers. Anarchy and chaos were fun. There was no incentive to move on, and if there was, where would they go? As the frontier closed, there was less room for cowboys and their wanton ways.

What if the Earps had just minded their own business? After all, they had come to Tombstone not to be lawmen, not even to be law-and-order advocates, but to pursue their own business interests in what might be the last big boomtown in the Lower 48. Virgil had become a deputy U.S. marshal from his connection to Crawley Dake only to have a salary of some kind, as fluctuating as it was. He ended up being marshal (then chief of police) of Tombstone only because the guy who beat him in the election, Ben Sippy, abruptly left town one step ahead of creditors and cowboys.

And in Virgil, Tombstone did not have a lawman who saw things in black and white, which was more Wyatt's view of the world. Virgil did have a strong sense of law and order but not a hard temperament, and his boundaries were not ironclad ones. George Parsons had disapproved of Virgil's coziness with Curly Bill at the McLaury ranch, but that was his way—defuse a situation, not escalate it. Virgil would have been the last one to force a confrontation with guns. In that shootout in Prescott when two outlaws died, Virgil had not instigated it but pitched in to help only after bullets began flying.

Morgan was a different matter. He was the less experienced lawman and a bit of a hothead, a combination that could provoke or at least agree to a confrontation. Wyatt had a more cool and measured disposition but was feeling a bit battered by events in Tombstone. As he would later testify, "I was tired of being threatened by Ike Clanton and his gang."

The family business interests had not produced as hoped. Cowboy pushover Johnny Behan had betrayed Wyatt and given the deputy sheriff's job to a political crony. He, too, had returned—reluctantly—to lawing for a paycheck, which he had not expected to do when he left Dodge City. And perhaps the ramrod-straight, teetotaling Wyatt saw more than his brothers that the cowboy outrages would only get worse if nothing was done, and that galled him. Plus, there was the whole mess involving that blabbermouth Ike Clanton and the Benson stage reward scheme, and that was damn irritating. Wyatt was anything but a hothead—however, when he did get mad, someone was going to pay. That was about to be demonstrated early on the afternoon of October 26.

Another influence was John Clum and the ad hoc vigilance committee that had resulted from the September meeting. With the podium of *The Tombstone Epitaph*, the editor railed against rancher and cowboy depredations and begged for better law enforcement, especially from Behan and his underlings. Clum was a supporter of the Earps, but his political posturing in his staunchly Republican newspaper was not doing them any favors. By repeatedly citing Virgil and his brothers as defenders of law and order and opponents of those fostering mayhem, Clum had created or at least promoted the scenario that the tensions in Tombstone boiled down to the Earps versus the ranchers and cowboys. This sure didn't make Virgil's job any easier. Wyatt, Morgan, and the tempestuous Doc Holliday were not keen on having such an inflated role in that scenario. True, Wyatt coveted Johnny Behan's job, but the next sheriff's election was over a year away; until then, best to focus on making a living.

Indeed, Doc Holliday was a wild card. He did not give a damn about Tombstone's politics and its ambitions for the future. His days were occupied with gambling and drinking. As Doc saw it, Ike Clanton had picked the fight with him, not the other way around, by dragging him into whatever deal he had with Wyatt and the Benson stage robbers. Doc could tolerate Johnny Ringo and Curly Bill as long as they did not bother him . . . or Wyatt. Still, especially after his return to Tombstone and the confrontation with Clanton, Doc knew the tensions were ramping up and that Wyatt and his brothers' backs were being measured for bull's-eyes. He was not good-natured like Virgil or patient and calculating like Wyatt. Doc flared quickly and fired first. If Wyatt felt threatened, Doc was threatened, too.

Then there was this other wrinkle: Wyatt coveted Behan's woman, or who had once been his woman. Some accounts suggest that by that autumn, Wyatt had her. Bob Alexander, in his biography of Johnny Behan titled *Sacrificed Sheriff,* states, "During August or September of 1881, a relationship developed between Josie and Wyatt Earp." Mattie had not been discarded, she remained at home in the company of the other Earp wives, but her increasing use of laudanum plus Wyatt's wandering eye equaled a "marriage" in its final stage. While self-preservation and the tax collection revenue the sheriff's job brought in were two very good reasons for Behan to be a subtle supporter of the cowboys, another was if they happened to kill Wyatt Earp, a rival for Josephine's affections was gone. And if Behan did not care about her anymore, simple revenge was good enough.

If there was to be a confrontation at all, the smart move for the ranchers and cowboys was to choose the place and the time. But the threats of Frank McLaury, the more aggressive of the two brothers, and those of Ike Clanton on the night of October 25 indicated spontaneity. This was no setup, just aggrieved men venting their irritation. A strategy would be the wise play, and the fact that they had yet to devise one to rid themselves of the meddlesome law-and-order advocates demonstrated they did not appreciate what they were up against. The Earps were not Mexican smugglers ambushed in a canyon but formidable adversaries when sufficiently riled.

Virgil was a Civil War veteran (as was James, if needed) who had seen action and a veteran lawman, and he had been credited with killing two men in that Prescott shoot-out four years earlier. George Hoy may have been Wyatt's only killing in Dodge City, but he had coolly drawn his gun or stared down opponents other times while a lawman there, and as Bat Masterson had written about him, Wyatt was "absolutely destitute of physical fear." Morgan was not as experienced and probably had not shot at a man before, but shoulder to shoulder with his brothers, there would be no backing down. Then add Doc Holliday to the mix: while his accuracy could be questioned, his eagerness to use a gun and his loyalty to Wyatt could not. The best chance the cowboys and ranchers had was sheer numbers or an ambush, which took some planning.

But planning was hard to do when someone as unstable as Ike Clanton was involved. Though he was not the only one, he played a significant role in the overall scenario that led to a violent confrontation. And his instability had become more pronounced in the weeks since his father's death. Though far from being the model patriarch, Old Man Clanton had been more circumspect in his behavior toward lawmen and discreet in his illegal activities. He understood that what the local law would allow, even the hands-off Johnny Behan, had its limits, and Newman Clanton tried to stay within them. It will never be known what impact he might have had on subsequent events, though it is possible no one could have reined in the cowboys and their increasingly confrontational ways. However, it is certain that his sudden death and absence took the shackles off his son Ike, whose normal boorish behavior ratcheted up to another level. Add to that more than a few dashes of alcohol . . .

Some accounts contend that directly after his altercation with Doc Holliday, while Wyatt was hustling the dentist away, Ike threatened that he and his cowboy friends "will be after you all in the morning." If so, that made his next actions even more odd. He probably found another open watering hole or two, then stumbled into the Occidental Saloon and joined a poker game that included Tom McLaury and Behan. The odd part was that another player was Virgil Earp—one of the "you all" to be dealt with later that morning.

The game continued for several hours. Ike had more to drink and more to say about Doc Holliday, none of it complimentary. Virgil could tolerate someone, even an annoying blowhard like Ike, grousing, and he may even have agreed with some of what Ike had to say. Still, Virgil was also a cautious man, and during the game he had his six-shooter resting on his lap.

The game finally broke up at dawn, and a worn-out Virgil was anxious to go home to bed. But once outside the Occidental, Ike delayed him, saying, "That damned son of a bitch has got to fight," referring to Holliday.

"Ike, I am an officer and I don't want to hear you talking that way at all," Virgil growled. "I am going down home now, to go to bed. I don't want you raising any disturbance while I am in bed."

"You won't carry the message?" Ike persisted.

"No, of course I won't."

"You may have to fight before you know it."

With his bed with Allie still in it waiting for him, Virgil turned away and went home.

Ike Clanton was too drunk or too dumb to heed Virgil's warning. It did not help that he had no place to stay. He had neglected to reserve a room in advance, and in his condition no one offered to take him in. Plus, it was morning. Ike must have gone back to the corral where his horse was being kept and guns checked because he was next seen wandering around town with a pistol and a Winchester rifle. To anyone who would listen, he promised harm to the Earp brothers and Doc Holliday.

At least a couple of witnesses thought it prudent to go to the homes of Wyatt and Virgil. An Oriental Saloon bartender named Ned Boyle had met Ike and been told, "As soon as the Earps and Doc Holliday show themselves on the street, the ball will open and they will have to fight," which Boyle conveyed to Wyatt. A. G. Bronk, one of Virgil's policemen, woke Virgil to give him an update on Clanton's wandering and threats.

But both brothers reacted the same way to such reports: Ike Clanton was an obnoxious drunk but probably not dangerous, and eventually he'd run out of steam. And they went back to sleep.

Another man the restless Ike encountered was John Clum. By this time it was late morning and the editor was leaving the *Epitaph* office to look at what the Grand Hotel's lunch special was. There at the corner of Fremont and Fourth was Ike Clanton. Spotting the Winchester, Clum called, "Hello, Ike, any new war?"

He was making light of it, but Clum would recall in his memoir, "The remarkable feature of the situation was that Ike actually was out on the war-path and was at that very moment seeking an opportunity to pot our valiant Chief of Police, and although I was mayor of the city, no hint of this serious situation had yet reached me."

There was a mixture of concern and amusement in downtown Tombstone about Ike Clanton's seemingly endless ramble. He encountered citizens who simply urged him to stop bothering people and go home. Others were alarmed by the drunken man carrying weapons and uttering dire warnings, and why wasn't the law doing something about it. This was an appropriate opportunity for Sheriff Behan to intervene, but to be fair, the city was just one part of his jurisdiction, it was really Virgil's problem, and Johnny may have been doing his job elsewhere in Cochise County . . . though it was more likely that he, too, was sleeping off the all-night poker game.

Apparently not satisfied with the reactions he was getting, Clanton made his way to the C. S. Fly boardinghouse, which Doc and Kate had checked into a few days earlier. "Carpe diem" was not one of Doc's mottoes, and he was still sleeping. Kate was up, however, and perusing pictures in the Fly photo gallery downstairs. Mary Fly, wife of Camillus (the "C" in C. S. Fly), was the one who greeted Ike when he arrived but wisely did not let him in. She summoned Kate, who, upon seeing Clanton with his weapons, rushed upstairs to warn Doc.

It would have made him irritable to see Ike Clanton at any time, but it being "early" in the morning and having his sleep disturbed made Doc mad as a hornet. "If God lets me live long enough to get my clothes on," he told Kate, sitting up on the side of the bed, "he shall see me." However, an impatient or forgetful Clanton drifted away from the boardinghouse.

For all his fulminations against his perceived enemies, Clanton may well have run out of people to annoy. Or he had run out of gas—he was, after all, on his second day without sleep—and gotten his horse and ridden back to his ranch. Perhaps the best thing to do was nothing. But after Virgil was woken again by a report of Ike's meanderings, and breaking the law while doing so by carrying the rifle and pistol, the chief lawman of the city became fed up enough that he got out of bed. This had to stop.

After Virgil dressed, he started for the downtown area on what was a chilly and windy midautumn morning. Along the way, he received fresh reports of an armed and drunk Ike Clanton. Finally, it dawned on Virgil that this could become a nasty situation, with people getting hurt. At about the same time, Wyatt, who had also reluctantly rolled out of bed, walked into the Oriental Saloon. There he was further informed of Ike's inebriated activities. With a sigh, Wyatt said, "I will go down and find him and see what he wants."

Morgan was also up and about, as was James, both having been told of trouble brewing. They ran into Virgil when they got downtown. The three brothers in turn met Wyatt when he emerged from the saloon. Where Clanton was now—except on his way home—was anyone's guess, so Wyatt went down Allen Street to locate him, and Virgil and Morgan went on Fremont. James, who was not armed, was advised to stay back.

In a farcical interlude, Ike spotted Wyatt, and while his eyes were fixed on him, the other brothers spotted Clanton, whose attention was so riveted on Wyatt that Virgil and Morgan simply walked up behind him.

When Ike turned, Virgil snatched the Winchester from him.

Ike reached for the pistol stuck in his pants. That led to a painful consequence. According to Virgil: "I hit him over the head and knocked him to his knees and took his six-shooter from him. I asked if he was hunting for me. He said he was, and if he had seen me a second sooner he would have killed me." Instead, the very much alive police chief arrested Clanton for carrying firearms inside the city limits.

The Earps had risked a shooting by confronting Clanton, but by acting—albeit tardily—they had, or so they thought, prevented a situation featuring an unstable actor that could have gone out of control. Lock up Ike, let him sleep it off, and by that evening or the next morning he could air his complaints to the heavens as he rode back to his ranch.

That is what makes what happened next so curious . . . and a gunfight almost a certainty.

Clanton's head was bleeding, but instead of bringing him to a doctor, Virgil and Morgan hauled him to the court of Judge Albert Wallace. However, the judge was not in his chambers, so Virgil left to locate him. Ike, his head throbbing, gave Morgan, who was left to guard Ike, an earful of his grievances, with the Earps and Doc Holliday being responsible for them. Wyatt and several citizens entered the courtroom, curious to see what would happen next and bolder now that the drunken miscreant was without weapons.

All Ike needed, and had really been seeking all morning, was an audience. He launched into a soliloquy: "You fellows haven't given me any show at all. You've treated me like a dog. Fight is my racket, and all I want is four feet of ground. If you fellows had been a second later, I would have furnished a coroner's inquest for the town. I will get even with all of you for this. If I had a six-shooter now, I would make a fight with all of you."

Wyatt may have been stifling a yawn, but Morgan had heard enough. Offering Ike his pistol back, he said, "Here, take this. You can have all the show you want right now."

There turned out to be no easier way to clear a courtroom. Expecting an explosion of gunshots, panicked onlookers fought one another to squeeze out the door. However, even assuming Clanton would have had the guts to grab the gun and get a "show" going, Wyatt intervened. What he said to Ike might have been more words the most taciturn Earp had strung together that entire week.

"You have threatened my life two or three times and I have the best evidence to prove it and I want this thing stopped," Wyatt stated. "You cattle-thieving son of a bitch, and you know that I know you are a cattle-thieving son of a bitch, you've threatened my life enough and you've got to fight. I will go anywhere on earth to make a fight with you, even over to the San Simon among your own crowd." One has to wonder when it was last, if ever, that Morgan had seen Wyatt so worked up.

Ike did not back down. "All right," he shot back, "I will see you after I get through here. I only want four feet of ground to fight on."

Virgil returned with the judge, and Wallace found Ike guilty and fined him $25. He was told his guns would be waiting for him at the Grand Hotel when he was leaving town, and Virgil walked the weapons over there.

That should have been plenty for one day, but something surprising and very serious had happened while court was in session. After his outburst, Wyatt had walked out and Tom McLaury had the misfortune to be in the street and in Wyatt's way. Wyatt should have kept walking, especially being the Earp with the steely self-discipline. But with Wyatt, once his emotions were let loose, there was no quick closing of the floodgates. Wyatt was sick and tired of the tensions with crooked ranchers and their cowboy allies and Ike Clanton in particular, and here was one of Ike's friends in the wrong place at the wrong time.

It is not known what Wyatt said, but McLaury's response was, "If you want to fight, I will fight you anywhere."

"Are you heeled?" Wyatt asked. "Right here, right now."

McLaury replied that he was not carrying a gun. This could have been true, because the rancher had checked his weapons at the corral when Clanton did the day before. However, McLaury had had plenty of time since to retrieve them, and because of ranch business to attend to he was carrying several thousand dollars in cash. In any case, Wyatt did not believe him. When he repeated the question and was not satisfied with the answer, Wyatt attacked Tom McLaury—first slapping him, then drawing his pistol and smacking the rancher in the head. McLaury fell to the ground, dazed and bleeding.

Witnesses heard Wyatt mutter as he stormed away, "I could kill the son of a bitch."

Another man in Tombstone, after such an act, might well have repaired to the nearest saloon to calm his nerves with whiskey. That was not Wyatt's way. He did march to Hafford's Saloon at the intersection of Fourth and Allen Streets, but to buy a cigar. After lighting it up, Wyatt stood outside, observing people and horses on the street. As he calmed down, Wyatt was not aware that Frank McLaury and Billy Clanton were about to arrive in Tombstone.

Chapter Twenty-Two

"THE FIGHT'S COMMENCED"

Frank McLaury and Billy Clanton rode into Tombstone a few minutes after noon on that almost wintry Wednesday, October 26, 1881. They were accompanied by a rancher and cattle-dealer neighbor John Randolph Frink, who intended to buy six hundred head from the McLaury brothers. When the trio stopped at the Grand Hotel, the first man they encountered was Doc Holliday.

Being that he had no quarrel that day with Frank or Billy, Doc shook hands with the latter and asked, "How are you?" Then, for Doc it was the time of day for breakfast, and he walked away to find some.

It was at the hotel bar, as he drank what was presumably his first drink of the day, that Frank learned of the attack on his brother. A friend of the Clantons, William Allen, found the older McLaury there and reported what Wyatt had done. Frank and Billy left the bar, took hold of their horses, and according to what Allen later reported, Frank said, "I will get the boys out of town."

Until around 3 P.M., the day would have many moving parts. And there would be many versions offered by a mixture of participants, witnesses, and gossips of what transpired, some of them at odds and other accounts being outright contradictions. With all the moving parts, if an "actor" on this day had said or done something differently, there may not have been the Gunfight at the O.K. Corral. One gets the sense, though, that it or something like it was bound to happen. Those involved appear to have had a let's-get-it-done attitude.

Certainly one contributing factor was that the older McLaury brother did not do what he said he would—"get the boys out of town." Instead, he and Billy Clanton ran into Billy Claiborne. Just turned twenty-one, he fancied himself another Billy the Kid. The other cowboys tolerated the pretension, and some even referred to him as "the Kid." Born in Mississippi, as a teenager William Floyd Claiborne was a cowhand for John Slaughter in Texas. In 1879, at the end of a cattle drive west, Claiborne decided to remain in Arizona, doing mining and cowboy work around Charleston. There, to get October 1881 going, he had shot and killed a man.

The name of the departed was James Hickey. Alcohol had been Hickey's best friend for three days, with his last stop being the Queen's Saloon. As he staggered out of it, he encountered Claiborne. Apparently, they had had a run-in before, and new insults were traded. When Hickey advanced on him, Billy whipped out his pistol and shot him just below his left eye, killing him. Claiborne's first trial ended in a mistrial, and in the second trial, which would take place only after the third attempt to collect enough jurors, Billy was found not guilty. It was believed that given the young gunman's quick-trigger temper, no juror wanted to vote otherwise.

Claiborne was in Tombstone that day for one of the hearings

on the Charleston killing, and when he had seen Ike Clanton and his battered condition, he had taken Ike to a doctor. At the Grand Hotel, Billy Clanton asked to be taken to Dr. Charles Gillingham's office so he could collect his brother and bring him to their ranch.

Ike, with his head bandaged, agreed to go. He told Billy and Frank McLaury that he had already asked the stableman at the West Coast Corral to hitch horses to his wagon. However, a decision was made not to leave and instead they walked over to Spangenberg's. While there may have been an innocuous reason for going there, such as needing fresh ammunition for their respective ranches, being seen at that particular store and with the events of that morning being talked about on the streets of Tombstone, assumptions were made that the men were buying guns in preparation to take on the Earps.

This assumption found Virgil. He also overheard a couple of cowboys talking about an impending fight. Things were getting more ominous. Virgil headed over to the Wells Fargo office and borrowed a 10-gauge shotgun. When he emerged, he may have looked for one or both of his brothers. As it happened, Wyatt was still working on the cigar outside of Hafford's Saloon. He had observed McLaury and the Clantons walk into the gun shop. After one last puff, Wyatt walked to Spangenberg's to see for himself what was going on within.

McLaury's horse must have been curious, too, because it got up onto the sidewalk and poked its head into the shop. Wyatt reached for the horse and pulled it back by its bridle. Suddenly, Billy Claiborne was in the doorway with his hand on the butt of his pistol. McLaury brushed past him and stepped outside. Wyatt informed him that a horse in a shop violated a city ordinance. If the tension in Tombstone had not been so high, McLaury might have laughed at the trivial transgression. Instead, he took his horse from Wyatt, backed it into the street, and tied it up more securely.

Meanwhile, Wyatt was looking through the now empty doorway. He saw Ike and Billy Clanton pushing cartridges into their belts, further evidence that there would be a confrontation. Wyatt had to conclude that this would be the day when the faction of ranchers and cowboys settled affairs with their nemeses, the Earps and the law-and-order system they reluctantly represented. As Casey Tefertiller observes, "When men hear the sound of death pounding in their ears, they assume every action or innuendo by their foes to have some hidden meaning."

Virgil was just leaving the Wells Fargo office when Bob Hatch, a friend of the Earps who owned a saloon and poolroom, hurried up to him. "For God's sake, get down there to the gun shop," he implored. "They are all there and Wyatt is all alone." Then he burst out, "They are liable to kill him before you get there!"

Virgil did not have to be told twice. He found Wyatt in the street outside Spangenberg's and the other four men back in the shop. He also saw cartridges being put into belts and had to assume the Clantons and Frank McLaury would emerge armed.* People in the street assumed the same thing. Word was being passed around that Tom McLaury, after a doctor had treated his head, had been seen on the street and it looked as if a pistol were stuck in his pants.

Wyatt returned to standing outside Hafford's, with Virgil beside him. To them, the scenario was that for once Ike Clanton had as much bite as bark and truly was fixing for a fight. In the brothers'

---

* Virgil and Wyatt could not have known that the elder Clanton had tried to purchase a gun but George Spangenberg, seeing Ike's boozy and battered condition, refused to sell one to him.

view, sometime that morning Ike had sent a message to the Clanton and McLaury ranches requesting help, and Billy and Frank had responded. They could not figure Billy Claiborne other than he was a young hothead aligned with the cowboys, and only a few weeks ago he had gunned a man down. The odds were not pretty if Tom, now armed, met up with the four men inside the shop. If the five men were about to leave Tombstone, they could keep their guns and go. But if they planned to stay, Virgil and Wyatt would have to attempt to arrest them.

Finally, the sheriff made an appearance. Behan had indeed slept late and had not begun the day until after 1 P.M. He was enjoying a shave at Barron's Barber Shop when a couple of men found him to tell him that a gunfight was about to happen. The half-shaved sheriff got up and hurried out of the shop. He ran into a visiting Charlie Shibell, who probably was relieved to no longer be wearing a badge with such a storm brewing. Together, they went in search of Virgil. On the way, a man named Coleman stopped them to say the Clantons and McLaurys were looking for a fight, and he advised Behan, "You should go and disarm that bunch."

They arrived outside Hafford's and asked Virgil what was happening. Virgil replied, "There are a lot of sons-of-bitches in town looking for a fight, and now they can have it."

For once, Virgil did not appear open to reason. Still, Behan suggested that he stick to his duty as police chief and ask the other men to give up their weapons. "I will not," Virgil stated. "I will give them their chance to make a fight."

This alarmed Behan. A situation out of control that could end with gunshots would not reflect well on any peace officer. It may have occurred to him that because of his decision, his deputies Billy

Breakenridge and Dave Neagle were still away chasing outlaws, so he would have to single-handedly stop a shoot-out. If he did not, with so many onlookers observing that afternoon's street theater, stray bullets could kill innocent people. Even Shibell, who still carried the stain of colluding with cowboys to steal the previous year's election for sheriff, did not want to see a worst-case scenario played out. To give Virgil a chance to cool off, he and Behan persuaded him to step into Hafford's Saloon. Virgil refused a whiskey, but Behan knocked one back.

By this time, Tom McLaury had joined his brother and Ike and Billy Clanton and Billy Claiborne. The five men stopped by the Dexter Livery and Feed Stable—ironically, co-owned by the enterprising Johnny Behan—where the younger Clanton had left his horse. However, they did not appear to be in any hurry to leave town or to do anything at all. They ambled to the O.K. Corral, which was across the way, on Allen Street between Third and Fourth Streets. There they dawdled, heatedly discussing what to do next. This was reported to the chief of police. "They mean trouble," one man told Virgil. "They are all armed, and I think you had better go disarm them."

Getting an impression of Tombstone on this Wednesday that most citizens did not want to provide was H. F. Sills, a railroad engineer who had just arrived in town. He saw several men standing around "talking some trouble they had had with Virgil Earp, and they made threats at that time, that on meeting him they would kill him on sight." One of them said that "they would kill the whole party of the Earps when they met them."

Stills walked up the street and asked who Virgil Earp and the Earps were. Virgil was pointed out to him, and he identified himself as the city marshal when Stills asked. The engineer reported what he had overheard, then like many others on the street, he stood aside and watched for what would happen next.

Since its informal activation in September, the Citizens Safety Committee had continued to exist. The head of it, William Murray, stepped into Hafford's. He took Virgil aside and confided, "I know you are going to have trouble and we have plenty of men and arms to assist you."

By this time, Virgil might have calmed down from his agitated state of a few minutes earlier, at least enough to realize that if men went for their guns, it could mean all-out war in the streets of the city. Right now the issue was limited to the long-simmering acrimony between the Clantons and McLaurys and the Earp brothers. But if there were dozens of armed citizens, the day could be a very bloody one indeed. Worse, if Ike Clanton's call for help had reverberated, a contingent of cowboys led by Curly Bill Brocius or Johnny Ringo could be on its way right now. As marshal and being Virgil, the last thing he wanted was chaotic violence and bodies bleeding into the dust.

"As long as they stay in the corral," Virgil told Murray, "I will not go down to disarm them. If they come out on the street, I will take their arms and arrest them."

This was still bold talk, considering that to avoid a more widespread confrontation it would be just Virgil and Wyatt against five armed men. But help was on the way, and it was not a vigilance committee.

As was his custom, after his early afternoon breakfast Doc Holliday had strolled to the Alhambra Saloon. There might already be a card game under way to join, or he would just amuse himself with solitaire. He would certainly be immediately recognizable to anyone who entered the saloon after him. As described by Gary L. Roberts, "Doc was dressed like a dandy in a gray suit and a pastel shirt with a stiff collar and tie. He wore a slouch hat and a long, gray overcoat and carried a silver-headed cane."

The Alhambra was where Morgan found Holliday. After being informed of that morning's events and perhaps regretting that in an unusual fit of bonhomie he had shaken Billy Clanton's hand, Doc accompanied Morgan to find Virgil and Wyatt. Citizens immediately directed them to Hafford's Saloon.

Wyatt was still standing outside, and Doc asked him what was going on. "We're going to make a fight," Wyatt replied.

The only other question Doc Holliday had was, "You're not going to leave me out, are you?"

"This is none of your affair."

"That is a hell of a thing for you to say to me."

"It's going to be a tough one."

Doc grinned. "Tough ones are the kind I like."

Inside Hafford's Saloon, Behan, the whiskey burning in his belly, told Virgil that he would ask the Clantons and McLaurys and Claiborne to give up their guns. "They won't hurt me," Behan declared, either boasting or with false courage. "I will go down along and see if I can disarm them."

To be fair to the sheriff, because a potential confrontation was within city limits, this was more the problem of the local police than his. And it was to Johnny Behan's credit that he offered to try to persuade armed men to stand down. On the other hand, he was a political animal. If he had stayed in bed that day or been called to business elsewhere in Cochise County, Behan would have been off the hook. But he was on the scene for all to see. If he abandoned the city marshal to his fate, the voters in Tombstone would remember that. And there was a big upside: if he did actually disarm the five men and violence was avoided, voters would remember that, too.

Virgil responded that the immediate issue was the men were wearing weapons within the city limits. If they surrendered their guns or got on horses and rode away, there would be no further trouble. And if they stayed in the O.K. Corral, they would be left to themselves, though Virgil was not about to wait all day to do his job or be able to concentrate on other matters.

He was approached by John Fonck, who had served as a police captain in Los Angeles. He offered to round up several men to stand with Virgil if he took on the ranchers and cowboys. The marshal responded that if those men were at the corral getting horses to leave, he would let them do so. But Fonck had just come from the O.K. Corral, and he told Virgil that the five men had left and were now on Fremont Street.

That tore it. Virgil could not allow them to roam all over downtown displaying weapons. But Behan interceded, saying he would meet up with those men and disarm them. Virgil nodded.

As he walked down the street toward where the Clanton and McLaury brothers and Billy Claiborne were reported to be, Behan was either quaking in his boots or picturing himself as a hero. When he reached them, he said, "Boys, you must give up your arms. You have got to give up your arms."

He was met with silent stares, so the sheriff pressed ahead: "Boys, you must go up to the sheriff's office and lay off your arms, and stay there until I get back. I'll go disarm the Earps."

Behan either did not say the last sentence or did say it—as he later testified—but he knew it was highly unlikely that his fellow lawman Virgil and his deputies would hand him their guns. If he said it, it was to further persuade the five men that there would be no fight and they could safely disarm.

But then he glanced up Fremont Street and saw the Earp brothers and Doc walking toward him. Now, whether Behan had meant what he said or not, getting the marshal's party to give up their guns or to at least stop in their tracks was the only way to avoid bloodshed. "Wait here," he told the others. "I will go up and stop them."

Virgil was a patient man . . . but Behan had taken too long. Standing outside Hafford's, he may have deputized Doc. Because of being so frequently called upon, Wyatt and Morgan were already designated as "special officers" and had law-enforcement powers. All four men had six-shooters stuck in their belts. Virgil took the walking stick and handed the borrowed shotgun to Doc, either because the latter's long overcoat might make his pistol hard to get to or because brandishing a shotgun at the cowboys might be like shaking a red cape at a bull. Plus, Virgil knew that Doc was no marksman with a handgun.

The four men waited another minute or two, then began marching down Fourth Street. Wyatt was on the left, and to his right were Virgil, Morgan, and Doc, with Virgil a couple of steps ahead. When they reached Fremont Street, they turned west, seeing Fly's boardinghouse and photo studio up ahead. Also up ahead, in a vacant lot next to Fly's property, were five men who, as far as the lawmen knew, were armed and demanding a fight.

When Behan saw the four lawmen steadfastly approaching, he hurried from the vacant lot to intercept them. They met in front of Bauer's Meat Market. "Gentlemen," Behan began, "I am sheriff of this county and I am not going to allow any trouble if I can help it."

The Earp brothers and Doc Holliday brushed past him. It was

abundantly clear that by this point the sheriff had lost all credibility with Virgil. Behan's passive approach to the cowboys was now coming back to haunt him; he was nothing more than someone to be ignored so the real work could be done. Behan followed behind the four men, practically begging them to halt, but he could no longer delay the inevitable. "For God's sake," the sheriff implored, "don't go down there or you will get murdered."

As they marched on, Virgil and Wyatt heard the sheriff add, "I have disarmed them all."

Behan would later deny he made that statement, but that is what Virgil and Wyatt heard and they relaxed a bit. Wyatt, Morgan, and Doc were still prepared to back Virgil's play, but if the sheriff had indeed taken the weapons from the five men, there would be no shooting. Virgil pushed his pistol into the left side of his pants and now in his gun hand he held the walking stick, as though he would wave it and the men in the lot would disappear. Wyatt and Morgan had their six-shooters in their right hands, but now they put them away on their right sides. Doc's pistol and the shotgun were hidden under the long gray coat, except when the wind pushed it open. Behan stopped trying to keep up with them as they strode down Fremont Street and dropped back.

Someone called out, "There they come!"

The Earp brothers and Doc Holliday arrived at the vacant lot, which was only fifteen feet wide, next to the Harwood House. As they came to a stop, Doc moved to one side. His role would be to prevent anyone from leaving the lot without having surrendered his gun. The Earps saw Ike Clanton in the middle of the lot, and closer to the Harwood House side stood the McLaurys and Billy Clanton and Billy Claiborne. The Earps were surprised to find another man present, Wes Fuller, a cowboy who had come to warn the others of the approach of the lawmen.

Also in the lot were horses belonging to Frank McLaury and the younger Clanton. The lawmen noted that in the horses' saddle boots were Winchester rifles, that Billy Clanton wore a gun belt and pistol, and that Frank McLaury had a six-shooter tucked in his right side. So, six men were there—and Behan had lied to them: none had been disarmed. "Son of a bitch," Wyatt muttered.

Virgil entered the lot with Wyatt behind him, Morgan remaining on the sidewalk but with a clear view of the other men. Raising his right hand and with it the cane, the marshal ordered, "Throw up your hands, boys. I intend to disarm you."

Wes Fuller wanted nothing to do with this, and he stepped away. Billy Claiborne looked as if he were fixing to do the same.

In an odd response, Frank McLaury said, "We will," as if he and the others would comply. At the same time, though, he stepped forward and grabbed the handle of his pistol. Billy Clanton reacted by placing a hand on his holstered gun. Tom McLaury tossed open his coat, apparently to grab one or perhaps two guns. There might well be shooting after all.

Wyatt pulled his gun out of his right coat pocket. Doc yanked the shotgun up out of his coat and pulled the hammers back. There was a sudden *click-click*—from either the shotgun or the hammers of two pistols being drawn back—and the sound was especially loud in the hushed silence of the vacant lot.

"Hold!" Virgil shouted. "I don't mean that!"

It was too late. What followed was an outburst of thirty shots in thirty seconds, destined to be the most famous gunfight in the American West.

Not wanting the five men to get the drop on them, Wyatt aimed and fired. As he later explained, "I knew that Frank McLowery [sic] had the reputation of being a good shot and a dangerous man." His bullet struck McLaury in the belly. Simultaneously, Billy Clanton had jerked his gun and fired at Wyatt but missed.

"I knew it was a fight for life," Wyatt would later state, "and I drew and fired in defense of my own life and the lives of my brothers and Doc Holliday."

But during the next few seconds there was a pause in gunfire. During it, Billy Claiborne took off, leaving four cowboys in the lot. The wounded Frank McLaury staggered away from Wyatt and Virgil. The marshal hurried to push the walking stick into his left hand and grab his gun with his right. Tom McLaury stepped behind one of the horses to grab a rifle. Doc walked into the lot. And suddenly, Ike Clanton ran at Wyatt.

He tried to wrap his arms around Wyatt. Wyatt could see that Ike was unarmed, so instead of shooting him, he managed to push him away. "The fight's commenced," Wyatt told the panicked man. "Go to fighting or get away." Ike chose the latter. He ran out of the lot and into Fly's and through it and kept running. After all the threats, this was all Ike Clanton could manage to do. He did not cease running until he reached Toughnut Street two blocks away.

Abruptly, the shooting began again. Both Frank McLaury, despite his grievous wound, and Billy Clanton pulled their triggers repeatedly. Virgil was shot in the lower leg and went down. Morgan was struck next, the bullet going through one shoulder and out the other. He, too, fell, calling out, "I am hit!"

"Then get behind me and keep quiet," Wyatt told Morgan, who stayed where he was. Of the lawmen, just Wyatt and Doc were left unhurt.

The latter advanced on Tom McLaury, who was reaching across the saddle. The agitated horse wanted to get away, and the moment McLaury was visible, Doc let loose with the shotgun, hitting his target in the right arm and side. McLaury tried to get out of harm's way—the horse had gotten loose and was dashing down Fremont Street—but he could get only as far as a telegraph pole in the corner of the lot before collapsing.

Doc threw down the used shotgun and yanked out his nickel-plated pistol. Billy Clanton continued to fire, even after taking two bullets. One was lodged in his chest and the other had hit him in the wrist. He slid down the wall of the Harwood House. Now with the gun in his left hand and balanced on his bent knee, he fired more shots.

Frank McLaury had grabbed the reins of the other horse and was behind it as he walked it out of the vacant lot. When he fired at Morgan, the horse bolted. Doc strode toward him and both men lifted their guns. "I've got you now," Frank said.

"Blaze away," Doc responded. "You're a daisy if you have."

They jerked their triggers. Doc's bullet tore into Frank's chest. Morgan, to try to protect Doc, had fired, too, and his bullet hit McLaury in the side of the head. The rancher's bullet passed through Doc's coat and grazed his hip. "I'm shot right through!" he announced. Then he approached McLaury, now lying on the ground and moving slightly. Doc said, "That son of a bitch has shot me and I aim to kill him."

But instead of more shooting it was suddenly quiet again in the vacant lot, except for the sound of Billy Clanton, one wrist smashed, futilely trying to reload his six-shooter. After a few moments, C. S. Fly approached and took the young man's gun. The gunfight was finished.

Chapter Twenty-Three

"IT HAD COME AT LAST"

As the last of the gun smoke cleared, people began to arrive from all directions. Some had not been far away but had sought cover when the shooting began. Others had heard the shots or reports of a shoot-out in the vacant lot off Fremont Street and made their way to it. Given how far Tombstone had progressed as a prosperous and growing city in only a few years, such a sudden explosion of deadly violence was indeed a remarkable event. Rather than a stage-coach holdup on a dark, remote road, this had been a bullet-riddled collision between the two forces competing for control of the city.

After some initial hesitation, several men picked up the McLaury brothers and Billy Clanton and carried them into a house on Third Street across from the vacant lot. Frank was dead; the head shot had taken care of that. Tom would soon join him thanks to the two barrels of shotgun pellets Doc had fired. Billy, also hit more than once but conscious, claimed he had been murdered and begged to be allowed to die in peace. In less than an hour, and after being quieted with a shot of morphine, his wish was granted.

Moments after the three men had been carried off, the whistles at the Vizina mine began to blow. Someone there had been told the gunfire was caused by an attack of Indians or vengeful cowboys were already riding rampant through the city. Dozens of men, many being members of the Citizens Safety Committee, carrying rifles and pistols, burst out of their homes and offices and shops and saloons and rushed toward Fremont Street.

Allie Earp recalled that she and Louisa, Morgan's wife, were sitting together sewing "when all of a sudden guns started roaring. The noise was awful it was so close. Lou laid down her hands in her lap and bent her head. I jumped up and ran out the door. I knew it had come at last."

Mattie was already outside. However, she had curlers in her hair and did not want to be seen, so she ran back into her house instead of joining Allie. As Allie described the next minute, she "flew up the street. People all over were running toward the O.K. Corral. The butcher's wife as I ran past caught me by the arm and slapped a sunbonnet on my head. One of the McLowery [sic] brothers was lying dead on the corner of Third Street." Allie was not distracted by the body: "All I had a mind for was Virge."

She pushed through the crowd of onlookers. "I knelt down beside Virge," Allie reported. "The doctor was bending over his legs, probing for the bullet. Virge was getting madder and madder from the pain. At last the doctor gave it up." Apparently, the bullet had gone through a fleshy part of the leg.

The only lawman not wounded was Wyatt. He was checking the conditions of Virgil, Morgan, and Doc when Johnny Behan came up to him. "I have to arrest you, Wyatt," he said.

The tall and slender man looked down at the sheriff and stated, "I won't be arrested. You deceived me, Johnny. You told me they were not armed." Behan may have looked confused, so Wyatt dismissed him: "I won't be arrested. I am here to answer for what I have done. I am not going to leave town."

The sheriff walked away. Morgan and Virgil were taken to the latter's house. No one seemed to notice Doc leaving the lot. He limped the short distance to Fly's boardinghouse and went to his room. Big Nose Kate was there, relieved he was alive. Doc appeared distraught and said, "This is just awful. Awful." She asked if he was hurt. He tugged his shirt up to expose on one hip a red streak two inches long. He had been luckier than Virgil and Morgan—and, of course, the three dead men.

Doc did not linger in the room. Possibly fortified by a shot of whiskey, he grabbed his nickel-plated pistol and went out again. He did not know how badly wounded the Earp brothers were. Another reason for returning to the lot was he had left Wyatt on his own and it occurred to Doc that at any moment a group of cowboys could ride into Tombstone seeking retribution.

Ironically, the first man arrested in connection with the gunfight was Ike Clanton, when he was located cowering on Toughnut Street. Ike was actually relieved to be arrested because he feared the Earps would come gunning for him. He would spend that night in jail, surrounded by ten men Behan had deputized to guard him. Phin Clanton would visit him there, after viewing the body of the youngest member of the family.

That evening, Sheriff Behan went to Virgil's house. When Allie informed him that Behan was walking toward the house, Virgil demanded, "Give me my gun." He was told that "it was only Johnny Behan," but he again demanded the Winchester rifle leaning against the wall. Allie gave it to him and also put Morgan's pistol within reach. For more protection, a mattress was stacked in front of the window. If anyone was going to get to Virgil and Morgan, they would have to enter the bedroom where the brothers lay. James Earp was there, too, and another one of the few times he wore a gun.

Behan was allowed in. The conversation was brief. Virgil, as both a deputy U.S. marshal and city marshal, had done his duty and was not about to submit to Johnny's authority. Behan said he had to arrest Wyatt and Doc. Virgil accused the sheriff of fixing to hang them instead, aided by a posse of vigilante cowboys. With the atmosphere becoming more hostile, and being outgunned, Behan left.

Wyatt arrived at Virgil's house later that evening. He told the others that Sheriff Behan indeed intended to arrest Doc and not just him but all three brothers, and Wyatt declared he would not stand for it. After he left, Morgan said to Allie, "If they come, you'll know they got Wyatt." She and Louisa locked the doors and stacked more mattresses against the windows, Then, Allie recalled, she "sat there with the six-shooter all night. I would have used it too, if they had come to kill Virge and Morg."

The night passed quietly, but there was much commotion in Tombstone the next day. George Parsons had been at work in the mountains the day before, and when he arrived on Thursday afternoon he noted, "Much excitement in town and people apprehensive and scary." Having been informed of the gunfight, Parsons commented, "Desperate men and a desperate encounter. Bad blood has been brewing some time and I was not surprised at the outbreak. It is only a wonder it has not happened before. A raid is feared upon the town by the cowboys and measures have been taken to protect life and property."

In a letter written October 29, Clara Brown told her San Diego readers of "the most tragic and bloody occurrence" of three days earlier. "The inmates of every house in town were greatly startled by the sudden report of fire arms, about 3 p.m., discharged with such lightning-like rapidity that it could be compared only to the explosion of a bunch of fire-crackers."

Taking a defiant tone was John Clum. The headline in the next day's *Epitaph* began, YESTERDAY'S TRAGEDY: THREE MEN HURLED INTO ETERNITY. The article was at first a pretty straightforward piecing together of how "the storm burst in all its fury yesterday." As it continued, however, Clum staunchly supported the actions of Virgil Earp to try to enforce the law. "Being fired upon they had to defend themselves, which they did most bravely," he told *Epitaph* readers. "So long as our peace officers make effort to preserve the peace and put down highway robbery—which the Earp brothers have done—they will have the support of all good citizens."

As to the rumors that there would be a raid on the town to get even for the deaths of the McLaury brothers and Billy Clanton, Clum insisted, "If the present lesson is not sufficient to teach the cow-boy element that they cannot come into the streets of Tombstone, in broad daylight, armed with six-shooters and Henry rifles to hunt down their victims, then the citizens will most assuredly take such steps to preserve the peace."

Also in his journal entry of October 27, Parsons had fretted, "It has been a bad scare, and worst is not yet over, some think." There was a clear demonstration that day such a concern was warranted.

After the bodies of the three dead men had been examined by the coroner, Henry Matthews, they were hauled by wagons to Ritter and Ream Undertakers. There, instead of being discreetly prepared for a funeral service, Frank and Tom McLaury and Billy Clanton in their open coffins were propped up in the firm's window. "Only twenty-four hours earlier, the faces of the three men had radiated pride, anger, fear, and despair as they had fought for their lives on a Tombstone street," writes Paula Mitchell Marks in *And Die in the West*. "Now their features shared the bland relaxation of death."

A sign above them blared in large capital letters, MURDERED IN THE STREETS OF TOMBSTONE. Should the cowboys gallop into town with guns blazing, they apparently had allies available.

An estimated three hundred people attended the funeral on Friday, October 28. The bodies of the three men were "neatly and tastefully dressed" and in "handsome caskets with heavy silver trimmings," according to the *Tombstone Daily Nugget*. A plate on each casket provided the occupant's name, age, place of birth, and "October 26, 1881." The McLaurys were in one hearse, Billy Clanton in another one. The wagon immediately behind the hearses contained Phin and Ike Clanton. Behind them were at least two dozen wagons and carriages and a stagecoach, plus individuals on horses or walking.

The two-block-long funeral procession was accompanied by the city's brass band playing mournful music. "It was a most impressive and saddening sight," *The Tombstone Epitaph* observed. Even the fallen marshal Fred White had not attracted so many mourners. It would seem that with this large a crowd for men who were not advocates of law and order in Tombstone, the gunfight two days earlier had not settled matters.

At the cemetery, Tom and Frank McLaury, aged twenty-eight and thirty-two, were buried together, nineteen-year-old Billy Clanton in a grave a few feet away. The crowd slowly dispersed. People returned to their homes and businesses. The saloons saw a surge of customers.

Clara Brown was mystified by the turnout, telling her audience of several days later in San Diego that "such a public manifestation of sympathy from so large a portion of the camp seemed reprehensible when it is remembered that the deceased were nothing more or less than thieves." She added, "The divided state of society in Tombstone is illustrated by this funeral."

The Earps and Doc Holliday were about to be arrested on warrants sworn out by Ike Clanton and Johnny Behan. Reluctantly, Mayor Clum agreed with others on the city council and suspended Virgil as chief of police, appointing James Flynn to the position. But the focus was mostly on Wyatt and Doc for having done the most damage and emerging the most intact. As the *Epitaph* informed readers about the gun battle, "Wyatt Earp stood up and fired in rapid succession, as cool as a cucumber, and was not hit. Doc Holliday was as calm as though at target practice and fired rapidly."

A court proceeding before Judge Wells Spicer was about to begin, and there was hope that a clear picture would emerge of what happened that Wednesday afternoon in the lot off Fremont Street. Many citizens worried, though, that what would become known as the Gunfight at the O.K. Corral was not a conclusion to the violence but a prelude of more to come.

"One must not judge the whole by a part," Clara Brown advised, "but it is undeniable that Cochise county started out upon its career hampered by a set of officials which might be improved; and doubtless will be at the next election."

This was an optimistic view some citizens shared. Perhaps the burst of violence of October 26 had bought time for tempers to cool off and Tombstone could begin its next chapter—a peaceful one with continuing prosperity. But that would not happen. Instead, the next chapter would be written in blood, and it flowed faster when Wyatt Earp was forced to seek vengeance.

ACT V

THE VENDETTA

Fifth and Allen Streets, 1882.
(COURTESY OF ARIZONA HISTORICAL SOCIETY)

*The bloody feud in Tombstone, Arizona . . . cost me a brave brother
and cost more than one worthless life among the murderous dogs who
pursued me and mine only less bitterly than I pursued them.*
—WYATT EARP

Chapter Twenty-Four

"IT WAS A FIGHT FOR LIFE"

The Earp brothers and Doc Holliday had fought for their lives in that vacant lot off Fremont Street on October 26. They would spend the next few weeks once more fighting for their lives, but this time in a courtroom. They had come to believe that the criminal justice system in southeast Arizona was too friendly to defendants. If true, they hoped that they would be the ones to benefit from it now.

From their point of view, however, they had done what they had to do under the law. Dozens of witnesses had seen and heard Ike Clanton threaten the lives of the Earp brothers and Doc Holliday. Soon before the confrontation, the McLaurys and Clantons had been observed loading up on ammunition. They had not left Tombstone when advised to do so. They had wandered about for a bit, then lingered very visibly in a vacant lot, illegally carrying weapons. Virgil Earp was the chief of police who was required—especially with the mayor and many constituents looking on—to enforce the law. There was the accumulated resentment against ranchers such

278 ★ TOM CLAVIN

as Frank and Tom McLaury and the three Clanton brothers and the rustling cowboys they harbored for running roughshod over communities in the region and robbing the stagecoaches and innocent passengers. It was too bad men had to die, but the Earps were not the ones who had set in motion the sequence of events that led to the deadly shoot-out. Sprinkle into the mix that an effective sheriff—one not giving priority to his political ambitions and fear of the cowboys (and possible jealousy toward one of the Earps)—might have found a way long before October 26 to reduce the risk of an outburst of violence.

Given all that, which most people except the most partisan understood, the matter could have ended when the funerals did. Tombstone had its eye on the future. The gunfight represented its unsavory past. It was time for all concerned to move on and begin planning for the twentieth century, only nineteen years away.

But that was not about to happen. As flawed as it was, there was a justice system in Tombstone, and certain steps had to be taken.

The first was a coroner's inquest convened on October 28 by Henry Matthews. During it, Ike Clanton, Billy Claiborne, and Johnny Behan established the positions they had chosen—that the Earps had forced the fight two days earlier, and those killed had been gunned down as they held their hands in the air and tried to surrender.

As damaging as this was from a public opinion standpoint, there was no legal impact. The inquest was not a trial, its purpose was simply to determine who died and why, which was "from the effects of gunshot wounds," Matthews ruled. Hardly a revelation, and the *Tombstone Daily Nugget* snidely commented about the deaths of Billy Clanton and the McLaury brothers, "We might have thought they had been struck with lightning or stung to death by hornets."

Because Matthews did not draw a conclusion about the legality of Virgil Earp's actions two days earlier, the door was left open for him and his brothers and Doc Holliday to be prosecuted for a crime, possibly murder.

As *The Tombstone Epitaph* reported, "The coroner's jury after deliberating for two hours in regard to the late killing of William Clanton, Frank and Thomas McLowry [*sic*], brought in a verdict that the men named came to their deaths in the town of Tombstone on October 26, 1881, from the effects of pistol and gunshot wounds inflicted by Virgil Earp, Morgan Earp, Wyatt Earp and one Holliday commonly known as 'Doc' Holliday."

Such a finding was not enough, however. As the newspaper added, "The verdict does not seem to meet with general approval, as it does not state whether the cowboys were killed by the marshal and his party in the discharge of their duty, or whether the killing was justifiable."

The ambiguity of the verdict allowed for more public criticism of the Earps and, as it immediately turned out, legal action. That got under way the day after the coroner's inquest when Ike Clanton went to Wells Spicer and swore out criminal complaints against Virgil, Wyatt, and Morgan Earp and Doc Holliday. The judge ordered that the four men be arrested but allowed Virgil and Morgan to remain at home because of their gunshot wounds. Instead of being regarded as upholders of the law, Wyatt and Doc found themselves behind bars.

Not for long, though. A consortium of Tombstone citizens, including Fred Dodge, Lou Rickabaugh, and James Earp, raised enough money for Wyatt's bail. Once he was free, he went around hat in hand—plus kicked in his own money—to collect enough cash to bail Doc Holliday out. The next step would be a hearing that Spicer would preside over to see if the case should be referred to a grand jury that would charge the four men with murder. Only a week after the gunfight, the defendants faced the possibility of having to save their necks.

Their supporters were chagrined that it seemed as though law and order itself would be on trial, and certainly the Earps were frustrated to find themselves in this position. "Met Wyatt Earp in hotel who took me in to see Virgil this evening," George Parsons recorded in his November 4 entry. "He's getting along well. Morgan too. Looks bad for them all thus far."

The hearing before Judge Spicer had begun on Monday, October 31. The district attorney, Lyttleton Price, would be assisted by Ben Goodrich and Marcus Aurelius Smith. Three days into the hearing this team would be expanded to include its most determined prosecutor, Will McLaury, the older brother of Frank and Tom, who had a law practice in Fort Worth, Texas.*

The defense attorney hired by the Earps was Thomas Fitch. This was an inspired selection. It demonstrated that not only were the Earps taking their precarious situation very seriously, but in Fitch they would have the best lawyer in the room. His very presence was a big asset.

The forty-three-year-old Fitch had been born in New York City and was a descendant of a colonial governor of Connecticut. Fitch's first occupation was as a newspaperman, which took him to Chicago, then Milwaukee, then San Francisco, where he married,

---

* Only thirty years old at the time, "Mark" Smith would go on to have a long political career, which included being one of two men appointed as the first U.S. senators representing the state of Arizona in 1912. Will McLaury was still grieving the death of his wife that summer, leaving him to raise three young children.

campaigned vigorously for Abraham Lincoln in the 1860 election, and was himself elected to the California State Assembly.* He then returned to the newspaper game, in Nevada. It was there he became friends with a young reporter named Samuel Clemens. The future novelist Mark Twain credited Fitch with giving him his "first really profitable lesson in writing."

Fitch became a lawyer and politically active in Nevada, was elected to one term in Congress, and while in Salt Lake City in 1871 was hired by Brigham Young. He and other top Mormon leaders had been arrested with "lewd and lascivious cohabitation with plural wives." Though not a supporter of polygamy—a position that, no doubt, Mrs. Fitch appreciated—Fitch did provide Young with a mostly successful defense. It is believed that he and Wells Spicer crossed paths while in Utah before the former returned to San Francisco. In 1877, Fitch moved to Prescott in Arizona to practice law, and two years later he was elected to the Arizona Territorial Legislature. He spent November 1881 in Tombstone defending the Earps and Doc.† That he and Judge Spicer knew and respected each other could not hurt.

When the first witness, William Allen, testified, it became immediately obvious that the coroner's hearing had been a prelude to the position the cowboys would take: The Clantons and McLaurys were innocent victims and the Earps and Holliday were cold-blooded killers. The victims had tried to surrender, but Holliday

---

* During his campaign labors, Fitch was dubbed "the silver-tongued orator of the Pacific." His skills had been on display in the summer of 1881 in Tombstone, when he had presented a rousing Independence Day speech.

† Specifically, Doc Holliday was represented during the Spicer hearing by U.S. Court Commissioner Thomas Drum, but Fitch was the lead attorney for the defense.

fired the first shot and the Earp brothers followed with a fusillade of bullets.

When it was Johnny Behan's turn, he echoed that version and presented himself as the voice of reason and real law and order who had been ignored. When the sheriff's testimony was reported in the newspapers, some citizens began to view the gunfight as more a planned murder than an arrest gone wrong.

There are three ways to account for the testimony that Behan gave. One was he told the truth . . . and that is the least likely explanation, with only his cowboy allies corroborating his version of events. The second explanation was that Behan had been "advised" by Phin Clanton or Will McLaury or even Curly Bill Brocius and Johnny Ringo that it was in his best interests and would promote continued good health if the Earps took the fall for the events of October 26. But the third may be the most plausible.

Nothing would serve the sheriff more than for the Earps to be convicted and imprisoned—or, even better, hanged—for murder. Behan's attempts to avoid gunplay on that windy Wednesday would be vindicated. The Earps and Doc, acting more as vigilantes than lawmen—that drunken gambler Holliday in particular—had pushed past the top officer in Cochise County to force a confrontation with men who could have been left alone until they lost patience with lingering and skulked out of town. With the Earps out of the way and the cowboys in control, Behan would be assured of reelection and continue to enjoy the largest piece of the tax revenue pie. And with Wyatt, specifically, buried in a cell or dangling at the end of a rope, Josephine Marcus might well reevaluate her prospects in Tombstone.

Thus, the sheriff's testimony was filled with fanciful details.

After stressing how hard he had labored to disarm both parties, which included scurrying "twenty-two or twenty-three steps up the street," he claimed that before shots were fired Doc Holliday had his nickel-plated pistol aimed at Billy Clanton, who cried out, "Don't shoot me. I don't want to fight." Tom McLaury threw open his coat to demonstrate that he did not have a gun. Doc fired first with the handgun, then the others joined in, with the cowboys clearly being victims. The Earps, the sheriff stressed, wanted the shoot-out to happen and had forced it.

During two days of cross-examination Behan's story was shaken but not broken. That he stuck to it allowed newspapers as far away as San Francisco to roast the Earps in print. "Public feeling, which at first was for the Earps and Holliday, seems to have taken a turn, and now nearly all the people of Tombstone condemn the murderers," commented the *San Francisco Examiner*, already convicting the defendants.

It did not help that Will McLaury became a frequent presence in the Tombstone saloons, railing against the defendants as he bought drinks for patrons who, no surprise, increasingly thought the angry and grief-stricken older brother was right. According to what he wrote a brother-in-law in Iowa, his late brothers Frank and Tom "were universally esteemed as Honorable, Peaceable, and Brave citizens never having been charged nor suspected of having committed any offense."

Wes Fuller's testimony supported Behan's, though Fitch, upon cross-examination, got the witness to admit that he had been drinking heavily the day and night before the gunfight and his recollections were fuzzy. Fuller could, at least, state with confidence that he did not have "a fit of delirium tremens."

Billy Claiborne swore that when asked to by Virgil, the Clantons and McLaurys raised their empty hands, but Doc Holliday and Morgan Earp began shooting at them anyway.

Things got worse for Wyatt Earp and Doc Holliday—they were returned to jail. Prematurely, the prosecutors declared that the evidence against them was sufficiently strong that they would be charged with murder, and they should be behind bars to prevent them from leaving the city and the state. Ominously, Judge Spicer agreed. A petition for their freedom submitted by Fitch to another judge was rejected. Will McLaury crowed his satisfaction. Wyatt and Doc fretted in their cells because being locked up meant less protection for the recovering Virgil and Morgan Earp should the cowboys become impatient with the hearing and act to resolve the case themselves.

One benefit of the jailing was it revealed that Wyatt and Doc still had supporters, because armed members of the Citizens Safety Committee turned out to guard the jail and Virgil and Morgan against any attempts on their lives.

The prosecution's star witness was the only surviving participant on the cowboy side. Ike Clanton swore to the accuracy of his testimony even though he had been absorbing alcohol during the twenty-four hours before the confrontation and had suffered a nasty blow to the head. He also testified that as soon as Wyatt and Virgil Earp spoke to them, he and his brother and the McLaurys raised their hands in surrender, but all four lawmen began firing anyway. Ike claimed that while Wyatt held him he fired, but somehow the bullet missed him and that bullets were whizzing by his head as he ran away. He speculated that the fight was caused by Doc Holliday having abused him the night before, and Holliday wasn't finished with him.

Before prosecutors could stop him, Ike further contended that Wyatt and Morgan had robbed the Bisbee stage back in March, and because Billy Leonard, Harry Head, and Jim Crane knew it, Wyatt wanted Clanton's help in killing them. Ike explained to the court that he had not revealed this explosive "truth" before because he had promised Wyatt "as a gentleman" not to do so.

The entirety of Clanton's testimony before Judge Spicer was parsed out during a brain-numbing four days. Much of it was self-serving perspective and opinion and some of it was outright preposterous. It would have been better if Clanton had not testified at all. As Casey Tefertiller points out, Ike had "presented a tale so contradictory, so permeated with evasions and fabrications, that his credibility was virtually nil." Just one more of his fabrications was that when the shooting began, his approach of Wyatt was not to beg for his life but to heroically attempt to push Wyatt out of harm's way.

Fitch and his colleagues did not have to work hard in their cross-examination to convince Judge Spicer that Ike Clanton was a liar as well as a fool and coward. Worse for the prosecutors who had allowed him to testify, Clanton's bizarre testimony and answers under cross-examination had called the prosecution's entire case into question. Almost two weeks into the hearing, the tide was turning.

When it was the defense's turn, the first witness on the stand was Wyatt Earp. Fitch tried an unusual gambit: instead of the typical question-and-answer followed by cross-examination, Wyatt would read a prepared statement detailing what he claimed had really happened. Fitch cited a statute in Arizona law that allowed for this. Over the strenuous objections of Lyttleton Price and his team, Judge Spicer agreed.

Though probably organized and at least partly written by Fitch, going a long way toward selling the statement to listeners was Wyatt's straightforward and earnest delivery. He explained the deal he had made with Ike Clanton, admitting that if successful, he hoped it would get him elected sheriff of Cochise County. Wyatt discussed the numerous depredations of the cowboys, including the Clantons and McLaurys, just one of them being the ambush in Skeleton Canyon. He described the events of the night before the gunfight, what had occurred the morning of it, and the unsought and sudden start of the shoot-out itself. He insisted that Sheriff Behan had deceived Virgil and his deputies and that the lawmen were surprised to be facing armed men.

Especially convincing was when he stated the family's motives. "I believe then, and I believe now . . . that Tom McLaury, Frank McLaury, and Ike Clanton had formed a conspiracy to murder my brothers, Morgan and Virgil, Doc Holliday and myself," Wyatt declared. "I believe I would have been legally and morally justifiable in shooting any of them on sight, but I did not do so. I sought no advantage when I went, as deputy marshal, to help to disarm them and arrest them. I did not intend to fight unless it became necessary in self-defense or in the rightful performance of official duty. When Billy Clanton and Frank McLaury drew their pistols, I knew it was a fight for life, and I drew and fired in defense of my own life and the lives of my brothers and Doc Holliday."

To further bolster his credibility, Wyatt offered two documents that were marked Exhibit A and Exhibit B. The first was a statement signed by prominent citizens in Dodge City attesting to Wyatt's integrity and effectiveness as a lawman and the second was a similar document from Wichita.

Other witnesses followed, including Virgil Earp, who was

interviewed at home. As expected, he repeated Wyatt's version of what had transpired. One by one, people such as H. F. Sills, Rezin Campbell, clerk of the Cochise County Board of Supervisors, and John Gardiner, an army surgeon in town that day, took the stand to dispute what Ike Clanton and other prosecution witnesses had said. Even Winfield Scott Williams, a Behan deputy, contradicted the sheriff's testimony. The prosecution team had let the case get away from them.

They might have redeemed themselves by cross-examining the volatile Doc Holliday, but he did little more than sit at the defense table and occasionally scribbled notes to his lawyer. Doc had been told that Big Nose Kate had left Tombstone, her getaway financed by Johnny Ringo, who during Doc's incarceration had become a frequent visitor to the rooms in Fly's boardinghouse. Just as well that Doc Holliday was behind bars, or he might have taken action very detrimental to the defense.

It is worth noting that to win their case—that is, to obtain a ruling that would move the case to a grand jury—prosecutors had to convince just one man. If this had been a trial before a jury, prosecutors might have been able to fill it with a combination of cowboy supporters and those who did not know or care about the Earps or maybe even resented them for their haughty law-and-order attitude. The "clannishness" that Allie had referred to could put some people off. But the only man in the courtroom who truly mattered was Wells Spicer. For more than four weeks he observed the caliber of prosecution witnesses and evaluated the plausibility of their stories and then did the same with the defense witnesses.

Finally, on November 29, the defense rested, and the hearing came to an end. Judge Spicer would not provide the participants and the city with days of tense waiting. By two o'clock the following afternoon, startling many of those involved, he was back in the courtroom to deliver his decision.

With a note of weariness, Spicer began, "The case has now been on hearing for the past thirty days during which time a volume of testimony has been taken and eminent legal talent employed on both sides." Citing the "great importance of the case," he declared that he would "be full and explicit in my findings and conclusions and should give ample reason for what I do."

Judge Spicer then laid out the basic scenario: On the morning of October 26, an inebriated Ike Clanton, armed with a rifle and pistol, staggered around downtown Tombstone letting everyone know he wanted to fight the Earps and Doc Holliday. Virgil, assisted by Morgan, did his duty and arrested Clanton. "Whether this blow [to the head] was necessary or not is not material here to determine." Ike was fined and there were some "hot words" between him and Wyatt, who in turn knocked Tom McLaury down.

Spicer's next statement was ominous for the defendants: "In view of these controversies between Wyatt Earp and Isaac Clanton and Thomas McLowry [sic], and in further view of the quarrel the night before between Isaac Clanton and J. H. Holliday, I am of the opinion that Virgil Earp, as chief of police, by subsequently calling upon Wyatt Earp and J. H. Holliday to assist him in arresting and disarming the Clantons and McLowrys [sic] committed an injudicious and censurable act."

However, the judge continued, while Virgil could have made a better decision, the county had been suffering from "lawlessness and disregard for human life," there was "a law-defying element in our midst," and there was a prevalence "of bad, desperate and reckless men who have been a terror to the county," so "I can attach no criminality to his unwise act." Spicer further stated, "In fact, as the results plainly prove, [Virgil] needed the assistance and support of staunch and true friends, upon whose courage, coolness, and fidelity he could depend in case of emergency."

The judge's ruling did not end there, as he went on to comment on the testimonies given by witnesses, but he had tipped his hand: Virgil and his brothers and Doc had done what needed to be done. Spicer finished up by stating, "I cannot resist the conclusion that the defendants were fully justified in committing these homicides; that it was a necessary act done in the discharge of official duty."

There would be no referral to a grand jury. In the eyes of the court, at least, the actions of October 26 were lawful and justified. Wyatt and Doc were immediately released.

Predictably, Ike and Phin Clanton and Will McLaury were outraged. Many people in Tombstone assumed Johnny Ringo and Curly Bill Brocius and their followers were already plotting their own means of justice. "Ike Clanton was peeved," understated John Clum. "He had gone back to his ranch and was busy reconstructing his pirate crew."

But there were also hopes that with Judge Spicer's definitive ruling, the ugly chapter that was the October 26 gunfight could conclude and Tombstone's story would return to focusing on a bright future. "The outlook for our camp is very favorable, and everyone seems in good spirits," wrote Clara Brown in her December 7 missive. "Two or three stages arrive daily loaded with passengers, houses are in demand, and there is a noticeable increase in activity in the branches of business." Sounding as though she had become head of the chamber of commerce, Brown added: "More capitalists are here than at any time heretofore, and they are manifesting lively interest in the mining property by which we are surrounded."

The rest of December and 1881 could be a second chance for the

Earp brothers and their wives and the seemingly ascendant law-and-order faction. But Mayor Clum had been right—the Clantons and the cowboys had other ideas. They were not done with Tombstone yet.

Chapter Twenty-Five

———◆———

"A SMOLDERING FIRE"

The Earp brothers were reasonably intelligent people, so it must have occurred to at least one or two of them that with the court case resolved, and with their release from jail, this was a real good time to leave Tombstone.

They could not doubt that Johnny Ringo and Curly Bill Brocius and their cowboy followers would want to avenge the shooting deaths of the McLaurys and Billy Clanton. The court proceedings may have been the best protection the Earps had, because while they were under way the remaining Clantons and the cowboys could hold on to the hope that justice would be done and the Earps, or at least Wyatt and Doc Holliday, would rot in jail or worse. However, Wells Spicer had robbed them of that hope and thus had unintentionally exposed the Earps to reprisals.

The Earp women were anxious to leave town. They had never been treated as wives there anyway. To them, California beckoned. Family awaited them there. When Virgil and Morgan were fully recovered from their wounds, they could pursue lawman jobs farther west or go back to being businessmen. Morgan was still young enough to start fresh at anything. The Earp brothers had done what they could to uphold law and order and almost gotten killed doing it. From now on, let Tombstone and its remaining peace officers do their own policing.

But the brothers were also stubborn and had that clannish pride. They did not want it to appear that the gunfight or the threatening presence of the cowboys chased them out of Tombstone. They still had business interests there, mostly the mines and Wyatt's faro games held in several saloons. It was still possible the mines would pay off, and if the Earps quit early, all that investment and work would have been wasted. For Wyatt there was the added incentive of having Josephine Marcus in town and available. She may have been further impressed hearing from witnesses that Wyatt had stood tall and in plain sight of his adversaries as he fired his pistol and was the only lawman to leave that vacant lot without a scratch . . . while Johnny Behan trotted back and forth like a dog trying to serve two masters.

And what if leaving town exposed others to harm? Judge Spicer had received death threats. One of them was in the form of a note, which began, "Sir, if you take my advice you will take your departure for a more genial clime, as I don't think this one healthy for you much longer, as you are able to get a hole through your coat at any moment. If such sons of bitches as you are allowed to dispense justice in this territory, the sooner you depart from us the better for you."

As had been true in Utah, Spicer was not one to cut and run because of a threat. In a letter published in the *Epitaph*, the judge proclaimed, "There is a rabble in our city who would like to be thugs if they had courage; would be proud to be called cow-boys, if people gave them that distinction; but as they can be neither, they do the best they can to show how vile they are, and slander, abuse, and threaten everybody. In conclusion, I will say that I will be here just where they can find me if they want me."

That went double for John Clum, being both mayor and anti-cowboy editor of the *Epitaph*. To the disbelief of some, Clum contended that he learned that Johnny Ringo, Curly Bill, and their comrades had created a "death list" containing the names of the men who would pay the price for the gunfight's victims. At the top were listed Wyatt, Virgil, and Morgan, followed by Doc Holliday and John Clum. His knowledge of such a list, or the very existence of it, had to be questioned when people read in the *Epitaph* that it "had been prepared with most spectacular and dramatic ceremonials, enacted at midnight within the recesses of a deep canyon, during which the names of the elect had been written in blood drawn from the veins of a murderer." What would be next, a headless horseman?

Clara Brown reported to her readers to the west that "a smoldering fire exists, which is liable to burst forth at some unexpected moment. If the Earps were not men of great courage, they would hardly dare remain in Tombstone."

The Earps could not slink away and put others in danger. And there was no doubt danger was present, with the brothers still in the thick of it. As George Parsons noted in his journal, "A bad time is expected in town at any time. Earps on one side of the street with their friends and Ike Clanton on the other side—watching each other. Blood will surely come."

It did not help the cowboy cause—such as it was, being that it was a desire for lawlessness—that Ike was its public face. Everyone knew that when the gunfight on October 26 began, his feet were his weapon, and they were reminded that he was a blowhard. He tried to sue the Earps for the damage the gunfight did and was rebuffed by the courts. And now people knew that he had agreed to a deal with Wyatt to betray the Benson stage robbers. Clanton was an embarrassment. However, he had lost a father and brother to violence within the last few months . . . and he simply would not go away.

Though in a limbo state as acting governor, John Gosper was concerned enough about the potential for more violence in Tombstone that he paid another visit there in November. After talking to Mayor Clum and others, Gosper realized that the gunfight the previous month had not resolved the overriding situation of the cowboys wanting control of Cochise County. If anything, they could be closer to that goal by having put Virgil, the police chief, and Morgan, one of his deputies, out of action, and the other two deputies that October afternoon, Wyatt and Doc, were in jail. James Flynn was only a caretaker in the marshal's chair, and the ineffectual and probably corrupt sheriff's department, headed by Johnny Behan, was a bit tarnished but otherwise as intact as it was before. The situation would only get worse. More violence would reflect badly on southeast Arizona and its ambitions and certainly reduce Gosper's chances of having the "acting" removed from acting governor.

"Fearful racket below—all night with nearly a fight," Parsons, who was living in an apartment overlooking Fifth and Allen Streets, recorded in his journal on November 29. "Shots fired once in a while. Am wondering when a bullet will come through floor or wall." And two nights later: "Fights at both saloons opposite and underneath last night. Quite a circus about one a.m."

As Clara Brown noted, "Many Easterners believe that Tombstone is appropriately named, and dare not venture into so criminal infested a locality."

Gosper turned to Crawley Dake for help. Essentially, the governor wanted the U.S. marshal to take the federal badge off Virgil and give it to a man "with proper discretion and courage" who would "go forward with a firm and steady hand [and] bring as rapidly as possible the leading spirits of this lawless class to a severe and speedy punishment."

Dake did not go for it. His response to Gosper came in a letter to the acting attorney general in the Chester A. Arthur administration, S. F. Phillips. The marshal stated that Virgil and his men "killed several cow boys in Tombstone and the sheriff's faction had my deputies arrested—and after a protracted trial my deputies were vindicated and publicly complimented for their bravery in driving the outlaw element from this part of our territory." Dake concluded: "I am proud to report that I have some of the best and the bravest men in my employ in this hazardous business—men who are trusty and tried, and who strike fear into the hearts of these outlaws."

Allie Earp, who had not wanted to come to Tombstone in the first place, was itching to leave. As Virgil's leg healed, "I knew it was time for us to be getting out of town. There was a feeling in the air. You couldn't put your finger on it, but it was bad just the same." She claimed to her nephew Frank Waters for his book published decades later that Virgil "felt like that too." However, "we kept putting it off, waiting till he could walk, and all the rest of our lives we wished we had gone, the way things turned out."

To be less exposed to attack, Virgil and Allie and Morgan and Louisa had moved into the Cosmopolitan Hotel. Mattie spent most of her time there, too, while Wyatt provided more of a moving target, sometimes staying there, sometimes in his own house, and other times bunking with the secret Wells Fargo agent Fred Dodge.

Doc continued living at C. S. Fly's boardinghouse. Once again, he was alone. During the Spicer hearing, Johnny Ringo had been paying attention to the reports about it and anticipated that Doc would be released from jail. That was when he told Kate Elder that living with a target of cowboy retribution would not be healthy. Kate was broke, of course, but Ringo had given her $50, and she had sought the safety of Globe.

Whatever its attributes, living at the Cosmopolitan was certainly not what Louisa had envisioned when she had finally joined Morgan in Tombstone. About staying there, she wrote her sister, "It is very disagreeable to be so unsettled."

This could have been true of Josephine Marcus, too, though "unsettled" in a different way. Josephine might be available but Wyatt was less so, and not just because of Mattie. "With Wyatt's every move being watched carefully by the Clanton faction, the lovers would have had little opportunity for a liaison or to make plans for the future," writes Ann Kirschner in *Lady at the O.K. Corral.* "Even exchanging greetings would have drawn Josephine into more danger. She could do nothing but wait."

Curly Bill Brocius continued to be an ominous specter haunting the dreams of some Tombstone citizens who feared that any moment he would come swooping into town at the head of a pistol-shooting cowboy army. They would have slept much better knowing that for most of November he was not in Arizona at all and some of that time away was spent under arrest.

It is not clear what Curly Bill was doing in New Mexico, but the November 10 edition of the *Arizona Daily Star* reported that he had been arrested in the mining town of Shakespeare along with a pal named Sandy King and a notorious outlaw, William "Russian Bill" Tattenbaum.* The charge was horse theft. After some time in jail, Brocius was able to argue in court that he was not a thief or rustler and was just in the wrong place at the wrong time. Remarkably, the judge bought this and let Curly Bill off with a small fine.

The cowboy had made his case in the nick of time. There was in Shakespeare a self-appointed vigilance committee whose members were angered by a recent rampage of cattle rustling. Curly Bill was shaking the dust of Shakespeare off his shoulders when a group of committee members, wearing masks, broke into the jail and grabbed King and Tattenbaum. They were immediately put on trial at a hotel, found guilty, and given a chance to plead for their lives. They did but apparently were not as persuasive as Brocius. King and Tattenbaum were hanged.

Prior to the hanging, King asked for a glass of water, explaining, "My throat is sore after talking so much to save my life." Their bodies dangled for days as a warning to other rustlers. The *Daily Star* lamented about Curly Bill, "'Tis a pity he had not been held so that he could have accompanied his friends."

Brocius returned to the relative safety of Cochise County and in December occupied himself with plotting against the Earps. This became obvious to some people when Brocius, Johnny Ringo, Ike Clanton, and Pony Deal began to be seen going in and out of the Grand Hotel. This establishment was near the Cosmopolitan Hotel. Clanton and the cowboys had rented a room from which

---

* The arresting officer was David "Dangerous Dan" Tucker. In his book *Deadly Dozen,* the western historian Robert DeArment includes Tucker in his profiles of the twelve most underrated lawmen of the American West. It would take such a man to corral Curly Bill.

they could spy on the Earps' comings and goings. It was impossible to keep doing this without the brothers learning of it, but they shrugged it off. Perhaps knowing where the cowboys were was preferable to having them suddenly show up out of nowhere.

The embattled mayor decided this was a good time to leave Tombstone, and unlike the Earps, he was not going to think twice. To be fair to John Clum, he was a widower with young children, so spending the holidays back east with extended family may have been necessary as well as understandable. And his life had gotten very uncertain. As he recalled, "I was still postmaster of Tombstone, and three times we picked up rumors that the outlaws were headed for town to rob the post office. Each time I invited two or three friends to spend the night with me sleeping in the post office well healed [sic] with guns and ammunition."

However, his getaway turned out to be more dangerous than remaining among friends in town. On December 14, he was one of six passengers on the 8 P.M. stagecoach taking him to Benson and the train station there. He would visit his brother in Tucson first, then turn east. On the dark road about four miles north of Tucson, the stage driver was startled by bursts of gunfire and the appearance of several masked men. Another driver, this one of a bullion wagon behind the stagecoach, Whistling Dick Wright, was hit in the leg.

"Ike and his bad boys evidently did not intend to let me get far from home," Clum concluded. "I knew enough not to stick my head out the window to see what was happening. In fact, I knew quite well what was happening and got my six-shooter in position where it would do the most good, or harm. Depending on the point of view."

Both Wright and the stage driver, Jimmie Harrington, refused to yield and they lashed their horses forward. The masked men fired several more shots. One of them struck a horse, which eventually slowed, then collapsed and died, but by then the would-be thieves had given up.

It seems that at this point, John Clum had had enough. He had lost his wife a year earlier, he'd had an extremely difficult tenure as mayor, during which the city had almost burned down and men were shooting and killing one another in the streets, and now that he was on his way to some respite, outlaws showed up to murder him. Clum climbed out of the stagecoach and simply wandered away into the night.

He turned up in Benson the next day, after walking for seven miles and borrowing a horse from a ranch.* Clum would later try to explain his odd nocturnal sojourn by saying he believed his continued presence on the stagecoach "only jeopardized the other passengers," as he considered the attack more an assassination attempt than a robbery. "I was much better off with my feet on the ground and no sidelights. I struck off through the mesquite and cactus on foot." It was, he added, "a precarious trek."

Virgil was feeling pretty much back to normal when he walked into the Oriental Saloon the next morning. There, Milton Joyce informed him of the attempted robbery of the Benson stagecoach. He added that he had been expecting such an event ever since Wyatt and Doc had been released from jail. The implied insult of Wyatt was not a good idea: with his right hand, Virgil slapped Joyce in the face. Immediately, others in the saloon restrained both men.

---

* Clum found his way to a mill, where the superintendent phoned Tombstone to say the mayor was safe. Telephone systems in Arizona were being installed late in 1881, with Tombstone being one of the first recipients.

After calming down and being released, Joyce started for the front door. Before exiting, he turned to Virgil and said, "Your favorite method is to shoot a man in the back, but if you murder me you will be compelled to shoot me in the front."

The dispute between the two hard-crusted men was not over. The next day, with Virgil and Wyatt and possibly Morgan, too, in there gambling, Joyce strode into the Oriental Saloon holding a pistol in each hand. He challenged the brothers to a fight. Displaying unusual initiative was Johnny Behan, who had spotted Joyce entering the saloon. He came up behind Joyce, grabbed him, and hauled him outside. There he was arrested for carrying the weapons and he wound up paying a $15 fine. The sheriff may have earned the grudging thanks of the Earps, but in Milton Joyce he had made a new enemy.

If nothing else, the ongoing enmity between the Earps and the cowboys helped to sell newspapers. Supporters of the brothers wrote letters that were published in *The Tombstone Epitaph*—which carried on during Clum's absence—and detractors had their screeds published in the *Tombstone Daily Nugget*. The clamor reached as far as San Francisco, where that city's *Daily Exchange* newspaper observed, "Tombstone seems to be in a nice condition of disorder."

It was about to get worse. With the next city elections set for January 3, Christmas season had to be shared with campaign season. Clum, understandably, would not seek reelection and was not in Tombstone for the campaign anyway. His supporters switched their allegiance to the lumberman Lewis Blinn, who would be opposed by John Carr. Virgil, not wanting to be a lightning rod and no doubt to Allie's relief, also decided not to run, and James Flynn took his place on the ballot for chief of police. His opponent was David Neagle, one of Behan's deputies.

The Earps resolved to keep as low a profile as possible. And, oddly, the man who was best able to stay above the fray was Doc Holliday. He was not out of a job—gambling continued unabated in Tombstone no matter who hated whom—and he was not viewed as a law-and-order figurehead. He did not have to be part of the Cosmopolitan Hotel enclave, he roamed the streets freely. He felt bad for Wyatt and his brothers, but there was nothing he could do about it.

"Doc [had] achieved something in the street fight," writes Gary L. Roberts, "but it was not something he sought or even wanted. If the reputation of the Earps were sullied in the street fight, the reputation of Doc Holliday grew as a man to be feared—and respected—for his courage if not his character. Men gave him room after that."

Christmas Day came and went, a somber one for the Earp brothers and their wives. Three days later, Virgil was ambushed.

On that night of December 28, the outgoing chief of police had, as usual, been playing cards at the Oriental Saloon. He left for "home" at the Cosmopolitan Hotel. As he ambled in the dark, shotgun blasts sounded. Virgil was hit hard enough to knock him to the ground. He later recalled that "three double-barreled shotguns were turned loose on me from about sixty feet off."

Incredibly, he got to his feet, then staggered back to the Oriental Saloon. Wyatt was still there, and when he saw his older brother, there was no doubt he had been shot up bad. The only question was whether he would bleed to death before a doctor could be found.

In his apartment, George Parsons heard the gunshots and apparently the assailants were spotted. "Cries of 'There they go,' 'Head them off,' were heard but the cowardly apathetic guardians of the peace were not inclined to risk themselves and the other brave men, all more or less armed, did nothing," he reported.

Allie and the other Earp women were still sitting at the table having dinner. She remembered that they were eating "some of the peppermint candy Virge liked" and waiting for him to return from the saloon. About 11:30, "we heard a sudden roar, loud but far off. Fifteen minutes later there was a knock on the door. I didn't have to open it. I grabbed my hat and coat and went running out."

Wyatt had sent word to find Dr. Matthews or Dr. Goodfellow or both. Then he and several other men carried his brother to his room at the hotel. Virgil was conscious, but that did not guarantee he would live. The damage was extensive, Dr. Goodfellow found. Shotgun pellets had penetrated Virgil's body and struck the liver, kidney, and spine. He had been hit in the thigh, too, but his left arm had gotten the worst of it. The doctor determined it could not be saved.

Allie nearly fainted at the sight of her husband's blood-soaked body. However, Virgil reassured her, "Never mind, I've got one arm left to hug you with."

When Dr. Goodfellow turned him over to examine the damage from that side, Virgil passed out. Moments after Wyatt walked in, he regained consciousness. Virgil told his brother, "When they get me under don't let them take my arm off. If I have to be buried, I want both arms on me."

Hoping for the best, Drs. Goodfellow and Matthews went to work. They removed 5.5 inches of humerus bone from the left arm and treated and closed up the other wounds as best they could.

It was determined that the shotgun attack had come from a construction site on the southeast corner of Fifth and Allen Streets. Ike Clanton's hat was found there, and Frank Stilwell had been seen entering the site soon before Virgil was ambushed. This could be just the beginning of violent reprisals for the October shoot-out.

Not knowing if Virgil would make it, in the early morning hours Wyatt headed to the telegraph office. There, he sent this message to U.S. Marshal Crawley Dake: "Virgil was shot by concealed assassins last night. His wounds are fatal. Telegraph me appointment to appoint deputies. Local authorities are doing nothing. The lives of other citizens are threatened."

Later that day, the *Epitaph* editorial writer wondered, "Who will be the next subject? And a further question, How long will our people stand this sort of thing?"

Wyatt Earp was not waiting to find out what other people would do. Dake replied with his appointment as a deputy U.S. marshal to take over the duties from Virgil. Right after his older brother weakly managed to administer the oath of office, Wyatt began putting a posse together.

Allie probably had the longest night of all. "All that night I sat there watching the blood drip, wondering why it had to be Virge again," she remembered. "I said my prayers. Then I didn't think or say or do anything. I just sat there. There was no getting away from Tombstone."

Chapter Twenty-Six

——◆——

"I'M YOUR HUCKLEBERRY"

It was bad enough that Virgil Earp was fighting to stay alive in the rooms he and Allie shared at the Cosmopolitan Hotel—then Wyatt got killed. Well, that was according to the *Las Vegas Optic*. Describing Wyatt as "a former Las Vegas slumgullion" and that he was "previously a policeman at Dodge City under Bat Masterson," the newspaper erroneously reported that he had "got his stomach full of buckshot at Tombstone three or four days ago and has been planted for worm feed." Normally, local residents would have little or no knowledge of what was printed in the *Optic*, but the *Tombstone Daily Nugget*, reverting to its anti-Earp ways, made sure to republish the fake news.

With John Clum and his grandiose prose absent, the *Daily Nugget* almost had the editorial field in Tombstone to itself as 1881 ended. The election for mayor was being hotly contested, with the *Daily Nugget* squarely against Lewis Blinn. The newspaper declared that "there is little doubt that a vote for [acting chief of police] Flynn is equivalent to a vote for a new lease of power for the

Earps." On election day itself, the *Daily Nugget* declared that the Earps and Doc Holliday "are solid for Blinn and Flynn. So is the Daily Strangler."

The turnout for the funeral of the McLaurys and Billy Clanton last October had been a harbinger of the voter turnout of January 3. John Carr defeated Blinn with ease, 830 to 298, and though the race for chief of police was closer, David Neagle won decisively over Flynn, 590 to 434. For the Earps, the city government would join the dominant newspaper voice against them.

Oddly, given that it was the Earps and Doc Holliday—and, by extension, their supporters—who were upholding the law during the confrontation with the cowboys ten weeks earlier, the *Tombstone Daily Nugget* opined that because of the result of the election there would be no "turbulence or violence on the part of the lawless elements of Tombstone in the future." The newspaper insisted that Mayor-elect Carr "will set down on 'em."

Not that the Earps were paying much attention to politics and the *Daily Nugget*'s fantasies. Their focus was on Morgan's ongoing healing and especially Virgil. As each day went by, it became likely that he would survive but also that he would be crippled for life. His career as a lawman was over, and the family had to wonder what this self-sufficient and proud man would be good for in the years to come. "Virgil Earp" and "shopkeeper" just did not seem to go together.

What the *Tombstone Daily Nugget* had predicted about the new administration preventing further lawlessness was immediately contradicted. On the Saturday morning just three days after the election, a stagecoach on the way to Bisbee was robbed and the outlaws got away with a good haul of Wells Fargo money.

It must have been a cold wait for the three thieves that was finally rewarded at around 3 A.M. when the stagecoach appeared. It may not have been coincidental that the holdup took place near the Clanton ranch, still run by Ike and Phin. The robbers fired several shots, and that led to a brief farce. The panicked driver and shotgun messenger simply jumped off the coach without even attempting to stop it. After hoofing it a short distance, the apparently more sensible horses came to a stop and waited for further instructions. The driver and messenger reappeared and clambered back up onto the stagecoach and took off, with the thieves trailing behind. They spurred their horses on and outrode the shuddering vehicle, whose passengers were nearly churned into butter. Once more in front of the stagecoach, the robbers fired again, and this time the stage came to a stop with all aboard.

The outlaws demanded that the wooden Wells Fargo strongbox be tossed into the road, where it was opened. The $6,500 inside was removed. Then the shotgun messenger and driver were told not to reveal any details about the robbers so they could not be identified, though later on the driver maintained that the leader was Johnny Ringo. Wells Fargo not only lost the money, which would have to be made good out of its own coffers, but some of its reputation.

That reputation was considerably more tarnished less than twenty-four hours later. Not only was there another stagecoach robbery, but, worse, one of the passengers was the veteran Wells Fargo detective James Hume.

On that Saturday night, January 7, he was one of nine people on the stage that left Benson, bound for Tombstone. An hour or so after midnight, after the stagecoach had passed Contention City, two men with guns and wearing black masks appeared on the road. Possibly because of Hume's presence, there was no shotgun messenger on this run. After the driver halted the horses, the thieves busied themselves with searching the frightened passengers, who were relieved of all cash and valuables. Hume had $75 and both his pistols taken along with some self-respect.

But he was a resilient detective. During the robbery itself, Hume had nonchalantly engaged the thieves in conversation, listening to how they spoke and observing how they dressed and any other physical details. Upon arriving in Tombstone, after doing a cursory summary for Sheriff Johnny Behan, Hume conferred with Fred Dodge. Hume knew what no one else in Tombstone did, that Dodge was an employee of Wells Fargo, working undercover. Unlike others who played partisan politics, Dodge knew that the Earps and the cowboys were the good guys and bad guys. Despite the occasional scattershot accusation, it was certainly not the Earp brothers who were robbing stagecoaches, and their whereabouts could easily be accounted for that weekend, when the two events had taken place.

It is possible, however, that by this time Wyatt knew of Dodge's true purpose in Tombstone, because Dodge was dispatched by Hume to find Wyatt, now a deputy U.S. marshal. Also possible, Dodge may have indiscreetly confided in Morgan when the two had been roommates. In any case, there could no longer be any doubt for Wyatt and by extension his brothers when Dodge escorted him to the Wells Fargo office to meet with Jim Hume, who briefed Wyatt on the robbery. Another indication that the Wells Fargo agents knew where their best law-and-order interests lay is that Hume told Wyatt many more details than he had offered Johnny Behan and, presumably, the newly elected chief of police.

Those details included, in addition to what Hume had heard and seen during the robbery, that since coming to Tombstone, Dodge had cultivated a ring of paid informants. One was a man named

Ayers who owned a saloon in Charleston. This same saloon was often frequented by cowboys who, feeling comfortable there, exchanged tales about their rustling and robbing activities. Odds were good the thieves could be found using their newfound wealth to buy drinks. That was where Wyatt, Dodge, and Morgan—chafing at the bit to do something—aimed to go. Hume was urged to stay behind.

However, when they arrived at the Ayers saloon, the small posse found that Hume had outridden them there. He was standing between and chatting with two men, and Hume blithely invited the "strangers" to join them for a drink. As Ayers served Dodge a beer, the proprietor, as Dodge recalled, "managed to indicate to me with his eyes the two men that were in the robbery." There was no direct evidence to be seen, though, plus, "This was not the safest place in the world for us to be in," so there was no move to arrest them. They had been identified, at least, and would be dealt with later. Most likely Wyatt Earp had been recognized by some in the saloon, and they may have known that he was now a federal marshal, so tight lips were all the visitors could expect.

It appeared that the October gunfight had not been a catharsis leading to less violence, and 1882 could be more trouble than the previous year. "In fact, the situation had only grown worse," writes Casey Tefertiller. "More and more no-accounts seemed to be drifting into Cochise County at a time when traditional crime had become less profitable." The Mexican army had effectively sealed the border, reducing the allure and safety of rustling. "The cowboy-criminals needed new targets, and everyone in Cochise County became a potential victim."

Mix in an unmotivated sheriff's department and cowboy-friendly city government and police department, and life was dangerous in and around Tombstone. "Many prominent townspeople lived in fear of every step," Tefertiller continues, "with any shadow in a dark alley providing the imagined potential for instant death." The situation had devolved to where Wyatt and anyone he deputized, and with the subtle backing of Wells Fargo, represented what was left of law and order.

As usual, U.S. Marshal Crawley Dake did not have the resources, especially financial ones, to be effective in southeast Arizona. But in the wake of the Wells Fargo embarrassments, he had an idea. Dake undertook the journey to San Francisco. There he met with company executives and requested that Wells Fargo lend him $3,000 to underwrite better enforcement. Instead of laughing Dake out of their offices, the executives agreed. Dake promised to repay the loan when $3,000 was sent his way by his superiors in Washington, D.C. This was certainly very dicey collateral, but Marshal Dake returned to the territory with a full pocket. If the cowboys could not be outnumbered, maybe they could be outspent.

There was not good financial news for Wyatt: his connection to the Oriental Saloon was severed when Milton Joyce became the controlling partner and, no doubt with some pleasure, shoved Wyatt out. His only priority, then, was to protect his extended family and wait for the right opportunity to identify the men who had bushwhacked his older brother and bring them to justice.

On January 17, Doc Holliday almost took that opportunity from him. That afternoon, as Gary L. Roberts puts it, "a fight between the two most feared men in Tombstone seemed certain," with that other man being Johnny Ringo.

There are numerous versions of what transpired, but one with some credence has Ringo and Doc encountering each other in front of the Occidental Saloon on Allen Street. Ringo wanted to settle the ongoing dispute right then and there with a duel. It is not known if the dispute was that between the cowboys and the Earps or their respective feelings about Big Nose Kate.

In any case, Doc's perplexing response was, "I'm your huckleberry. That's just my game."

As was often the case, George Parsons was an observer: "Much blood in the air this afternoon. Ringo and Doc Holliday came nearly to having at it with pistols. Bad time expected with the Cowboy leader and D.H. I passed both not knowing blood was up. One with hand in breast pocket and the other probably ready."

During the confrontation he did not hear what Ringo said, but Doc retorted, "All I want of you is ten paces out in the street."

As the two men squared off, James Flynn arrived. He had not yet officially turned his police chief responsibilities over to David Neagle, and as a lame duck he could easily have sat this one out. But as Virgil would have done before him, he interfered to prevent bloodshed. Flynn grabbed Ringo's arm and held it even as a few of the onlookers who had gathered called, "Let him loose!" Wyatt arrived on the scene, grabbed Doc's arm, and pulled him through the crowd.

Not done with his lawing, Flynn arrested Ringo for carrying a weapon, then followed Wyatt and Doc and did the same. Ringo and Doc were released after paying their fines, and Wyatt was simply released because he was a deputy U.S. marshal and could carry a gun anywhere. It wasn't as easy for Ringo—three days after the confrontation with Doc, the cowboy leader was behind bars again. The aggressive judge William Stilwell had revoked Ringo's bail for a previous offense, the robbery he had been accused of in Galeyville. This aggravation gave Ringo just one more reason to hate Holliday and his Earp pals.

For Wyatt, with Virgil recovering and Morgan's nasty wound a memory, it was time to go after the outlaws, who perhaps by now believed they had gotten away with the December 28 ambush. He went before Judge Stilwell—remarkably, no relation to the cowboy Frank Stilwell—and received arrest warrants for Pony Deal and Ike and Phin Clanton. In an unanticipated show of support, or at least neutrality, the new mayor, John Carr, had the two newspapers publish a proclamation asking citizens to not interfere with Wyatt's duties.* His next step was collecting men to ride with him.

Wyatt did not exactly have the pick of the litter, but that was fine with him. He was gearing up for a pursuit of men who would kill if they had to, not for a picnic in the mountains. More than stagecoach robbers, they were assassins. Morgan was first to sign up, and with Warren back in Tombstone, he was immediately recruited. (Even though his brother had been shot, it was best for all that James keep tending bar.) Doc Holliday, of course, got on a horse, and also saddling up were Sherman McMasters, Turkey Creek Jack Johnson, and Texas Jack Vermillion.

One can only speculate as to why these men agreed to ride with Wyatt on a mission unlikely to prove popular in a cowboy-friendly environment. Quite simply, it may have been because Wyatt asked and there was the promise of a reward. He may not necessarily have wanted these men, given that their shady pasts did not make them poster boys for law and order, but he had little choice.

The twenty-eight-year-old McMasters had been born in Illinois but wound up in Texas, where he became, briefly, a Texas Ranger. In 1878, he helped Curly Bill Brocius escape from a jail there and

---

* Not sharing the mayor's attempt at fairness, the *Nugget* hid the proclamation among its legal notices.

followed him to Arkansas. Two years later, McMasters was a suspect in a stagecoach holdup near Globe in Arizona. It was the same story in 1881, and in September when he was in Tombstone, Virgil Earp had attempted to arrest him, but he escaped. However, several months later, after the attack on Virgil, McMasters and Wyatt were allies.

It is believed that the thirty-three-year-old John "Turkey Creek Jack" Johnson, who hailed from Missouri, first met and was befriended by Wyatt in Dodge City. Around this time, in 1876, he was also in Deadwood, South Dakota, where in a gunfight he killed two men. Sometime after, he teamed up with Curly Bill, McMasters, and Pony Deal but does not seem to have been a hard-core cowboy busy with rustling and robbing. Johnson made his own way to Tombstone, where he reunited with Wyatt.

Of the three, the only one who would make it to the twentieth century was John Wilson "Texas Jack" Vermillion.* Born in 1842, he served in the Confederate army under Nathan Bedford Forrest. After the war he moved to Missouri, married, had two children, and served as a territorial marshal. When both his children died in a diphtheria epidemic, the grief-stricken Vermillion went west, first to Kansas, then eventually to Tombstone. He became acquainted with the Earps and sometimes served as one of Virgil's special deputies.

This group—possibly with a couple of other men—led by Wyatt, rode out of Tombstone on January 23 in search of thieves and bushwhackers. Leaving soon afterward was Johnny Ringo.

---

* The origin of Vermillion's nickname is murky, as he was not known to have spent much time, if any, in Texas. Once, when asked why he was called Texas Jack, Vermillion replied, "Because I'm from Virginia."

Reinstating his bail had been taking too long and the cowboys had to be warned, so Ringo demanded to be let out and Johnny Behan complied. When word also got out, James Earp went to the court and had a warrant sworn to rearrest Ringo, and another posse was pulled together. This one left Tombstone on January 24. The riders found Ringo easily enough, in Charleston, and without fuss he set off with them back to Tombstone. However, the damage was done—he had let the cowboys and the Clanton brothers know that the Earp posse—which had been expanded by an influx of more men from Tombstone—was trying to hunt them down.

As a result, when it was Charleston's turn to be visited by Wyatt's group, there was no one to give up. Not that the citizens seemed inclined to, anyway. A telegram signed "Charlestonian" and sent to Behan on January 26 complained, "Doc Holliday, the Earps and about forty or fifty more of the filth of Tombstone are here armed with Winchester rifles and revolvers, and patrolling our streets, as we believe, for no good purpose." And to no avail.

Actually, "patrolling our streets" was an understatement. Approaching Charlestown, Wyatt and his posse were met by Ben Maynard, a cowboy, who declared the men being sought were not there. He was not believed. Wyatt took his guns and Maynard was pushed ahead into town and forced to knock on doors, acting as a human shield in case the knocks were met by gunfire. A much-relieved Maynard watched the disappointed posse leave.

Wyatt and his posse were back in Tombstone later that day. Ironically, a second posse, this one headed by Charley Bartholomew of Wells Fargo, found the Clanton brothers four days later. Ike and Phin were taken to Tombstone and charged with ambushing and attempting to kill Virgil Earp. This was unexpected, but defiantly the Clantons demanded their day in court.

314 ★ TOM CLAVIN

It came on February 2. The evidence presented included the finding of Ike's hat at the construction site and being overheard later that night in Charleston saying that if Virgil was not dead, Ike "would have to go do the job over." But there were men who took the stand to claim that the Clanton brothers were in Charleston at the time of the shooting. Ike's hat was in Tombstone, but it could not be convicted. The verdict was not guilty, and Ike and Phin were set free.

That tore it as far as the Earps were concerned. A letter from Virgil and Wyatt was published in both the *Epitaph* and *Nugget*, declaring that "there has arisen so much harsh criticism in relation to our operations, and such a persistent effort having been made to misrepresent and misinterpret our acts. In order to convince the public that it is our sincere purpose to promote the public welfare," they were resigning as deputy U.S. marshals.

This was a rather astounding move. The brothers appeared to be accepting that maybe they were indeed part of the problem, so best to step aside. And yes, there was frustration that the legal system had not backed them up, but these were the only two paying jobs Virgil and Wyatt had left, supporting the view that they were trying to do the right thing. As it turned out, a few days later, when Crawley Dake visited Tombstone for an update, he refused to accept their resignations.

Instead of the city calming down, what followed was something like a comedy of errors. As Wyatt prepared to form another posse and take to the trail again, he was arrested. So were Virgil, Morgan, and Doc Holliday. All except Virgil were brought back behind bars. Ike Clanton, showing a lot more fight than he had done in the vacant lot off Fremont Street, and Phin had new murder charges filed in Contention City against the four men.

Ike boasted to a friend, "I have got the Earps in jail, and am not going to unhitch. I have got them on the hip and am going to throw them good."

During the next few days, the defendants hired a lawyer (Thomas Fitch was away). The judge, J. T. Drum, refused to hear a motion of habeas corpus because he had once been Doc's lawyer, so the Earps and Doc were hauled to Contention City for a hearing. But the judge there sent them back to Tombstone. On February 15, the case was postponed and Wyatt, Morgan, and Doc were released. The Contention City judge had obviously punted upon getting a look at the small army that accompanied the defendants. As George Parsons put it, "Quite a posse went out. Many of Earp's friends armed to the teeth."

Free to go, Wyatt set out on February 17 with the same posse, this time joined by Charlie Smith, also known for obvious reasons as Harelip Charlie. He was a long way from his place of birth, Litchfield, Connecticut. The thirty-seven-year-old had been a gambler and briefly a lawman in Texas, then had come to Tombstone because of the silver strikes. In this endeavor Smith and the Earps crossed paths and became friends. When Wyatt put out the call for more help, Smith answered it.

Further searching by Wyatt and his posse the rest of the month and into March proved frustratingly unfruitful. Wherever they looked, the cowboys seemed to have disappeared like water being absorbed by the desert sand seconds after a rainfall. No doubt they were being tipped off regularly by ranchers and other supporters. Conceivably, the fact that the posse existed with arrest warrants in Wyatt's pocket would be enough to bring peace to Cochise County and Tombstone in particular.

Clara Brown thought so: "The turbulent condition of affairs . . .

has for some time subdued, though exactly in what manner I cannot say, as the movements of the posses sent from here almost daily at that time were secret. There being a lull in cowboy criminality (which we hope is something more than temporary), and the Indians apparently having left the Dragoons, Tombstone people have been obliged to look to other causes of excitement."

That lull was about to end in a spectacular way. While the cowboys were not willing to reveal themselves, they were no longer going to be passive. They came into Tombstone with murder on their minds.

Chapter Twenty-Seven

"A BAD CHARACTER SENT TO HELL"

Compared with Virgil and Wyatt, Morgan was the more restless Earp brother. The younger man was more impetuous. He also no longer had a woman to keep him company. Because of the constant threat of violence, her discomfort at the Cosmopolitan Hotel, and her fragile health, several weeks earlier Louisa Earp had been sent back to Colton in California to live with Nicholas and Virginia. Now, in mid-March, Morgan was feeling antsy.

And it did seem as though the cowboy conflict had calmed down. With spring almost officially here, there was real work to be done on the ranches and time to be spent finding new and clever ways to continue rustling cattle on the Mexican side of the border. When Morgan declared that he wanted to see a performance of the play *Stolen Kisses* at Schieffelin Hall, there was some risk, but he would be among other people, not alone on a dark street, as was the case when Virgil was ambushed. Morgan bought a ticket for the show for Saturday, March 18.

Most likely, as he headed to the theater that evening, Morgan did not know about the conversation that Wyatt had with Briggs Goodrich late that afternoon. The attorney had represented cowboys in court, yet he was also on friendly enough terms with the Earp brothers. Just checking, Wyatt had approached him to ask if he had heard of any ominous cowboy activity. Goodrich said he had not, but he had seen a few cowboys he did not recognize in Tombstone, so something could be up. Coincidentally, Johnny Ringo had given the lawyer a message to convey to Wyatt: "If any fight came up between you all, he wanted you to understand that he would have nothing to do with it; that he was going to take care of himself, and everybody else could do the same."

If this message was meant to reassure the Earps, it was a misfire. Fine, Ringo, one of the two cowboy leaders, would not be part of an attack on the Earps . . . but the implication was, some kind of action was in the works, and if Ringo was not leading it, maybe Curly Bill Brocius was.

"Are we in danger?" Wyatt asked.

Goodrich reiterated that he knew of no specific threat, but that the Earps might "get it" at any time.

Not long afterward, Goodrich was also on his way to the performance of *Stolen Kisses*. En route, he saw more cowboys he did not recognize. As it happened, Goodrich encountered Morgan Earp and Doc Holliday. He reported to them what he had just observed and warned, "You fellows will catch it if you don't watch out." However, for Morgan and Doc, it was a Saturday night and they were out on the town.

After the conversation with the attorney, Wyatt went to his rooms at the Cosmopolitan Hotel. He could not shake a feeling of foreboding, so when he figured the play was over, he walked to the theater. When Morgan emerged, Wyatt said he would escort him back to the hotel. Still fidgety, his younger brother wanted to stay out a little longer and suggested they visit the Campbell & Hatch Saloon and Billiard Parlor.

Wyatt was troubled by the suggestion. "It's just a hunch, Morg, but I want you to come along to the hotel and go to bed."

"I want to have one game of pool with Bob Hatch," Morgan responded. "It won't take that long. Then I'll go to bed."

Reluctantly, Wyatt agreed. They headed to Campbell & Hatch, accompanied by Sherman McMasters and Dan Tipton. The latter had served as a Union sailor during the war and had become an occasional member of Wyatt's most recent search parties.

The three men and others in the establishment looked on as Morgan and Hatch competed at the pool table. At one point, Morgan lined up a shot with his back to the rear of the room, where there was a glass door. To anyone in the alley behind, he would have been easily visible in the well-lit parlor. As Morgan leaned forward, the glass exploded as two bullets were fired from a rifle into the room.

The first bullet struck Morgan, entering his right side and shattering his spinal column. The bullet then exited his body and wounded another man in the room, George Berry, in the leg. The second bullet fired through the back door penetrated the opposite wall, where Wyatt was sitting, missing his head by only a few inches.

There was immediate confusion as others in the parlor dove to the floor and hunched behind chairs. Morgan initially collapsed atop the pool table, then slowly, his right hand weakly reaching for his holstered pistol, slid off it to the floor, his blood and life seeping out of him.

Though exposing themselves to another volley, McMasters and

Hatch ran out the rear door and searched the alley. They returned to report whoever it was had taken off. By then, Wyatt had straightened his younger brother out on the floor . . . and realized that the wound was a mortal one. A call had gone out for a doctor, but no one could save Morgan.

Morgan glanced down at his legs and whispered to Wyatt, "Take my shoes off." After Wyatt did, Morgan's next request was, "Lay me straight."

"You are straight, Morgan," Wyatt replied, "just as straight as you can be."

"Then my back is broken."

Wyatt, helped by Tipton and McMasters, lifted Morgan up and brought him into the adjacent card-playing room and onto a couch. It took him another half hour to die. By then, he was surrounded by Wyatt, James, Warren, and Virgil, who'd had to be helped getting dressed and to leave the hotel. Also there were Bessie and Allie and possibly Mattie. When Doc Holliday was informed, he immediately rushed to the pool hall.

Morgan may have been making one last attempt at humor when he said to the others, "This is the last game of pool I'll ever play."

At the very end, Wyatt promised to find the men who had shot his brother. "That's all I ask," Morgan said. "But Wyatt, be careful." After that last request, Morgan died. The time of death was a few minutes after midnight. The new day was Wyatt's thirty-fourth birthday.

The news spread fast in Tombstone that another Earp had been shot and this time killed. With Morgan's death, any hope of a new and peaceful season faded. "The calm of the last two months was but the precursor of a storm such as we hope will never again visit the camp of Tombstone," lamented Clara Brown.

"Another assassination last night about eleven o'clock," reported George Parsons. "I heard the shots, two in number, but hearing so many after dark was not particularly startled. Poor Morgan Earp was shot through by an unknown party." He added, "Bad time ahead now."

Especially for Wyatt, because of the guilt he felt over not insisting that Morgan return to the hotel and the burden of being the one who would have to pursue the cowardly assassins. As Don Chaput observed in his Virgil Earp biography, "The West became a different place when Morgan Earp died. The famous shootout itself had gotten Tombstone—and the Earps—national notoriety. Now Wyatt would move to a larger stage. Deputy U.S. Marshal Wyatt Earp made a vow to make things right for the Earp family by slaying the men responsible . . . [he] set out on a personal vendetta without parallel in the American West."

He would not have to look far for help. When the chips were down, Doc would be there, and they were sure down now. A tale concocted much later has Doc going on a furious rampage that night, but there is no truth to it. However, "at the very least," writes the Holliday biographer Gary L. Roberts, as Morgan lay dead, "he and Wyatt came to an unspoken agreement. Something had to be done. It was a solution that a man reared on the antebellum Southern code of honor like Doc could appreciate, with the law seemingly impotent, and it likely took no more than a glance at Wyatt to confirm the next step."

First, though, there were family responsibilities to attend to. On Sunday, March 19, with Doc and members of the posse who had often doubled as bodyguards in recent weeks, Wyatt traveled to Contention with Morgan's body. One can only wonder if the turnout would have been anything like that of the previous October, for the funeral of Frank and Tom McLaury and Billy Clanton, had it been decided to bury Morgan in Tombstone. The coffin was placed on a train, and James Earp accompanied it to Colton, California, where Nicholas and Virginia would bury their son. Mercifully, Louisa had not been present to witness her husband's death, small comfort that it was.

Wyatt was saying a lot of good-byes lately. That day of his thirty-fourth birthday it was to James and his slain brother, Morgan. The previous month, much more discreetly, he had said good-bye to Josephine Marcus. Any hope of deepening the relationship between them had vanished. In February, she had quit Tombstone and returned to live with her parents in San Francisco. Wyatt would do what he had to do and then, with luck, go and find Josephine there.

This did not mean that Mattie once again had Wyatt all to herself. On March 24, she and Bessie would leave Tombstone. With Wyatt and Warren the only Earp brothers left there, and their lives being in jeopardy, it was thought best for those two remaining Earp wives to be sent to the expanding family compound in Colton. Mattie, too, would wait in California until Wyatt's business was completed.

Wyatt's "business" was now more urgent than ever—find those who had ambushed Virgil and then Morgan, not only to bring them to justice but before there was another ambush. He would likely be the prime target, but Wyatt had been targeted by gunmen before. He was more concerned about the family members remaining in Tombstone. The most vulnerable was Virgil. Though still weak from his wounds, he was alive, and that could prove irresistible to those who recalled he was in charge the previous October when the shoot-out took place. Allie stood guard night and day, but she was no gunman.

Two days after Morgan and James were sent west, Wyatt and his party were again on their way to a train station, this time the one in Benson. The plan was to put Virgil and Allie on the next train there so that they, too, would be safe in Colton. However, sometime along the way Wyatt received disturbing information: Ike Clanton, Frank Stilwell, and at least two cowboys were in Tucson, keeping watch as trains pulled in from Benson. There could be little doubt that another ambush was in the works for when Virgil and Allie were in Tucson for a brief layover.

Wyatt told his posse that he and Warren would get on the train at Benson and take it to Tucson to guard his brother and Allie. Not hesitating, Doc Holliday and the others climbed on the train right behind him.

When it came to a stop at the Tucson station, Doc was the first man off the train, and he held two shotguns. Waiting to greet him and the others was J. W. Evans, like Virgil and Wyatt a deputy U.S. marshal. After a short conversation with him, Doc, probably with some reluctance, checked the shotguns at the railroad station. Across the tracks was Porter's Hotel, and the Earp entourage went there for dinner. So far so good—no sign of cowboy assassins, and another federal marshal was providing a pair of eyes.

After eating and with the train soon to depart, Wyatt and the others escorted Virgil and Allie to the train. They paused only for a minute to talk to Evans, and Sherman McMasters, at Doc's request, retrieved the shotguns. After Wyatt made sure that Virgil and Allie were seated as comfortably as possible, a passenger mentioned that he had seen two men lying on a flatcar near the engine. When Wyatt looked, he spotted Stilwell and Clanton. Clearly, they were waiting until the train pulled out and then they would find Virgil and finish what one or both of them had begun in December.

Wyatt, now carrying one of the shotguns, got off the train and walked toward the flatcar. The two men jumped off it and began running. Wyatt took off in pursuit. Behind him were Doc, Warren, McMasters, and Turkey Creek Jack. The strides of Wyatt's long legs closed the gap between him and Stilwell, who began to stumble. Ike kept running. Thus far, when confronted by the Earps, Clanton had demonstrated world-class speed.

Once more, Ike escaped. Wyatt, at least, was able to catch up to Stilwell. "He couldn't shoot when I came near him," Wyatt recalled. "He stood there helpless and trembling for his life." Stilwell grabbed the barrels of the shotgun, causing Wyatt to jerk the triggers. The outlaw was killed instantly.

However, the more likely and supported scenario was more complicated. In all likelihood Stilwell died when Wyatt fired the shotgun, perhaps inadvertently. But witnesses later reported hearing more gunshots. The way George Parsons heard it the next day in Tombstone, Stilwell's body was "riddled with bullets and buckshot." The clear implication is that the entire Earp group had made sure Stilwell had breathed his last and paid in full for Morgan's murder.

On the train, Virgil and Allie had heard the gunshots. Because the former marshal was still hurting, Allie wore his gun belt around her waist. She would have sat close to Virgil anyway, but in this instance she did so to give him easy access to his pistol should there be a last-minute attack. But the only person they spied approaching the train was Wyatt emerging out of the darkness. They saw him hold up a finger and mouth, "One for Morgan," as the train left the station.

That night, Wyatt and Doc and the others walked to the Papago

Station, where they eventually boarded a freight train that took them to Benson. They retrieved their horses and rode to Tombstone.

Stilwell's cold and bullet-riddled body was not discovered until after sunup. While gunshots had been heard the night before, in a remarkable coincidence, that night for the first time Tucson was putting gas streetlights into operation, and it was assumed the shots were part of the celebration. When railroad workers found Stilwell, they saw someone who had indeed been shot multiple times, including a close-range shotgun blast. A saloonkeeper named George Hand, after catching a glimpse of the body, commented that Stilwell "was shot all over, the worst shot-up man I ever saw."

When word reached Tombstone, there was shock at the killing, but the victim did not elicit much sympathy. "A quick vengeance, and a bad character sent to Hell, where he will be the chief attraction until a few more accompany him," George Parsons recorded in his journal.

It would not have been difficult to make a case that Stilwell's presence in Tucson and his skulking around the train station, especially in the company of Ike Clanton, indicated he was part of another attack planned against the Earp family—Virgil, with Wyatt next on the list.*

If this had been the end of the violence, Wyatt and his accomplices would probably have escaped any legal retribution because he

---

* Earp detractors pointed out that Stilwell did have a legitimate reason to be in Tucson, which was to appear in court on robbery charges. And Clanton was supposed to be a witness in a murder trial. However, this does not explain why two enemies of the family were together at the train station that evening when the Earps arrived.

had avenged a brother's death, one obviously committed by cowards who had shot Morgan in the back.* Even as "advanced" as the justice system was on the frontier in 1882, such a motive was very persuasive.

"I repeat, and bear witness that it was not the Earps who first disturbed the quiet," Clara Brown insisted to her San Diego readers, "and that their criminal actions since have been from the determination to avenge the murder of a dearly beloved brother."

On the other hand, the headline above the story in the *Tombstone Daily Nugget* about the Tucson shooting was, COWARDLY AND BRUTAL ASSASSINATION OF FRANK STILWELL. It was also possible that once ensnared in the legal system, Wyatt, along with his brother Warren and Doc, might never get out.

Further proof of that arrived shortly: Wyatt, Doc, Warren, McMasters, and Johnson were wanted for murder, and it was Sheriff Johnny Behan's job to arrest them.

---

* In August 1876, even though he had snuck up on him and shot him in the back of the head, Jack McCall was acquitted of murdering Wild Bill Hickok in Deadwood after claiming Hickok, while marshal of Abilene, Kansas, several years earlier, had killed his brother. Only later was it learned that McCall never had a brother.

Chapter Twenty-Eight

"A BLOODY, WRETCHED BUSINESS"

It was a coroner's inquest in Tucson that had resulted in the new arrest warrants for Wyatt and Warren Earp, Doc Holliday, Sherman McMasters, and Turkey Creek Jack Johnson. If these men had remained in Tucson, it would be the responsibility of the Pima County sheriff, Bob Paul, to arrest them. But because they had left, a telegram was sent to the Cochise County sheriff to be on the lookout for the fugitives. The avengers had become the hunted.

There had been another coroner's inquest, and this one had a more direct impact on Tombstone—the investigation into the murder of Morgan Earp. The star witness turned out to be Marietta Spence. Stuck in a marriage in which she often served as a punching bag, she was not reluctant to reveal damaging details about her husband.

Under questioning, she stated that the men who shot and killed Morgan Earp were her husband, Pete, Frank Stilwell, Frederick Bode (another cowboy), and two men she identified as Indians, one of whom was named "Charlie." He was believed to be Florentino Cruz,

328 ★ TOM CLAVIN

a veteran of local cattle rustling and related illegal activities. According to Marietta Spence, the previous week she and her mother were standing outside their house chatting with Pete Spence and Indian Charlie. When Morgan walked by, Pete nudged Charlie and said, "That's him."

Then on the night of Saturday, March 18, Marietta testified, she and her mother were inside the home when they heard gunshots. Soon after, the house was filled with Pete Spence, Charlie, Stilwell, Bode, and the other "Indian." They were very excited about something that had happened, and her husband warned her that if she said anything to anybody about that night, he would kill her and, adding insult to injury, dump her body in some remote location on his way to Sonora. For good measure, he would shoot her mother, too.

The prospect of having her corpse ravaged by wild animals did not have the effect her husband desired. "Spence didn't tell me so," Marietta declared, "but I know he killed Morgan Earp."

The Tombstone inquest concluded that the five men had conspired to murder Morgan Earp and carried out the execution. Learning of the results when back in Tombstone, Wyatt now officially knew whom to track down. Frank Stilwell, of course, had already met rough justice. It was time for the others to meet a similar fate.

However, there was that telegram sent from Tucson by Justice of the Peace Charles Meyer instructing Johnny Behan to locate and arrest Wyatt Earp and Doc Holliday and their co-conspirators. If citizens of Tombstone knew of the telegram, they could have expected a confrontation that afternoon that might have been more violent than the one in October. The Earp party was back from Tucson, so it remained to be seen how quickly the sheriff and his deputies acted and how many cowboys would provide eager assistance.

But for several hours after the telegram arrived, the only man who knew of its contents was the telegraph office manager. It was not completely true that in the aftermath of the October gunfight, and especially after Morgan's murder, the Earps had little support in Tombstone. It was true that the cowboys and their bullhorn, the *Tombstone Daily Nugget*, were the noisiest in their antipathy toward the Earp brothers. Wyatt, Doc, and the others had mostly kept their heads down and did what they thought they had to do. And so, too, did their many remaining friends in the city. One of them was the telegraph office manager, who believed that delaying the delivery offered Wyatt and his crew the opportunity to leave town before the sheriff sought them out.

However, when Behan was finally given the telegram from Judge Meyer early that evening, Wyatt and his men were still in Tombstone. They were leaving the Cosmopolitan Hotel, well armed and ready to ride. Hearing of this, the sheriff hurried to the hotel. As Wyatt exited and strode toward his horse, Behan told him that he wanted to see him. Wyatt replied, "Johnny, if you're not careful, you'll see me once too often." He added that if he were going to surrender to anyone, it would be the Pima County sheriff and friend Bob Paul . . . but he was not going to wait around for Paul to arrive.

Behan backed off. To be fair, he was overwhelmingly outmanned and outgunned. He had sent word for his deputy Billy Breakenridge and the new police chief, David Neagle, to grab guns and come back him up, but they had not yet arrived. Wyatt got onto his horse, and he and his men left Tombstone. The sheriff had been publicly humiliated. What he did next only made it worse for him.

"Behan claims that they resisted arrest, but the bystanders claim that this was all that passed, and nothing was said about an arrest," reported Clara Brown. "He also asserts that every one of the party drew their guns on him, which is denied by the spectators."

Even the pro-cowboy *Daily Nugget* found Behan's behavior hard to swallow, offering that "it is possible [Behan] was a little hasty or over confident in the authority vested in him."

The night of Tuesday, March 21, the Earp party camped at Watervale, just three miles west of Tombstone. Given such proximity, at any time Behan could have gathered his deputies and any available cowboys and gone to arrest Wyatt and Doc. He did go so far as to form a posse. It consisted mostly of cowboys, some of whom had warrants out on them and had more reason to be in jail than Wyatt and Doc, including Johnny Ringo. But the posse did not venture out of Tombstone.

Wyatt and the members of his posse knew that Pete Spence had a wood camp in the South Pass of the Dragoon Mountains, so the next morning they rode to it. Upon arriving, Wyatt asked about Spence's whereabouts. A teamster, Theodore Judah, told him Spence was not there. The next query was about Indian Charlie. Wyatt was given the same answer. He grew more frustrated when Judah, who was offering the truth as he knew it, could not tell him when Spence would return.*

Wyatt was not done with the camp just yet. He scanned the Mexican laborers there, asking questions about spotting any saddled, riderless horses at the camp that would indicate someone

---

* Only afterward did Wyatt learn that a terrified Spence, having heard of Frank Stilwell's grisly death, had presented himself to Behan and was in the Tombstone jail under the protection of the sheriff.

hiding. Wyatt was met with shrugs. The posse began to leave the camp, but they did not go far before encountering Florentino Cruz, otherwise known as Indian Charlie. Judah and one of the laborers had begun to follow, and as he later testified, "We had not gone 20 feet, before we heard shooting."

It was at this moment that Wyatt's pursuit of those who had shot his brothers truly became a vendetta ride from Hell.* One could argue that this transition had already taken place, in Tucson with the killing of Frank Stilwell, especially the brutal manner of it. However, Wyatt and Doc and the others had not gone to that train station to kill anyone, they had gone to protect Virgil from assassination. And when Stilwell and Ike Clanton were discovered on that flatcar, preparing for an ambush, they had weapons and clearly planned to use them. Yes, when Wyatt caught up to Stilwell and Ike had disappeared, he could have arrested the former and hauled him back to Tombstone for trial. But Wyatt had seen how ineffectual the judicial system had become with the cowboys as defendants. Or, possibly, this was one of the few instances— such as his beating of Tom McLaury—when emotions got the better of him.

When Wyatt spotted him, Florentino Cruz was unarmed. And he was running away. Deputy U.S. Marshal Earp did not pause to think that a terrified Cruz, surrounded by weapons, might have been only too happy to reveal details and accomplices in the shoot-

---

* It has been attributed to Wyatt Earp that at the Tucson train station he declared, "Tell 'em the law's coming. You tell 'em I'm coming, and hell's coming with me." If only he had been that loquacious. The declaration is found only in the screenplay of the 1993 feature film *Tombstone*, written by Kevin Jarre and with Kurt Russell portraying Wyatt.

ings of Virgil and Morgan. Instead, Wyatt's blood was up and the fleeing man was in the gunsights of an avenging brother.

Believing that bullets would be coming at him at any moment, Cruz was described by one of the wood camp workers as running erratically and "jumping from side to side." There was a burst of gunfire. Judah and other observers saw him fall, and moments later the posse rode off. When Cruz's body was found lying facedown, camp workers discovered he had been shot four times.

There was no doubt that being in Behan's custody saved Pete Spence's life. That same day, sheriff's deputies encountered and arrested Frederick Bode and Hank Swilling, the latter believed to be the other "Indian" cited by Marietta Spence. They were only too happy to stretch out inside a jail cell instead of a grave.

Now calling the federal marshal's mission "the Earp vendetta," newspapers around the United States provided their wide-eyed readers with daily updates. Generally, the pursuit was pilloried, though the cowboys were regarded as hooligans and outlaws. The *San Francisco Daily Exchange* went so far as to intone, "When the cowboys and Earps meet a sanguinary conflict is inevitable. It may fortunately happen that the slaughter on both sides will leave but a few survivors, and a big funeral, with the Earps and cowboys to furnish the remains." That, the newspaper predicted, "would be the lifting of a great weight from the minds of the citizens of Tombstone."

On Thursday, the day after the killing of Cruz, two members of the vendetta posse, Dan Tipton and Harelip Charlie, were back in Tombstone. The hope was that the Earp-friendly businessman E. B. Gage would give or at least advance Wyatt $1,000 for food and supplies for the posse, and he would be repaid when the Wells

Fargo money arrived. And while they were in town, try to glean what Johnny Behan was up to.

Unfortunately for Wyatt's mission, the sheriff was up to arresting Tipton and Smith for having resisted his attempt to arrest them outside the Cosmopolitan Hotel. Behan may not have been lawman enough to try to put Wyatt behind bars, or Doc Holliday, but two followers were a different story. Before nightfall, after a judge threw the case out, Tipton and Smith were back on the dusty street, but Gage had stayed clear of them.

Curiously absent from the events of the past week was Curly Bill Brocius. The reason was probably that he was wanted for stealing cattle and did not want to be seen in Tombstone. But Brocius was about to be back onstage. Somehow, a desperate Behan deputized Curly Bill to go find Wyatt and his posse. He had proved effective as a tax collector, maybe Brocius could be the lawman Behan was not. He collected a band of cowboys who eagerly interpreted the arrest warrant as dead or alive, and they went off to pick up Wyatt's trail.

It did not take long at all to find it. The confrontation between Wyatt Earp and Curly Bill Brocius, building for a year, was finally about to happen.

On the morning of Friday, March 24, Wyatt's posse stopped for breakfast north of Contention, near the San Pedro River. Their next destinations were the ranches along the Babocomari River, along the way keeping their eyes peeled for cowboys, especially ones who may have been involved in or have knowledge of one or both Earp shootings. Another part of that morning's mission was to meet with Harelip Charlie and Dan Tipton at Iron Springs in the Whetstone Mountains about twenty miles west of Tombstone.

The belief was they would have the money Wyatt had sent them to get.

The search along the river produced no results. Unless the cowboys could put together a strong force, they did not want to take on the two remaining Earp brothers, Doc Holliday, and their gunmen out in the open. However, predictably, an ambush was more to their liking—one organized by Curly Bill.

Wyatt and Doc had to have wondered what Brocius's role had been in recent events. He had not been mentioned by Marietta Spence as participating in Morgan's assassination and was otherwise keeping a very low profile. That coupled with the uneventful search along the river meant the Earp posse was not as vigilant as it should have been. Wyatt, for one, had even loosened his gun belt to ride with a little less discomfort. He hoped his men were waiting at Iron Springs with the $1,000. Instead, that was where Curly Bill and his cowboys had set up.

The posse approached with Wyatt and Texas Jack in the lead. Suddenly, the air was full of bullets and Wyatt counted nine cowboys firing six-guns. Texas Jack's horse was shot out from under him and he was trapped beneath it. Wyatt jumped off his horse and yanked out his shotgun. Bullets tore holes in his coat, but he was not hit. Doc Holliday and the others scattered, scrambling for cover.

Wyatt recognized Curly Bill in the forefront of the ambush, and he let loose with the shotgun. Brocius was hit full in the chest and nearly torn in half, dying instantly.

But the other cowboys kept up a steady fire, though one of them, Johnny Barnes, was wounded. Embarrassingly, Wyatt's gun belt had slipped down off his hips to his thighs and he could not climb back up onto his petrified horse. As he struggled to tug the gun belt back up, more bullets tore through his coat, one struck his boot, and the shoehorn on his saddle was blown away, making it even more difficult to remount.

Wyatt finally did, though. Given that he was now even more of a clear target, it was astonishing that he was not shot. Back in the saddle, instead of taking off, Wyatt reached down and helped Texas Jack get out from under his horse. When both men were out of the line of fire, Doc and the others opened up with shotguns and rifles.

Assisting Wyatt out of the saddle, Doc said, "You must be all shot to pieces," then he and the others were shocked that the only injuries were a shredded coat and a missing shoehorn and boot heel.

"Let's mount up and go at them," Doc suggested.

Wyatt was not keen on that, just having come close enough to ending up like Curly Bill. "If you fellows are hungry for a fight," he said, "you can go on and get your fill." The rest of the posse chose to stay where they were.

"Our escape was miraculous," Doc would recall. "I think we would have been killed if God Almighty wasn't on our side."

One can only speculate what happened to the corpse of Curly Bill. It was never found. His bloody and bedraggled body could have been left at Iron Springs when the cowboys left and animals took care of it. Or his remains may have been taken by the others to be buried somewhere, apparently in an unmarked grave. Some citizens believe that Curly Bill had not been killed at all, although *The Tombstone Epitaph* stated emphatically that he was "as dead as two loads of buckshot can make him." That the attention-loving, rampaging Curly Bill Brocius was never heard from again anywhere leads to only one conclusion.

With news about the Earp posse escaping an ambush, it was

time for the sheriff to stop sitting around Tombstone and ride after the men many residents in Cochise County considered outlaws. With the prevalence of that perception, Johnny Behan had no trouble adding more men to those who had already volunteered, including Ike and Phin Clanton. From their point of view, a successful outcome for this posse was sweeping the Earps and Doc off the Arizona map. With them out of the way—preferably dead, but otherwise behind bars indefinitely—the Clantons, Johnny Ringo, and the cowboys faced no real opposition.* They would have their way in Cochise County. Behan would be reelected the following November, thanks to having led this posse on a successful mission. Also for the Clantons, of course, there was the satisfaction of avenging their brother Billy.

The next day, Saturday, Harelip Charlie returned to Wyatt and the posse, but he had been unable to meet with Gage and thus had empty pockets. At least he was another loaded gun. They camped that night close enough to Tombstone that they could see the lit lamps of the city and the light of the saloons streaming out into the streets. Wyatt considered trying to work his way into town under the cover of darkness to meet with Gage, but there were too many riders about. No sense making life any easier for Johnny Behan.

Charlie Smith had brought back with him news of the rogues who passed for deputies in the sheriff's posse. These men had every reason to want Wyatt Earp and Doc Holliday dead. In his version of events, Billy Breakenridge wrote that his boss "took those men knowing that the Earp party would resist arrest" and that Behan "believed the cowboys would stay and fight."

---

* An added benefit for Ringo was that with the death of Curly Bill he was now the undisputed cowboy leader.

By this time, Bob Paul had arrived in Tombstone, and the sheriff invited his Pima County counterpart to come aboard. Paul refused. He saw Behan's posse as something like a lynch mob. The *Arizona Daily Star* explained that Paul could not accompany the deputized cowboys "inasmuch as they are most all hostile to the Earps and a meeting simply meant bloodshed." With twenty-five men in the Behan posse, the Earp party could well be wiped out.

Referring to "Excitement again," George Parsons recorded in his journal, "Sheriff went out with a posse supposedly to arrest Earp party, but they will never do it. There is a prospect of a bad time. Terrible thing, this, for our town, but the sooner it is all over the better." He added: "Went to church tonight."

About Wyatt and Warren Earp, Clara Brown wrote, "They are evidently determined to wreak their vengeance on all who were implicated in the murder of their brother." Not that they were viewed as honorable avengers: "Divided as the sentiment of the place has always been, there are many now who denounce the Earps in the strongest language, and look upon the murder of Morgan and the attempted assassination of Virgil and Wyatt as 'good enough for them.' It is a bloody, wretched business throughout, which every peaceable, honest citizen must deplore."

And it was not yet finished. The next morning, Behan and his two dozen men left Tombstone on what was expected to be a collision course with Wyatt, Doc, and the other vendetta riders.

Wyatt had not waited around. He and his men had already been on the move when the sheriff and the cowboys mounted up. Turning in the saddle, Wyatt watched Tombstone recede from view. What he did not know was that it would be the last time he would see the city that would forever be linked to his name.

Chapter Twenty-Nine

"MURDERERS AND OUTLAWS"

The death of a man Wyatt Earp and Doc Holliday may not have known worked to their advantage by making it seem that the ride for revenge they were leading was less a vigilante effort and more a law-enforcement mission.

Martin Peel was murdered on the night of Saturday, March 25, while at the Tombstone Milling and Mining Company, which was near Charleston. For unknown reasons, there had been a confrontation with a group of cowboys, and two of them, Zwing Hunt and Billy Grounds, had shot Peel. The victim's father happened to be Judge Bryant Peel. The killing of a judge's son was enough to draw more unwanted attention to the cowboys and their continued lawlessness, but Judge Peel rubbed readers' noses in it with a letter published in *The Tombstone Epitaph*. "There is a class of cut-throats among you and you can never convict them in court," the letter stated. "You must combine and protect yourselves and wipe them out, or you must give up the country to them, or you will be murdered one at a time, as my son has been."

George Parsons speculated that the Peel murder was "an attempt at theft, and perhaps simply thirst for gore on account of the company against the outlaw element. Now that it has come to killing of upright, respectable, thoroughly law abiding citizens—all are aroused and the question is now, who are the next."

Only one day after Peel was gunned down, Clara Brown wrote that "it was not the Earps who first disturbed this quiet . . . there are certainly extenuating circumstances to take into consideration."

And two days after the Peel murder, the new governor, Frederick Tritle, arrived in Tombstone. Before his appointment by the Chester A. Arthur administration, Tritle had been the law partner of William Murray, who was head of the pro-Earp Citizens Safety Committee. While in Tombstone—staying with Milton Clapp of the Safford, Hanford & Co. Bank, who was helping to fund the Earp posse—the governor was given an earful by Murray and others with similar sympathies.

One result was a telegram Tritle sent to President Arthur in which he declared that "business is paralyzed and the fairest valleys in the territory are kept from occupation by the presence of the cowboys." A second immediate result was the formation of yet another posse.

Clearly having no faith in Johnny Behan as a lawman, this new posse would be headed by John Jackson, who was a deputy U.S. marshal, as Wyatt still was. Its mandate was to capture cowboy outlaws, which could even include members of the sheriff's posse, who were more intent on the continuing chase of Wyatt and his men than the killers of Martin Peel.* Jackson picked his posse and off they rode.

---

* On March 29, upon the orders of (acting) Sheriff E. M. Harley, Deputy Sheriffs Billy Breakenridge and John Gillespie rode to Chandler's Milk Ranch, where it was believed that Hunt and Grounds were hiding. This turned out to be true. In

Wyatt and Doc and their posse were wandering a bit. They did not know for sure where the next cowboy suspected in Morgan's death was, but with a sheriff's posse after them they could not sit around and wait for information. They had probably heard of some of the "cut-throats" in it and had to think that, especially with the ineffectual Behan in charge, they would shoot first and think about the law later. Not that it mattered: Wyatt was not about to let himself be arrested under any circumstances.

The rest of the posse might not have been so keen on being killed rather than arrested, but Wyatt knew Doc Holliday was in his corner no matter what, and probably his brother Warren, though he had little to no experience in such matters. Doc had to wonder, though, how far the vendetta ride would go. This was not the same Wyatt he had known from Dodge City days. "Doc saw the changes in his friend," writes Gary L. Roberts. "Nothing in Wyatt Earp's life, before the vendetta or after it, ever hinted that he was homicidal by nature. The vendetta was the great anomaly in a life as devoid of vigilantism as it was of murder." Wyatt "took the law into his own hands because he believed the law had failed. He believed that the legal system was so corrupt and impotent that he had no other way to keep his promise to his brother but to go after Morgan's killers himself."

Now, Frank Stilwell, Florentino Cruz, and Curly Bill Brocius were dead. There had to be others involved with Morgan's murder, plus those who had gone unpunished for Virgil's near-fatal ambush. There was no choice but to push on, and it was to the north they rode. In addition to Doc and Warren, Wyatt's party included

---

the ensuing gun battle, Grounds and Gillespie were killed and Breakenridge arrested a wounded Hunt.

Harelip Charlie, Texas Jack, and Turkey Creek Jack. Sherman Mc-Masters had been wounded in the fight with Curly Bill and his cowboys—not seriously, but enough to sideline him for a bit.

On Saturday, having left Tombstone behind and the day Peel was murdered, the posse entered the Dragoon Mountains, where they stopped and boarded a train. The hope was that a messenger sent by E. P. Gage was on board, carrying the $1,000 promised to Wyatt to underwrite the ongoing search. However, there was no such person. The posse continued to a ranch owned by two brothers, Hugh and Jim Percy.

Here was another instance where hospitality prevailed. The Percys feared that the cowboys might come after them for harboring Wyatt and Doc and their men, but they could not be turned away. The brothers also feared gunplay: two men they were already hosting overnight were Barney Riggs and Frank Hereford, and the latter was a deputy sheriff. However, wisely choosing not to try being a hero, Hereford, with Riggs right behind him, raced into the corncrib and hid from the posse through the night. The Percys fed the posse and the men slept there, though they left at three o'clock on Sunday morning, March 26, to reduce the risk to the Percys of being seen there.

The next place to shelter the posse was the ranch of Henry Clay Hooker. For the fifty-four-year-old owner, southeast Arizona had turned out to be a land of fulfilled promise. Born in New Hampshire, Hooker had lived in New York City and Kansas City before joining thousands of other young men in the California Gold Rush. He founded and operated a successful mercantile business in California until fire destroyed it along with much of Hangtown. Hooker and his wife and three children were left with $1,000.

He put it to use in an extraordinary but smart scheme. He bought five hundred turkeys, and with two dogs to keep the herd in formation, he drove them over the Sierra Nevada to Carson City, Nevada, near the Comstock Lode and sold them for $2.50 a head. Hooker turned his profit into ten thousand longhorns and drove that herd up from Texas. Along the way, in 1872, he found Sulphur Springs Valley and realized it was perfect for raising his own cattle. He established the Sierra Bonita Ranch there, about thirty miles from what would become Tombstone, and as he acquired more land and cows—over 40,000 of them—Hooker became known as the Cattle King of Arizona.* He would die on his ranch in 1907, a month before his eightieth birthday.

On that Monday, March 27, the posse led by Wyatt and Doc arrived at the Sierra Bonita Ranch. As part of his report about recent events, Wyatt told about the grisly death of Curly Bill, to which Henry Hooker replied, "Good work, Wyatt." Hooker had no concerns about cowboys or lawmen knowing of the posse's presence at his ranch, and they were welcome to stay as long as they liked. This was probably an appealing invitation, given how long the posse had been on dusty trails. But there was still unfinished business. Instead, Wyatt asked to buy fresh horses. These were provided, but Hooker refused any money.

The posse enjoyed more of Hooker's generosity by way of a big meal, during which Wyatt allowed himself some alcohol. They would ride the next day, resuming the search for outlaws.

---

* As the Hooker operation expanded, one of his ranch hands was seventeen-year-old William Bonney. He did not remain employed there long, and shortly afterward, at a saloon near Fort Grant, Billy the Kid killed his first man.

But that next day, Tuesday, was when Sheriff Johnny Behan's posse caught up with the Earp posse. Or almost did.

Hooker's offer to stay must have been tough for Wyatt to reject. His host employed loyal ranch hands and had a defendable main house and plenty of supplies and ammunition. Clearly, the Behan posse had the Earp one outmanned and outgunned, so the Hooker ranch would reduce that disadvantage. If the sheriff wanted to make a fight, do it now and get him and his cutthroat cowboys out of the way. Wyatt, if he survived, and whoever survived with him, could then complete the vendetta ride without further interference.

But this was not Henry Hooker's vendetta, it was Wyatt Earp's. It was finally time for him and Johnny Behan to have it out. So late that afternoon of March 27, Wyatt, Doc, Warren, Dan Tipton, Harelip Charlie, Turkey Creek Jack, and Texas Jack left the Hooker compound and rode up into the hills. After three miles and while there was still enough light, Wyatt selected a bluff that offered expansive views and a defensible high ground. Seven men were still not enough, but height would shorten the odds considerably. The posse camped on that bluff overnight, no doubt checking and rechecking their pistols and rifles and ammunition.

The next morning, Behan led his men to the Hooker compound, where the owner greeted him. What transpired was reported in *The Tombstone Epitaph* based on an account provided by one of the ranch hands. It is worth noting that the deputy Harry Woods rode with Behan, yet a similar article did not appear in the *Tombstone Daily Nugget,* the anti-Earp newspaper he once edited.

Following frontier custom, Hooker offered to feed the men and their horses . . . but that was as far as his hospitality went. When the sheriff asked where the Earp posse had gone, Hooker said he did not know. "And if I did, I would not tell you," he added.

An affronted Behan said, "Then you must be upholding murderers and outlaws."

"No, sir, I am not," responded Hooker. "I know the Earps and I know you and I know they have always treated me like a gentleman. Damn such laws and damn you and damn your posse. They are a set of horse thieves and outlaws."

From behind Behan, a posse member called out, "Damn the son of a bitch. He knows where they are and let us make him tell."

The ranch foreman, Billy Whelen, joined his employer in confronting the posse, holding a Winchester rifle. "You can't come here into a gentleman's yard and call him a son of a bitch," Whelen declared. "Now you skin it back. If you are looking for a fight and talk that way, you can get it right here before you find the Earps."

To the sheriff, Hooker observed, "These are a pretty set of fellows you have got with you, a set of horse thieves and cutthroats." His gaze lingered a little longer on Ike and Phin Clanton and Johnny Ringo.

Behan claimed that these men were not friends and frequent riders. Accordingly, when Hooker fed them, he had one table for the sheriff and his deputies and separate tables for the Clantons and the cowboys. During the meal, Behan explained, "If I can catch the Earp party it will help me at the next election," a strange reason to give Hooker to gain his cooperation. And it did not come close to working.

When the meal was over, Behan and his posse mounted up and, after some deliberation, rode back the way they had come. As Hooker would later put it, Johnny and his men "were willing to ride in any direction in Arizona except where the Earps were waiting for them."

Though his posse far outnumbered Wyatt's, Behan set off to get help. He and his men rode to Fort Grant and asked the commander there to loan him Indian scouts. He even offered $500 to pay for them. Colonel James Biddle, however, refused. If Henry Hooker had chosen not to aid the sheriff, the U.S. Army would also mind its own business.

After watching the tiny figures of the posse ride away, Wyatt and his men spent the rest of the day and night preparing for the fight they expected to commence when Johnny Behan returned. The next morning, the sheriff did. Again, he and his men entered the Hooker compound. Again, the ranch owner greeted Behan, though even less cordially than the day before. Plus, what else could he tell the sheriff? It was now Behan's play.

What differed this time is that Henry Hooker did tell Behan where he believed the Earp posse was. Having sized the sheriff up and knowing his recent history as a lawman, and seeing the sketchy composition of his posse, Hooker figured they would be no match for a well-armed and entrenched Earp party. If there was to be a showdown, now was a good time for it.

The sheriff was not so sure. Instead of leading his men toward the hills, he complained that his pursuit of the Earp party, now in its second week, was costing a lot of money. He might have to disband the posse rather than have the taxpayers of Cochise County be further burdened by it. Hooker was nonplussed: Was the sheriff looking for financial help? Whatever Behan hoped to achieve, he did not get it. Once more the posse rode away—again, not in the direction of the Earp brothers, Doc, and their men. They moseyed around in the valley for a couple of hours, pretending they had no idea where the Earp posse was, then traveled back to Tombstone, having done nothing more than add to the taxpayers' tab.

Wyatt now understood there would be no confrontation. Johnny

Behan simply did not have the stomach for one. Wyatt and Doc led their men back down out of the hills to the Hooker compound. There they rested, with no one expecting to see the dust of a couple dozen approaching horses. A horse that did approach bore Dan Tipton, who had been sent into Tombstone to try again for the $1,000 collected by Gage. This time he had been successful. Another rider who arrived during that week's respite was Lou Cooley, a Tombstone stagecoach driver. He carried with him another $1,000, donated by Wells Fargo.

"All things considered, it was a remarkable moment," Gary L. Roberts writes about the sudden infusion of funds. "While Earp and his riders were enjoying the hospitality of one of Arizona's most prominent ranchers, he received money from one of Tombstone's leading mining men and from Wells Fargo. Such a dramatic demonstration of the establishment's support of Earp and his mission was striking."

The posse was still at the Hooker ranch on April 4 when Doc Holliday put pen to paper. The letter would be published in *The Tombstone Epitaph*. Filled with sardonic language—such as a frugal meal "we ate with relish" and being "cheerfully furnished" with the best a freighter's camp had to offer—it was Doc's account of the Earp party's adventures during the last week in March. He refers to "Sheriff Behan and his posse of honest ranchers," and Doc claims his posse was hot on the trail of outlaws. "We are confident that our trailing abilities will soon enable us to turn over to these 'gentlemen' the fruit of our efforts, so they may not again return to Tombstone empty-handed." Doc signed the letter, "One of Them."

This document turned out to be the last salvo in the Earp vendetta. The posse checked and rechecked various locations but found no more suspects in the attacks on Virgil and Morgan, and Behan stuck close to Tombstone. There was even a fourth posse formed, this one by Jack Stilwell, another one of Frank's brothers, who had earned a good reputation as an army scout. He recruited former members of Behan's posse, including Ike Clanton and Johnny Ringo, and they spent a few listless days trying to find the Earp posse. With no promising results, the Stilwell posse disbanded, and some of the cowboys, finding Cochise County increasingly unfriendly and not wanting to encounter Wyatt and Doc, sought their futures in Mexico.

The city and its surroundings were moving on. "Killing business over for the present," noted George Parsons, adding that the news occupying everyone's attention now was the arrival on April 7 of General William Tecumseh Sherman, as part of an inspection tour of the Department of Arizona. There would be no more matters involving the Earp posse to report as the month progressed.

Probably there would have been, though, if Wyatt Earp and Doc Holliday had returned to Tombstone. But for both of them, the city that once promised much was no longer a place in which to live and try to prosper. For Wyatt, it would be too sad to continue where one brother had been crippled and another murdered. No family members remained in Tombstone. Mattie waited for him in Colton and perhaps Josephine in San Francisco. For Doc Holliday, if Wyatt Earp was moving on, so would he.

There would actually be two more casualties of the Earp vendetta ride. First, though, the posse had to disband. Wyatt had previously let Bob Paul know that he would either surrender to him or leave the state. Choosing the latter, the posse left Arizona and on April 15 it arrived in Silver City, New Mexico. The local newspaper noted their arrival and that they "were all well mounted and armed to the teeth." The next day, Harelip Charlie decided to return to Arizona, but Wyatt, Doc, Texas Jack, Turkey Creek Jack, a returned Sherman McMasters, and Dan Tipton sold their horses and boarded a train for Albuquerque.

The riderless posse remained there for two weeks in a sort of limbo state, and then it was decided that Colorado would be the next destination. Right before leaving, though, came the next casualty—the tried-and-true friendship of Wyatt Earp and Doc Holliday. There have been varying accounts of what happened, but the one with the most credence is that an argument occurred when Wyatt and Doc were having dinner at an eatery called Fat Charlie's. Wyatt probably mentioned something about going to find Josephine in San Francisco. Perhaps Doc had met her in Tombstone and disliked her or was taking Mattie's side,* but in any case Doc called Wyatt "a damn Jew boy." Wyatt, furious, left the saloon.

Doc and Dan Tipton took a train to Trinidad, Colorado. That would allow for a return to gambling and some cooling off. Probably, Doc had no idea that this absence from Wyatt would last years. McMasters and Turkey Jack soon left Albuquerque, too, probably to find a steadier and safer form of employment. The Earp party was down to Wyatt, his brother, and Texas Jack.

As Wyatt told an Albuquerque newspaper—which had to promise it would not publish the interview until after he had left town—the purpose of the posse's stay was to await a pardon from

---

* Armchair psychologists might point out that the supposed love of Doc's life back in Georgia was his cousin Martha Anne Holliday, who had been called Mattie. After Doc went west, she entered a convent and became Sister Mary Melanie. There was a Holliday family connection to the author Margaret Mitchell, who based the character Melanie Hamilton on Mattie Holliday.

President Chester A. Arthur, which, he contended, Governor Tritle and other Earp defenders were working on. It was reasonable to think one was forthcoming. If nothing else, it would be a smart move because, Wyatt vowed, he and his men "were [still] being sought by their foes, and they would not give themselves up to Arizona officers without resistance."

However, there would be no need for resistance or for a pardon, either. While various newspapers and officials in and out of Arizona continued to debate if the Earp vendetta ride had been a vigilante hunt or a federal marshal's justified pursuit of outlaws, for Wyatt it was over. There was only the future to pursue now.

When nothing had happened by the end of April, Wyatt and Warren and Texas Jack also took a train to Trinidad, Colorado. They would feel safer there—farther from Cochise County, and, perhaps more important, Bat Masterson was the city marshal. If Wyatt was experiencing something like what is called PTSD today after the uncharacteristic killing spree and his break with Doc Holliday, being with the loyal and ebullient Bat would be the best medicine. Afterward, Wyatt moved on to Gunnison, also in Colorado, where he settled in as a faro dealer. He still planned on looking up Josephine in San Francisco, but he was not about to do so empty-handed.

That one other late casualty of the vendetta ride was Johnny Ringo. His death has produced a plethora of conspiracy theories since July 14, 1882, when his body was found in an isolated spot in the Chiricahua Mountains. There was a single bullet wound in his head. The romanticized theory was that Doc Holliday and Ringo had finally had it out, over both Wyatt and Big Nose Kate. Two days earlier, Doc had appeared in court in Pueblo, Colorado, so it is very unlikely that he would have found transportation swift enough to put him in southeast Arizona in time to kill anyone. Plus, it is even more unlikely that Doc, noted for his inaccuracy with handguns, would have managed to dispatch the cowboy with a single shot to the head.

Acquaintances knew that Ringo had suffered from bouts of severe depression. More likely he had seen the fading future of the cowboy in Cochise County, and with no prospect of being welcomed elsewhere, he had sunk very low. Drunk and despondent, Ringo had raised a Colt .45 to his head and pulled the trigger. He was found lying against the trunk of a tree. He had removed his boots, which were found tied to the saddle of his horse, grazing two miles away. Johnny Ringo was buried near the base of the tree, and today the grave is an Arizona historic landmark.

Citizens of Tombstone expressed surprise and relief upon hearing of the cowboy leader's death. With both him and Curly Bill Brocius gone, along with most of the rest of the cowboys and all of the Earps, a page had been turned in Tombstone. The mines surrounding the city had begun to flood with water, meaning their remaining production of valuable ore was limited. The city's prospects were also fading.

But for now, in the typically hot and dusty summer of 1882— and after surviving a second devastating fire in May—there were more mundane and pleasant matters for the citizens of Tombstone to attend to.

"This a season of church benefits," Clara Brown had informed her readers to the west. "*Pinafore* by the Episcopalians was preceded by the Floral Mythological Concert for the Presbyterians, and necktie party and dance given by the Catholics, while the Methodists are arranging for a strawberry festival. Adios."

EPILOGUE

The only reason Tombstone would be remembered today is as one of many American boomtowns that came and went—if not for the Earp brothers and Doc Holliday teaming up to win a gunfight there and Wyatt and Doc's revenge ride that followed. In order for those events to happen, the city had to be founded in the first place, in the most unlikely manner by Edward Schieffelin, and then allowed for a time to prosper.

Though by then better dressed, Schieffelin had left Tombstone to go on more prospecting expeditions. Not satisfied enough with his "Eureka!" moment, he wanted another one. Along the way, when in San Francisco, he met Mary Brown, and after they married the couple lived in Los Angeles. Eventually, he found the city too crowded and confining and resumed his explorations. In 1897, two decades after the first one, he did indeed make another big strike—though this one would have an unhappy twist.

Schieffelin had gone to Oregon and was living in a remote cabin while searching for gold. One night in May he was at a table working on a sample of gold ore. He was prompted to write in his journal, "Struck it rich again, by God." He had a massive heart attack and died. His body was found slumped over the table. The samples would test at $2,000 to the ton. If there was a map or directions to the site where he extracted the gold, it was never found.

According to his wishes, he was buried in Tombstone, in prospector's clothing and his pick and canteen in the coffin with him. He had died four months shy of his fiftieth birthday. The monument above the grave of Edward Schieffelin states, "A dutiful son, A faithful husband, A kind brother, A true friend."

Alas, the widow of the man whose discoveries had produced millions of dollars in valuable ore in southeast Arizona was not left in a comfortable financial condition. In the will, Mary Schieffelin was left properties in California that had already been sold off. She frittered away what was left of the original fortune after heeding poor financial advice. Ill health put her in the Los Angeles County Hospital, which had been built on land donated by her husband. Mary later returned to San Francisco, where she died in 1918.

Many of the more prominent citizens of Tombstone during the Earp period did not remain long in the city, for one reason or another. In the justice system, no one proved to be more important than Judge Wells Spicer. Despite the threats on his life, he had no harm visited upon him in Tombstone following the hearing on the October 26, 1881, gunfight. However, Spicer must have lost some interest in the law because he chose to return to prospecting. His journey began in Pima County, took him to Sonora in Mexico, and then to the Quijotoa Mountains near Tucson. There he found a deposit of silver, filed a claim, and invested most of his money in working the expanding mine . . . which went bust. What Spicer had initially found was apparently all there was in silver, but there was plenty of misery extracted.

Despairing and destitute, Judge Spicer quit prospecting and quit on life, too. In January 1887, he set off into the Arizona desert and was never seen again.

After his holiday visit with his young children, John Clum returned to Tombstone. However, he did not stay long. On May 1, 1882, exactly two years to the day that he had first published *The Tombstone Epitaph,* he sold it and left. Clum roamed the country. He lived in Nevada, California, and Alaska, where during a gold rush he once again became a postmaster. It was there he encountered Wyatt Earp, who was still seeking his fortune.

When Clum did go to Arizona again, it was to settle in Tucson. And there he was reacquainted with Johnny Behan, still hoping for political redemption. Somewhat reluctantly, the two men became friends. Clum outlived him and just about everyone else he had known, not dying until 1932, in his eighty-first year.

Another Earp supporter, Bob Paul, who was no doubt relieved at not having to arrest Wyatt and Warren Earp and Doc Holliday, continued a sterling career in law enforcement. He was the Pima County sheriff for four more years, became a railroad detective, and in 1890, President Benjamin Harrison appointed him the U.S. marshal for the entire Arizona Territory. He was usually seen carrying a shotgun, and sometimes, not respecting borders, he crossed into Mexico to get his man. Paul was serving as a justice of the peace in Tucson when he died of cancer in March 1901 at age sixty-nine.

Thomas Fitch, who had successfully headed the defense team during the Spicer hearing, took to traveling, both in the United States and in Europe. He lived for a time in San Diego and then

San Francisco, taking on law cases that interested him, including Hawaiian sake makers who wanted their product classified as beer instead of liquor to more easily get through U.S. Customs.

In 1909, at age seventy-one, Fitch moved to Los Angeles to return to being a newspaperman. He worked as a reporter for the *Los Angeles Times,* and he held that position for seven years. He was eighty-five when he died in November 1923.

In 1887, with the boom period in Tombstone over, George Whitwell Parsons resigned his position as the first librarian of the Tombstone Library. He went in search of greener pastures, or at least more profitable ones, by relocating to Los Angeles. The incessant journal keeper would consider himself "a prominent and important, but little remembered, citizen." He was active in the YMCA, Episcopal Church, California Academy of Sciences, Los Angeles Chamber of Commerce, Committee on Mines and Mining, and Committee on Railroads and Transportation. As a lobbyist, he fought for laws at the city and state levels to curb corruption.

It seems George Parsons never married. He died of a heart ailment at age eighty-two in San Bernardino in January 1933. That city's newspaper described him as a "desert pioneer" for his efforts to erect signs at watering holes for thirsty travelers and their automobiles and as a "veteran of the wildest days of Tombstone . . . much employed in later years by noted writers in search of information and color."

Clara Spalding Brown's last letter to her readers in San Diego from Tombstone was dated November 14, 1882. When she and her husband moved back to California, it was to Los Angeles. She became a prolific writer of articles for magazines, not slowed at all by the death of Theodore Brown in the early 1890s. She cofounded the Southern California Woman's Press Club, published a novel, and reported for regional newspapers.

After several years of being a widow, Brown married the best-selling author Edward Sylvester Ellis and moved in with him in Upper Montclair, New Jersey. As with her first one, her second marriage did not hinder her writing output. She continued to churn out articles for magazines and newspapers, including ones in New York, Detroit, and Denver. And she became a member of the Woman's Press Club of New York City. When Ellis died in 1916, Brown went back to the West Coast and, among other activities, became corresponding secretary of the press club she had cofounded there. Her full life ended at age eighty, in July 1935, from pneumonia.

There were two survivors of the five men the Earps expected to square off against them that Wednesday afternoon off Frontier Street. One was Billy Claiborne. He escaped death that day, but not for very much longer. After testifying for the prosecution at the Judge Spicer hearing, he left town to escape the derisive comments about him seeking cover rather than confront the Earps and Doc. Claiborne worked in the mines near Globe for much of 1882, then that November he returned to Tombstone with a surly attitude. He had gotten it into his alcohol-addled head that "Buckskin" Frank Leslie had killed his friend Johnny Ringo.

On the night of November 14, already drunk, he entered the Oriental Saloon to wash down more whiskey. When he began cursing other patrons, the bartender told him to stop. Conveniently, the bartender that night was Leslie. Claiborne kept up his tirade, and Leslie grabbed him by the collar and tossed him out. "That's all right," Billy said, "I'll get even with you."

He was not about to take much time doing it. A patron entering the Oriental informed Leslie there was a man outside waiting to shoot him. Displaying more courage than sense, Buckskin Frank stepped out the door. He saw the barrel of a rifle protruding from the end of a nearby fruit stand. "Don't shoot," he said. "I don't want you to kill me, nor do I want to have to shoot you." Claiborne responded by firing the rifle. He missed. Leslie had a pistol, and he used it. Billy took a bullet in the chest. When Leslie advanced on him, he pleaded, "Don't shoot again, I am killed." Six hours later, that proved to be true. Billy Claiborne was only a month past his twenty-second birthday.

The other survivor of the famous gunfight was the man whose actions had instigated it, Ike Clanton. Once the vendetta was over and the Earps and Doc Holliday were gone from Arizona, Ike returned to ranching with his brother Phin and as much rustling as he could get away with. But the old ways of a dishonest man making a living in the territory were less tolerated. In June 1887, both Ike and Phin were in trouble again.

They had been charged with cattle rustling. A detective named J. V. Brighton was on their trail. He and his posse found the outlaws at a ranch on Eagle Creek, south of Springerville. Phin surrendered; Ike did not. Brighton's bullets put an end to his disreputable life, and Phin wound up in prison. Ike was given a cursory burial in an unmarked grave on the Clanton ranch property, and his remains were not discovered until 1996 by a family descendant, Terry "Ike" Clanton.

As his wife's testimony alleged, Pete Spence quite likely was involved in the murder of Morgan Earp and may have even pulled the trigger. However, he enjoyed the protection of Sheriff Behan's jail during the period of Wyatt's revenge and never had to account for his perfidy. Incredibly, by June 1883, Spence was serving as a deputy sheriff in Georgetown, New Mexico. Not so surprisingly, he pistol-whipped a man to death. He served eighteen months of a five-year sentence and was pardoned by the territorial governor. Back in Arizona, he joined up with Phin Clanton to run a goat ranch. When his partner died, he married Phin's wife, Laura Jane. Spence lived to age sixty-two, dying in 1914, and was buried in a Globe cemetery next to Phin Clanton.

It should surprise no one that in November 1882, Johnny Behan was not reelected Cochise County sheriff. More humiliating, the local Democratic Party refused even to nominate him. He would spend the rest of his life as a political hack, depending on patronage for employment.

He left Tombstone in 1887 and held positions including superintendent of the Yuma Penitentiary (being accused of financial improprieties); a customs inspector in El Paso, Texas, where he hunted down illegal Chinese immigrants; and when the Spanish-American War began, the fifty-three-year-old Behan volunteered, eventually serving overseas, not in the Philippines but in the Boxer Rebellion in China in 1900. Upon his return, he lived in Tucson.

Behan was sixty-seven when he died in June 1912 of heart disease and syphilis that dated back to his Tombstone days. His grave can be found in the Holy Hope Cemetery in Tucson.

Of the steadfast members of the Wyatt Earp vendetta ride posse, the least is known about cowboy/outlaw Sherman McMasters. Will McLaury, in a letter to his father, reported McMasters had been killed by cowboys. Decades later, Wyatt Earp claimed that McMasters had died while serving in the Philippines during the Spanish-American War. In 1906, a probate record filed by a sibling stated McMasters had died in Colorado in 1892, which would have made him thirty-nine.

Turkey Creek Jack Johnson also had a short life. After parting with Wyatt in Colorado, he wandered to Texas and then, after marrying, to Salt Lake City. He died there of tuberculosis and may have been only thirty-five years old.

Texas Jack Vermillion reunited with Wyatt Earp in June 1883 during the Dodge City War. While there he shot a card cheat and acquired another nickname, "Shoot-Your-Eye-Out Jack." Seven years later he returned to his native Virginia, settling near Big Stone Gap and serving as a Methodist preacher. With his second wife, he had two children, Opie and Minnie. Vermillion died peacefully at sixty-eight in 1911.

Harelip Charlie Smith was the only member of Wyatt's revenge posse to return to live in Tombstone. He teamed up with Fred Dodge, who had revealed himself as a Wells Fargo agent, in the hunting of outlaws. When illness forced Dodge off the trail, Smith succeeded him as a special officer. In September 1888, a man who had previously engaged in a fistfight with Smith shot him in the street, shattering his hip, and his outlaw-chasing days were over. Still, he was a deputy sheriff in Pinal County when he died at age sixty-three in 1907. Along the way he had married a widow and become stepfather to her two young sons.

Perhaps never recovering from the brutality of the vendetta his brother Wyatt involved him in, Warren experienced a much more troubled life as time passed, thanks in part to alcoholism. He drifted from town to town across the frontier, not returning to Arizona until 1891, when he found work as a driver of stages that transported the U.S. Mail, interspersed with stints as a range detective. Warren acquired the reputation of being something of a bully and exaggerating the exploits of Wyatt and Virgil, probably for free drinks and other favors.

In July 1900, Warren was doing some detecting work for Henry Hooker. Because of an interest in the same woman and that they simply rubbed each other the wrong way, Warren and Johnny Boyett, Hooker's range boss, were often in conflict. One day in Brown's Saloon in Willcox, Arizona, the two men argued. The argument reignited that night in the same saloon, and this time both men were drunk. Warren said he had a gun and that Boyett should get one of his own. He went and got two, both .45-caliber Colts. When Warren appeared in the saloon, Boyett fired several times and missed. Finally, Warren was struck squarely in the chest, and moments later he was dead, the second Earp brother to meet a violent end.

After the events in Tombstone, James and Bessie Earp stayed put in California. She died only six years later, in 1887. James lived quietly and well into old age, dying in January 1926 at eighty-four. He was buried in the Mountain View Cemetery, near his sister Adelia and sister-in-law Allie.

After arriving in California in March 1882, Virgil and Allie Earp decided to remain in Colton. As he recuperated, he was able to get regular medical attention in San Francisco. In an interview with the *Examiner* that May, he explained what had led to the now famous gunfight in Tombstone: "My brother Wyatt and myself were fairly well treated for a time, but when the desperate characters who were congregated there, and who had been unaccustomed to troublesome molestation by the authorities, learned that we meant business and were determined to stop their rascality if possible, they began to make it warm for us."

Virgil opened a detective agency in Colton, and in 1886 he was elected constable there, with his seventy-three-year-old father being justice of the peace. The following year, Virgil became the city's marshal. But in 1893, now fifty and no doubt to Allie's dismay, he became restless. The couple moved to the mining town of Vander-bilt, California, and built Earp's Hall, a gambling emporium that also featured Saturday boxing matches and Sunday church services. When the Vanderbilt boom went bust, Virgil reunited with Wyatt in Cripple Creek, Colorado, but it already had all the liquor and gaming it could handle, so Virgil and Allie returned to the familiar environs of Prescott. He invested in what was called the Grizzly Mine, which promised to produce profits, until one day in November 1896 when it collapsed with Virgil in it. Several broken bones and bad bruises required months of recuperation.

He had a much more enjoyable experience in 1898, when he was fifty-five. That autumn, a letter from a woman with the delightfully coincidental name of Jane Law, mailed from Portland, Oregon, found him. Virgil was informed that she was his daughter, the one born in 1862. A few months later, he and Allie traveled to Oregon and father and daughter and his first wife, Ellen, were reunited. Virgil also met his three grandchildren for the first time.

Virgil and Allie divided their time between Prescott and Colton, where his mother, Virginia Ann Cooksey Earp, had passed away in January 1893. Nicholas had remarried nine months later. In 1901, at eighty-eight, he was placed in the Veterans Home in Sawtelle, which was on the western fringe of Los Angeles. In February 1907, shortly after being elected to the Los Angeles County Court and having outlived six of his ten children, Nicholas Earp died at ninety-three.

Two years earlier, in 1905, Virgil had become a peace officer again when he was appointed a deputy sheriff of Esmeralda County in Nevada. And even with just one functioning arm, he also served as a bouncer in one of the saloons in Goldfield. Next door was the

Northern, built by Tex Rickard, and it soon became very successful, boasting of having the longest bar in the West.* Virgil did not
keep both positions very long because his health became more fragile. He was just plain worn out, and a bout of pneumonia tipped the
scales.

Lying in bed in a hospital in Goldfield, Virgil asked Allie for a
cigar. Then he asked her to place a grandniece's letter to him under
his pillow, "light my cigar, and stay here and hold my hand." On
October 19, 1905, at age sixty-two, Virgil Earp died. He was buried in the Riverview Cemetery in Portland, where he could be near
his daughter when her turn came.

Allie outlived Virgil by forty-two years. For some of those years
she lived in San Bernardino and was a close friend to Adelia Earp
Edwards; then she moved to Los Angeles. She died there in November 1947 at age ninety-eight, and she and Adelia share a grave
in the Mountain View Cemetery in San Bernardino.

Mattie can be said to be another casualty of events in Tombstone. She believed that after the bloody business there was finished,
Wyatt would come to Colton to collect her. She was mistaken.
Leaving Tombstone meant the end of her life with Wyatt. Mattie
remained at the Earp farm until August 1882, when she boarded
a train to begin a return journey to Arizona. There she looked up
Big Nose Kate, who took her in. The two women occupied the re-
built Globe boardinghouse. The first three years of her stay, Mattie
lived a quiet life and her use of laudanum may have diminished or

* George Lewis Rickard would become the most successful boxing promoter in
the United States, with Jack Dempsey his most notable star in the ring. Rickard
also built the third incarnation of Madison Square Garden and founded the New
York Rangers hockey team.

stopped. But in 1885, she spied Wyatt and Josephine in Globe and went into a tailspin.

She began to drink heavily and returned to using opium and laudanum in ever-increasing doses. Mattie remained in Globe until October 1887, when she boarded a stage for a smaller Arizona town, Pinal. The only aspect that may have appealed to her about the dusty and derelict post-boom mining community, with ghost town being its future, was anonymity. No one would care what or how much she drank, and there was one doctor who could prescribe laudanum. By the late winter of 1888, Mattie was in severe pain, and this time it was more physical than emotional—increasing abdominal anguish and decreasing appetite indicated she could have cancer, cervical or intestinal, or there was the possibility of a late-stage sexually transmitted disease. On the night of July 3, Mattie mixed an overdose of laudanum with whiskey, drank it down, passed out, and did not wake up.

As detailed in the book *Dodge City*, Doc Holliday, not Wyatt or Warren, would be the one arrested for the Earp vendetta, in Colorado. It was Bat Masterson, as a favor to Wyatt, who extricated him from jail in Denver and deposited him in Pueblo. Doc spent the rest of his days in Colorado. Being away from the dry air of Arizona allowed his lung disease to progress, and increasing amounts of alcohol greased the skids. In May 1885, Doc and Wyatt were reunited, at the Windsor Hotel in Denver. As Jeff Guinn writes in *The Last Gunfight*, "Whatever disagreement [they] might have had three years earlier was forgotten. They talked quietly together, and the habitually taciturn Wyatt had tears in his eyes when they said goodbye for what both men knew would be the last time."

Doc was living in Leadville when he had his last gunfight. A man named Billy Allen, looking to earn a reputation, challenged him in a saloon. Doc demurred, but when Allen drew his gun Doc drew faster, firing twice and hitting Allen in his shooting arm. Doc could have killed him, but the last thing he needed was more trouble from the law . . . or he had indeed tried to kill him and the best he could do was hit Allen in the arm.

Entering 1887, Doc was gravely ill and he moved to Glenwood Springs, hoping the sulfurous waters would offer some relief. However, they failed to extend his life. According to Kate Elder, it was here the longtime lovers said their good-byes. She claims to have nursed Doc during his last weeks that autumn, which were mostly spent in bed because he was too weak to do anything else, even drink alcohol. But on November 8, Doc asked a nurse for whiskey, and he drank it down in two gulps. He looked at his feet and said, "Damn, this is funny," probably thinking of the prediction given to him years earlier that he would never die in bed with his boots off. By dying that day, he proved the prediction false. Dr. John Henry Holliday was thirty-six. Wyatt's most devoted friend was buried at the Linwood Cemetery.*

Josephine Marcus was indeed waiting for Wyatt in San Francisco, and soon after he arrived there to collect her, she became his fourth wife, though it is unclear when or if that became official. He called her Sadie, after her middle name of Sarah, even though that was also the name of his second wife and the one Josephine had used as a pseudonym while being courted by Johnny Behan and possibly being a prostitute.

The couple began a wandering journey through the West, a combination of an ongoing search for wealth and the inherent Earp

---

* Kate Elder would die fifty-three years later, in November 1940, in the Arizona Pioneers' Home in Prescott, five days before her ninetieth birthday.

restlessness. During the 1880s they spent time in Galveston, Texas, Salt Lake City, Los Angeles, San Francisco, and Idaho, where for a time Wyatt owned a saloon. In San Diego, Wyatt was a real estate speculator and he owned racehorses, none of which were fast enough to be consistent winners. Around this time Sadie developed her own addiction, this one being gambling. Wyatt was constantly buying jewelry back from pawnshops and re-gifting them as presents to his wife.

In the 1890s, Wyatt heard about the gold strikes in the Klondike area of Alaska and decided that would be their next adventure. He did not find gold, but a saloon he owned in Nome did a brisk business. In 1901, he cashed out and he and Sadie relocated to Los Angeles, where one newspaper referred to him as "the well-known sporting authority," alluding to his controversial connection to boxing. The Earps lived in Nevada and Colorado, where there was the last get-together with Virgil, then it was back to California. Wyatt and Sadie finally settled down for good in Los Angeles.

Over the next two decades, Wyatt was approached to cooperate on writing projects. He cooperated with John Flood, a writer and friend, but this much-exaggerated "biography" was never published. Next up was Stuart Lake, and he and Wyatt exchanged letters throughout 1928, until Wyatt was too unwell to continue. When the new year began, he was very ill. He had prostate cancer, and whatever treatment existed at the time would have been too late anyway given its recent diagnosis. One day that January, Wyatt could not get out of bed, and that is where he remained, with his wife of forty-seven years at his side.

Sadie continued her vigil day after day. At one point, Wyatt woke up. He appeared thoughtful and said, "Supposing . . . supposing."

He was quiet for a few moments, then added, "Oh well," and fell back asleep. He died on January 13, 1929.

The services were held at the Pierce Brothers chapel in Los Angeles. Among those who attended was John Clum, almost forty-eight years since what had become known as the Gunfight at the O.K. Corral. Wyatt's body was cremated. Six months later, Sadie brought the ashes to the Marcus family plot at Hills of Eternity, a Jewish cemetery in Colma, California. She would join him there in December 1944, after succumbing to a heart attack at eighty-three.

We will never know what Wyatt meant when he murmured, "Supposing." And we can only wonder what he thought that day in late March 1882 as he gazed for the last time at the town to which he had brought his dreams from Dodge City. Now he was a grieving and avenging brother, a lapsed lawman still loyal to law and order and possibly hours away from being killed. Finally, and maybe with a sigh—the most emotion the taciturn man would display—Wyatt Earp turned away from Tombstone and rode off, into American history.

Acknowledgments

I've long maintained that without staffers and volunteers at librar-
ies, historical societies, and other research centers I would not have
a career. I mean this most sincerely. Once more, this time with
Tombstone, my thanks go to those at such institutions in Arizona—
especially Erika Way and Joanna Brace—and in Kansas and elsewhere who helped me along the arduous research road and whose
unflagging courtesy made the trek less of a slog. I am always both
delighted and humbled by the expertise and enthusiasm of these
professionals. A big thank-you to Rebekah Tabah Percival at the
Arizona Heritage Center for her generous assistance in the gathering of images. I am also grateful for the efforts of staffers at the
John Jermain Memorial Library for their long-standing assistance
and kindness.

My thanks also to the journalist Kitty Merrill and Hollis Cook,
a retired park ranger at the Tombstone Courthouse State Historic
Park, for reading the manuscript and alerting me to errors. For
ones that still managed to slip through, they are on me.

This book would not have originated, let alone been completed, without the encouragement and steadfast support of my editor, Marc Resnick. Others at St. Martin's Press have also made the journey a happy and productive one, including Sally Richardson, Rebecca Lang, Hannah O'Grady, Danielle Prielipp, Tracey Guest, Steve Cohen, and Sona Vogel. Another "founder" of *Tombstone* is Nat Sobel, a friend as well as agent, and I appreciate everything done for me by his staff, especially Adia Wright. Thanks also to Scott Gould, who helped me begin the trip west.

My dear friends continue to wait for me to not work so much so we can get together more often. The support of Mike, Tony, John, Bob, Heather, another Bob, Phil, Ed, Joe, yet another Bob, Ken, Dave, Lynne, and a bunch of others is a big reason why every day matters. And finally, my love to Leslie, Katy, and Brendan for . . . well, keeping me around.

Selected Bibliography

BOOKS

Alexander, Bob. *John H. Behan: Sacrificed Sheriff.* Silver City, NM: High-Lonesome Books, 2002.

Bailey, Lynn R., ed. *A Tenderfoot in Tombstone: The Private Journal of George Whitwell Parsons: The Turbulent Years: 1880–82.* Tucson: Westernlore Press, 1996.

———. *The Dragoon Mountains.* Tucson: Westernlore Press, 2008.

———. *Henry Clay Hooker and the Sierra Bonita.* Tucson: Westernlore Press, 1998.

———. *A Tale of the "Unkilled": The Life, Times, and Writings of Wells Spicer.* Tucson: Westernlore Press, 1999.

———. *The Valiants: The Tombstone Rangers and Apache War Frivolities.* Tucson: Westernlore Press, 1999.

Ball, Larry D. *The United States Marshals of New Mexico and Arizona Territories, 1846–1912.* Albuquerque: University of New Mexico Press, 1999.

Barra, Allen. *Inventing Wyatt Earp: His Life and Many Legends.* New York: Carroll & Graf, 1998.

Bell, Bob Boze. *Classic Gunfights.* N.p.: Tri-Star Boze Publications, 2003.

Boyer, Glenn, ed. *I Married Wyatt Earp: The Recollections of Josephine Sarah Marcus Earp.* Tucson: University of Arizona Press, 1996.

Breakenridge, William M. *Helldorado: Bringing the Law to the Mesquite.* Edited by Richard Maxwell Brown. Lincoln: University of Nebraska Press, 1992.

Brown, Clara Spalding. *Tombstone from a Woman's Point of View.* Edited by Lynn R. Bailey. Tucson: Westernlore Press, 2003.

Burns, Walter Noble. *Tombstone: An Iliad of the Southwest.* New York: Grosset & Dunlap, 1927.

Burrows, Jack. *John Ringo: The Gunfighter Who Never Was.* Tucson: University of Arizona Press, 1987.

Chafin, Carl, ed. *The Private Journal of George Whitwell Parsons.* Tombstone, AZ: Cochise Classics, 1997.

Chaput, Don. *"Buckskin Frank" Leslie.* Tucson: Westernlore Press, 1999.

———. *The Earp Papers: In a Brother's Image.* Encampment, WY: Affiliated Writers of America, 1994.

———. *Virgil Earp: Western Peace Officer.* Encampment, WY: Affiliated Writers of America, 1994.

Charles River Editors. *Legends of the West: Gunfight at the OK Corral.* Columbia, SC: 2018.

Chrisman, Harry E. *Fifty Years on the Owl-Hoot Trail.* Chicago: Sage Books, 1969.

Clavin, Tom. *Dodge City: Wyatt Earp, Bat Masterson, and the Wickedest Town in the American West.* New York: St. Martin's Press, 2017.

———. *Wild Bill: The True Story of the American Frontier's First Gunfighter.* New York: St. Martin's Press, 2019.

Clum, John. *Apache Days & Tombstone Nights.* Edited by Neil B. Carmony. Silver City, NM: High-Lonesome Books, 1997.

Cox, William. *Luke Short and His Era.* New York: Doubleday, 1961.

Craig, R. Bruce, ed. *Portrait of a Prospector: Edward Schieffelin's Own Story.* Norman: University of Oklahoma Press, 2017.

DeArment, Robert. *Bat Masterson.* Norman: University of Oklahoma Press, 1979.

Devere, Burton, Jr. *Bonanzas to Borrascas: The Mines of Tombstone, Arizona.* Tombstone, AZ: Rose Tree Museum, 2010.

Dworkin, Mark J. *American Mythmaker: Walter Noble Burns and the Legends of Billy the Kid, Wyatt Earp, and Joaquín Murrieta.* Norman: University of Oklahoma Press, 2015.

Earp, Wyatt. *My Fight at the O.K. Corral.* Edited by H. P. Oswald. CreateSpace Independent Publishing, 2012.

Eppings, Jane. *Around Tombstone: Ghost Towns and Gunfights.* Charleston, SC: Arcadia Publishing, 2009.

———. *Images of America: Tombstone.* Charleston, SC: Arcadia Publishing, 2003.

Faulk, Odie B. *Land of Many Frontiers: A History of the American Southwest.* New York: Oxford University Press, 1968.

———. *Tombstone: Myth and Reality.* New York: Oxford University Press, 1972.

Gatto, Steve. *Curly Bill: Tombstone's Most Famous Outlaw.* Lansing, MI: Protar House Books, 2003.

———. *Johnny Ringo*. Lansing, MI: Protar House Books, 2002.

———. *The Real Wyatt Earp*. Silver City, NM: High-Lonesome Books, 2000.

Gray, John Plesant. *Tombstone's Violent Years, 1880–1882*. Edited by Neil B. Carmony. Tucson: Trail to Yesterday Books, 1999.

———. *When All Roads Led to Tombstone: A Memoir*. Edited by W. Lane Rogers. Mahtomedi, MN: Tamarack Books, 1998.

Guinn, Jeff. *The Last Gunfight*. New York: Simon & Schuster, 2011.

Hand, George. *Next Stop: Tombstone*. Tucson: Trail to Yesterday Books, 1995.

Herring, Hal. *Famous Firearms of the Old West*. Guilford, CT: Globe Pequot Press, 2011.

Hickey, Michael M. *The Death of Warren Baxter Earp: A Closer Look*. Honolulu, HI: Talei Publishers, 2000.

Hornung, Chuck. *Wyatt Earp's Cow-boy Campaign: The Bloody Restoration of Law and Order Along the Mexican Border, 1882*. Jefferson, NC: McFarland, 2016.

Isenberg, Andrew C. *Wyatt Earp: A Vigilante Life*. New York: Hill and Wang, 2013.

Jahs, Pat. *The Frontier World of Doc Holliday*. New York: Hastings House, 1957.

Kirschner, Ann. *Lady at the O.K. Corral: The True Story of Josephine Marcus Earp*. New York: HarperCollins, 2013.

Lake, Stuart N. *Wyatt Earp: Frontier Marshal*. New York: Houghton Mifflin, 1931.

Lubet, Steven. *Murder in Tombstone: The Forgotten Trial of Wyatt Earp*. Yale University Press, 2004.

Marks, Paula Mitchell. *And Die in the West: The Story of the O.K. Corral Gunfight*. New York: William Morrow, 1989.

Martin, Douglas D. *Tombstone's Epitaph: The Truth About the Town Too Tough to Die*. Albuquerque: University of New Mexico Press, 1951.

Masterson, W. B. (Bat). *Famous Gunfighters of the American Frontier*. Mineola, NY: Dover Publications, 2009.

Metz, Leon Claire. *The Encyclopedia of Lawmen, Outlaws, and Gunfighters*. New York: Facts on File, 2003.

Meyers, E. C. (Ted). *Mattie: Wyatt Earp's Secret Second Wife*. Blaine, WA: Hancock House, 2010.

Millard, Candice. *Destiny of the Republic: A Tale of Madness, Medicine and the Murder of a President*. New York: Doubleday, 2011.

Miller, Nyle, and Joseph Snell. *Why the West Was Wild*. Norman: University of Oklahoma Press, 2003.

Monahan, Sherry. *Mrs. Earp: The Wives and Lovers of the Earp Brothers*. Guilford, CT: Globe Pequot Press, 2013.

———. *Taste of Tombstone: A Hearty Helping of History*. Mesa, AZ: Royal Spectrum, 1998.

Nash, Jay Robert. *Encyclopedia of Western Lawmen & Outlaws*. New York: Da Capo Press, 1994.

O'Connor, Richard. *Bat Masterson*. New York: Doubleday, 1957.

O'Neal, Bill. *Encyclopedia of Western Gunfighters*. Norman: University of Oklahoma Press, 1991.

Parsons, George Whitwell. *A Tenderfoot in Tombstone*. Tucson: Westernlore Press, 1996.

Roberts, David. *Once They Moved Like the Wind: Cochise, Geronimo, and the Apache Wars*. New York: Simon & Schuster, 1994.

Roberts, Gary L. *Doc Holliday: The Life and Legend*. New York: John Wiley & Sons, 2006.

Rosa, Joseph G. *Age of the Gunfighter: Men and Weapons on the Frontier 1840–1900*. Norman: University of Oklahoma Press, 1995.

Schieffelin, Edward. *Destination Tombstone: Adventures of a Prospector*. Mesa, AZ: Royal Spectrum, 1996.

Shelton, Richard. *Going Back to Bisbee*. Tucson: University of Arizona Press, 1992.

Shillingberg, William B. *Tombstone, A.T.: A History of Early Mining, Milling, and Mayhem*. Spokane, WA: Arthur H. Clark Co., 1999.

Slotkin, Richard. *Gunfighter Nation: The Myth of the Frontier in Twentieth-Century America*. New York: Atheneum, 1992.

Steckmesser, Kent Ladd. *The Western Hero in History and Legend*. Norman: University of Oklahoma Press, 1997.

Sweeney, Edwin R. *Cochise: Chiricahua Apache Chief*. Norman: University of Oklahoma Press, 1991.

Tanner, Karen Holliday, and Robert K. DeArment. *Doc Holliday: A Family Portrait*. Norman: University of Oklahoma Press, 2001.

Tefertiller, Casey. *Wyatt Earp: The Life Behind the Legend*. New York: John Wiley & Sons, 1997.

Traywick, Ben T. *The Chronicles of Tombstone*. Tombstone, AZ: Red Marie's Books, 1986.

True West, eds. *True Tales and Amazing Legends of the Old West*. New York: Clarkson Potter, 2005.

Turner, Alford E., ed. *The Earps Talk*. College Station, TX: Creative Publishing, 1980.

———. *The O.K. Corral Inquest*. College Station, TX: Creative Publishing, 1981.

Utley, Robert M. *Geronimo*. New Haven, CT: Yale University Press, 2012.

Wagoner, Jay J. *Arizona Territory, 1863–1912*. Tucson: University of Arizona Press, 1970.

Waters, Frank. *The Earp Brothers of Tombstone: The Story of Mrs. Virgil Earp*. Lincoln: University of Nebraska Press, 1976.

Young, Roy B. *Cochise County Cowboy Wars: A Cast of Characters*. Self-published, 1999.

ARTICLES

Bell, Bob Boze. "Geronimo!: Tombstone Posse vs. San Carlos Apaches." *True West*, November 2013.

———. "Hell's Comin' with Me!" *True West*, March 2018.

———. "Shootout at Cottonwood Springs: Wyatt Earp vs. Curly Bill Brocius." *True West*, May 2009.

Boardman, Mark. "The Forgotten Vendetta Rider." *True West*, March 2018.

Boessenecker, John. "They Rode for Wells Fargo." *Wild West*, December 2018.

Bommersbach, Jana. "Sitting with Wyatt Earp." *True West*, February 2018.

Brand, Peter. "10 Earp Vendetta Ride Myths." *True West*, March 2018.

———. "Wyatt Earp's Vendetta Posse." Historynet.com, January 29, 2007.

Chaput, Don. "Triggered." *Wild West*, February 2019.

Hayden, Kenneth W. "The Winding Trail of Curly Bill." *Wild West*, October 2001.

Hocking, Doug. "From Blood Brother to Broken Arrow." *True West*, September 2017.

Larew, Marilyn, and William Brown. "Sierra Bonita Ranch/The Hooker Ranch." National Park Service, June 20, 1977.

O'Dowd, Peter. "Clerk Finds Papers from 1881 Gunfight at OK Corral." NPR, April 22, 2010.

Powell, Eric A. "On the Range." *Archaeology*, March/April 2019.

Rose, Vicky J. "Tombstone Courthouse State Historic Park." *Roundup Magazine*, June 2019.

Russell, Mary Doria. "Sins of the Father." *True West*, March 2018.

Tefertiller, Casey, and Jeff Morey. "O.K. Corral: A Gunfight Shrouded in Mystery." *Wild West*, October 2001.

Trimble, Marshall. "Doc's Last Duel." *True West*, January 2016.

Utley, Robert M. "The Bascom Affair: A Reconstruction." *Arizona and the West* 3, no. 1 (1961).

Weiser, Kathy. "Fred Dodge: Undercover Detective." *Legends of America*, October 2017.

———. "John Chisum: Cattle Baron of the Pecos." *Legends of America*, September 2017.

———. "New Mexico's Lincoln County War." *Legends of America*, July 2017.

———. "Scott Cooley: Texas Ranger Turned Killer." *Legends of America*, October 2017.

———. "William 'Billy' Breakenridge: Lawman, Surveyor, Author." *Legends of America*, September 2017.

Index

Meyer, Charles, 328–29
Meyers, E. C., 78–79, 107–8
Miles, Nelson, 231
Monahan, Sherry, 14–15, 79, 89, 95
Mormon Rebellion (Utah War), 217–18
Morton, William, 40
Mountain Meadows massacre, 217–18
Mrs. Earp (Monahan), 14–15, 79
Murphy, Lawrence, 38–39
Murray, Frank, 73
Murray, William, 260, 339

Naiche, 226
Narváez, Pánfilo de, 21–22
National Police Gazette, 172
Nauvoo Legion, 217–18
Neagle, David, 214, 237–38, 259, 300, 310, 329
Neri, Francisco, 204
New Mexico Territory, 11, 18, 33
    Arizona Territory separated from, 38
    cowboys and, 132–33
    Gadsden Purchase and, 35–36
    Gold Rush and, 34–35
    Lincoln County War and, 38–41, 132–33
Nez Percé, 31
Nicollet, Joseph Nicolas, 65

O.K. Corral, Gunfight at, 241, 255, 259–69
Olney, Joseph Graves (Joe Hill), 136, 147, 189–91, 201
Oriental Saloon, 138–39, 157–58, 165, 166, 169–75, 188, *209,* 299–301, 309, 355–56
O'Rourke, Michael (Johnny-Behind-the-Deuce), 162–63

Parsons, George Whitwell, 96–97, 125, 152, 160–61, 180, 186, 192, 202,
208, 228–30, 243, 271–72, 280, 293–94, 301–2, 310, 315, 321, 324–25, 337, 339, 347, 354
Patterson, Frank, 111
Paul, Bob, 145–47, 168, 169, 174, 177–81, 185, 211–12, 214, 337, 353
Peacock, A. J., 182–85
Peel, Bryant, 338
Peel, Martin, 338–39
Peppin, George, 40
Percy, Hugh, 3–4, 341
Percy, Jim, 3–4, 341
Phillips, S. F., 295
Philpot, Eli, 177–78, 185
Phoenix Rangers, 227
Pierce, Franklin, 35
Pike's Peak Gold Rush, 36
Polk, James, 66
Prescott, Arizona, 70–77, 84
Prescott, William H., 71
Price, Lyttleton, 199, 280, 285

railroads, in Arizona Territory, 42–43
Randall, Alder, 86, 151
Redfield, Hank, 179
Redfield, Len, 179
Reilly, James, 139–40
Rickabaugh, Lou, 169–71, 174
Rickard, George Lewis (Tex Rickard), 361, 361*n*
Riggs, Barney, 3–4, 341
Ringo, John Peters, 5, 126, 133, 147, 187, 204, 211–12, 287, 289, 291, 296, 306, 318, 336, 344, 347
    arrest of, 310
    cattle rustling and, 137
    death of, 349–50
    Holliday's fight with, 309–10
    violent crime and, 134–37
Ritter and Ream Undertakers, 272–73
Robbins, Marty, 127